# THE SALAMANCA DIARIES

*For Annalisa*

# THE SALAMANCA DIARIES

## FATHER MCCABE AND
## THE SPANISH CIVIL WAR

## TIM FANNING

MERRION
PRESS

First published in 2019 by
Merrion Press
An imprint of Irish Academic Press
10 George's Street
Newbridge
Co. Kildare
Ireland
www.merrionpress.ie

9781785372773 (Cloth)
9781785372780 (Kindle)
9781785372797 (Epub)
9781785372803 (PDF)

British Library Cataloguing in Publication Data
An entry can be found on request

Library of Congress Cataloging in Publication Data
An entry can be found on request

Typeset in Minion Pro 11.5/15 pt

# CONTENTS

NATIONALISTS

REPUBLICANS

FRANCE

Gijón   Llanes   Pendueles   San
Oviedo   Santander   Sebastián   Hendaye
ASTURIAS   Covadonga   Bilbao
Santiago de
Compostela

Vallodolid

Zaragoza

Barcelona

Salamanca

Madrid

Navalcarnero   Ciempozuelos

Cáceres   Toledo

SPAIN
*(July 1936)*

PORTUGAL

Valencia

Mallorca

Lisbon

Seville

Granada

Málaga

Gibraltar

MOROCCO

ALGERIA

# ACKNOWLEDGEMENTS

I spent countless hours reading the diaries of Alexander McCabe in the Manuscripts Room of the National Library of Ireland in Dublin. I would like to thank all the staff for their courtesy and help. Mary Broderick and James Harte, in particular, made every effort to facilitate my requests. Many thanks to former archivist Susan Leyden, current archivist Anna Porter and the staff of the Russell Library, St Patrick's College, Maynooth for their help in guiding me through the Salamanca Archive. I am also grateful to Noelle Dowling of the Dublin Diocesan Archives.

I am thankful to Regina Whelan Richardson, who has written about the Irish College and Asturias, for sharing her own research. The late Monica Henchy was a close family friend of Alexander McCabe and also wrote about the Irish College in Salamanca. I am indebted to her for sharing her memories of Padre Alejandro. I would also like to thank Professor Dermot Keogh for his recollections of Fr McCabe.

I owe a special debt of gratitude to Bridie Smith, who went out of her way to show me around Fr McCabe's homeplace in County Cavan and put me in touch with people who knew him and the McCabe family. I would also like to thank the following for helping me with my research in Counties Cavan, Leitrim and Waterford: Noreen Clarke, Kathleen Conaty, Edmund Connolly, Fr Michael Cooke, Prin Duignan, Fr Liam Kelly, Fr Dónal Kilduff, Br Joseph Killoran, Felix Larkin, Ann Lynch, Donal McCabe, Fr Ultan McGoohan, Fr Tom McKiernan, Mgr PJ McManus, Liam McNiffe, Gráinne Mhic Aonghusa, Mgr Michael Olden, Annette Smith and Fr Thomas Woods.

Thanks are also due to Joan Bennett, Kieran Fagan, Fr Dermot Fenlon, Fr Stewart Foster, the late Dermot Gallagher, who pointed out the John McGahern reference, John Horgan, Dr. Michael Kennedy, Máire Mac Conghail, Máire Mhac an tSaoi and Professor Eunan O'Halpin. I also wish to thank Michael Lillis for his observations on the manuscript, which were invaluable, given his experience of Spain.

Many thanks to Professor Antonio R. Celada of the University of Salamanca for his enquiries on my behalf and Agustín Sánchez for his guided tour of the Colegio Fonseca. The Sanmartín family in Pendueles has been looking after the *Casa de los Irlandeses* for almost a century. I am especially appreciative to Conchi Sanmartín Pidal, whose uncle, Domingo, was one of the many victims of the Spanish Civil War, and her husband, Miguel Rodriguez Cofiño, for their warm hospitality to an unexpected visitor. I must also make mention of Álvaro Reynolds for his help in translating some enquiries and requests into formal Spanish.

I am deeply grateful to Ian Gibson and Professor Paul Preston, both of whom took the time to read the typescript. It was their pioneering work which first provoked my interest in the Spanish Civil War.

Many thanks to Conor Graham and Fiona Dunne of Irish Academic Press and Jonathan Williams for his unstinting efforts to ensure the book was published.

I would also like to acknowledge the debt I owe to my late parents. My father, Ronan, grew to share my fascination with Fr McCabe and was a welcome companion on research trips to the border counties. My mother, Virginia, was always enthusiastic about my projects, whether doomed or fruitful.

Finally, thank you, Annalisa, for your constant good humour, patience and loving encouragement, and, of course, Chiara.

*I started to keep a Diary in January, 1927, when I was in England. Since then, I have written 1,600,000 words. The best Diaries and the most faithfully kept were those for 1938, 1939, 1940, 1941, 1942, 1943, 1944 and 1945. I never missed a day and sometimes, I wrote several pages to a day. I put down everything that I thought to be interesting about life in the College, in Salamanca, and in Spain during those eventful years. They would make an interesting record of all this period. But there were some crudely bitter pages, especially about the cruelty of the Spanish Civil War, and so, before I went to Ireland at Xmas, I brought all these journals down to the furnace and burned the whole record. Perhaps, nobody would have the patience to read it, and if somebody had, he might be shocked at my comments and judgements on all this tragic period, and at the baldly-expressed cynicism, with which I regarded certain aspects of it. … In all, I destroyed about 800,000 words, and it was time wasted, when I might have been learning German or revising Greek. Anybody reading some of the pages would feel that there is very little hope left for Western Europe and I expressed a fierce hatred for the German Nazis, who seem to have been the 'scourge of God' of the 20th Century. Perhaps, my views were a bit lurid at times, but so were the flames that destroyed so many European cities, and have dissipated the wealth that had been accumulated for over a century.*

Fr Alexander J. McCabe, Salamanca,
13 June 1946[1]

# INTRODUCTION

I first came across the diaries of Fr Alexander Joseph McCabe, the rector of the Irish College in Salamanca during the Spanish Civil War, while weighing up the idea of writing a book about the Irish Brigade that fought for Franco. McCabe's perceptive observations about the colourful leaders of the brigade, including the quixotic figure of General Eoin O'Duffy, were intriguing, not least because McCabe possessed a rare ability to sum up in a line or two an individual's key characteristics – be they physical or psychological, intellectual or emotional. These brief sketches were not confined to O'Duffy's raggle-taggle band of adventurers. Franco chose Salamanca as his GHQ in the early stages of the civil war and McCabe met and scrutinised the generals, diplomats, journalists and spies from many nations who passed through the city. He was the perfect eyewitness: cool, detached and measured.

As I dug a little deeper, I became interested in his own life and character. From Drumkilly, a small rural townland in County Cavan, McCabe left Ireland when he was nineteen. For the next thirty-one years of his life, bar a brief period during 1929 and 1930, he lived abroad, first in Spain, as a clerical student, then as a curate in London and Essex, before he returned to Spain as first vice-rector and then rector of the Irish College in Salamanca. He was just thirty-five when he was appointed rector. A year later, in 1936, the Spanish Civil War began and the Irish clerical students were evacuated. For thirteen long years, McCabe was in charge of a college that had no students, until, in 1949, disillusioned, he returned home to Ireland.

He spent the next dozen years of his life as a curate and parish priest in his native diocese of Kilmore. They were not particularly happy ones. His drinking had become a problem, and he fell victim to a diocesan policy of punishing alcoholic priests by transferring them to poor, remote parishes. McCabe drifted across the Ulster and Connacht borderlands. The grey, overcast skies and inundated fields of Cavan and Leitrim must have seemed a long way from the bright sunshine and sandstone of the Castilian *meseta*. After a brief period as parish priest in Ballaghameehan in County Leitrim, in 1961 he was removed from ministry and sent to Belmont Park in Waterford city, a hospital run by the Brothers of Charity. A telling sign of his fall from grace was the fact that his name ceased to appear in the *Irish Catholic Directory*, where once it had been proudly heralded as a college rector. By the late 1960s, however, McCabe had undergone a successful rehabilitation and his name once again appeared, in 1970, in the aforementioned ecclesiastical publication as chaplain to St Joseph's Nursing Home in the Cavan town of Virginia. Here he spent the last two decades of his life, reading, writing and occasionally receiving visitors.

McCabe was discreet, stubborn, and often hot-tempered, but also charming, erudite, a good conversationalist and a warm host. In 1936, the Irish war reporter Francis McCullagh observed of him that he was 'precise, practical, not at all imaginative or sentimental'.[1] This is undoubtedly the image that McCabe wished to convey, but, though an enemy of sentimentalism, not least of bleary-eyed nationalism in all its guises, to describe him as lacking imagination is unfair, as any reader of his diaries, which are now housed in the National Library of Ireland in Dublin, will know.

Much of what is written here is based on what those diaries contain. As may be seen by the entry at the beginning of this book, McCabe tended to consign his journals and notebooks to the flames, most notably the diaries that cover 1938 to 1945. These were destroyed at the end of 1945 at a time when McCabe had despaired of the butchery he had witnessed during the Spanish Civil War and the Francoist repression that followed. Contained within the surviving diaries, however, is not only an invaluable depiction of life in Salamanca before, during and after the civil war, but also of a rapidly changing Western society, in which technology – the radio, cinema, the aeroplane – were advances to be both embraced and feared.

This book is primarily concerned with McCabe's perception of the events and personalities of the Spanish Civil War, and, in particular, his contact with the Irish Brigade, but it also contains his thoughts about the wider political and social changes that he witnessed in Ireland, and farther afield, in the first half of the last century. As an adult in Salamanca and later in Ireland, McCabe, who had an excellent memory, wrote of his earliest days in rural County Cavan, when labour-saving devices were few and the automobile was still an oddity on the roads. He recalled the first time he saw a moving picture as a child and the impression it made on the local community. He remembered the mule-driven coaches picking up passengers from the railway station in Salamanca in the 1920s, and how, a decade later, they had disappeared and been replaced by motorised taxis. He harked back to an Edwardian era in rural Ireland when boys were fed on a diet of British imperial adventures and the tumultuous years after the 1916 Rising. He recalled the young boys going off to sign the Ulster Covenant in 1912 and the traumatised men coming back from the Great War. Not only did he witness the Spanish Civil War, he was in the East End of London during the General Strike of 1926 and in New York during the early days of the Great Depression.

His diaries contain his impressions of some of the great works of European architecture, art and literature and the many, varied places he saw. McCabe spent most of his free time travelling. In the 1930s he visited the United States, North Africa, Turkey, Greece, Germany, France and Switzerland. His description of the class and racial divisions on board the liner that took him to the United States are particularly revealing. The few broken bits of masonry from ancient wonders such as the Parthenon that lie in the boxes of material that he left to the National Library of Ireland are poignant souvenirs from his travels, the names of the places from where they had been looted scrawled on them with marker pen.

And, of course, McCabe travelled long and far throughout Spain. He had many Spanish friends and spoke the language fluently. He was critical of the country's social, political, educational and religious deficiencies in the 1920s, 1930s and 1940s but also recognised its cultural achievements.

McCabe's political attitudes were shaped by his Anglophilia, which became pronounced during his early years as a curate in the south of England. He had little sympathy for Irish cultural nationalism and was hostile to the Irish language and efforts to create a new, romantic Gaelic past. He believed that the archetypal Irishman was to be found among the honest, plain, uncomplaining soldiers who down through the generations had fought and died in foreign armies, especially the British. He was undoubtedly proud to be an Irishman but, before the illusion was destroyed by the Second World War, he believed that the British Empire was the world's greatest civilising project.

Of strong opinions, academically gifted and possessing a shrewd, capable mind – the shame is that he did not study for a degree, since it might have helped him find a job suited to his talents when he left Salamanca – his learned observations on history and politics are fascinating, not least because he happened to be in the right place at the right time (or, perhaps, the wrong place at the wrong time).

The factors that led to the Spanish Civil War are complex and were rooted in Spanish conditions. Both sides were a motley crew of parties, interests, factions and ideologies. Even though we know now the grisly truth behind the rhetoric, there was something inherently romantic about the idea of the Spanish Civil War which inspired so many men from abroad, including the Irishmen who joined both the International Brigades and O'Duffy's brigade, to fight in Spain. McCabe knew differently. Though broadly sympathetic to the nationalist cause, he was critical of the intransigence of the Spanish aristocracy and their inherent hatred of the working classes. Indeed, he found it ironic that Irishmen, many of whom had fought to rid their own country of landlordism, should, a few decades later, be in Spain fighting to protect it. He was also shocked by the brutality of the nationalist repression behind the lines. During and after the war, he could hear the lorries containing prisoners passing outside the Irish College in Salamanca – and the echo of the rifle shots as those same prisoners were executed against the wall of the municipal cemetery.

Some of McCabe's prejudices are undoubtedly jarring to a modern reader – though they should be seen in the context of an era when such views were common among Europeans. But McCabe had a flexible mind and was unafraid to change his opinions as times moved on. He would later reflect on his first impressions of events. These scribbled notes in the marginalia of his diaries show a shifting perspective.

Rather than regretting the fact that McCabe chose to destroy those volumes covering the crucial years from 1938 to 1945, we should rejoice that his remaining diaries have survived, giving us an invaluable eyewitness account of the Spanish Civil War, the political instability from which it emerged and the repressive postwar regime that followed. Occasionally cynical, often melancholic, the diaries are prescient, lively, informed, acerbic, humorous and highly entertaining.

# Chapter 1

# DRUMKILLY

In a hilly piece of soft ground in Drumkilly, County Cavan, lie the remains of the McCabe family. James McCabe, his wife, Katie, and nine of their eleven children are buried in the family plot beneath a Celtic cross. Another child, Patrick, emigrated and is buried in the United States. Alexander, the eldest, as befitting his exalted status as a priest, both in life and death, is buried in a separate grave. His last resting place in the 'new' cemetery is marked by a simple piece of black marble, on which are inscribed the dates of his birth, his ordination and his demise. The house where Alex (or Alec), as he was commonly known, was born and raised overlooks the graveyard, although it was not yet in use when he was a boy. Today, one can see his grave from his old bedroom window. He dreamt of seeing the world but this patch of Cavan was where he wished to be buried when he returned.

The townland of Drumkilly is in the parish of Crosserlough in the diocese of Kilmore. The nearest village to the McCabe family home was Kilnaleck. In the early part of the nineteenth century, the tenant farmers living in Drumkilly were reliant on Ulster's thriving linen industry. It was a cottage industry with all members of the family involved in its production, from planting to weaving. In 1821, nearly every resident of Drumkilly of working age participated in the linen industry, as spinners, knitters or weavers; every girl in the village was spinning flax by the age of twelve, probably even younger. By the 1830s, though, the small farmers could no longer compete with the great linen mills along the Lagan valley, and the decline in the local industry meant that these farmers were increasingly reliant on subsistence farming. By the early 1900s, east Cavan was an area of small farms and heavy tillage. The main crop was oats, and in early autumn the fields would be covered in yellow grain.

In 1886, James McCabe, then in his mid-twenties, moved to Drumkilly from his native, neighbouring parish of Denn to become the first master of the new national school, one of eight that had been built by Fr John Boylan, Crosserlough's energetic parish priest for thirty-three years during the Irish Catholic Church's sustained period of church- and school-building in the latter part of the nineteenth century. In 1898, aged thirty-five, James McCabe married Katie Fitzpatrick, the 26-year-old postmistress. They lived in the comfortable two-storey house opposite the school which was provided by the parish for the master. On the same side of the road was the Catholic chapel, where the local curate said mass.

Alexander was born on 12 May 1900, in the last year of Queen Victoria's reign. In 1901, less than a year after his birth, there were thirteen families living in the townland. As the local teacher, James McCabe held an important position in the small rural community's hierarchy: the McCabes lived in one of the best houses in Drumkilly, he was the secretary of the chapel committee, and many of his neighbours would turn to him for help in writing letters and wills. Initially, however, his neighbours had regarded him with some suspicion because he did not come from Crosserlough. When he arrived in Drumkilly, James McCabe laid out his small garden according to a plan contained in some agricultural textbooks. 'My father hadn't much imagination, but he was scrupulously exact, and conformed rigorously to what was laid down, whether it were instruction, rule or plan,' his eldest child wrote later in his diary. 'But some of the neighbours didn't like all these nonsensical innovations, which they regarded as "swank".'[1] So one night they dug up James McCabe's garden, spoiled the plots and covered the walkway with earth.

Bright, hard-working and curious, James McCabe was a frustrated man with a short temper. He had wanted to be an engineer but had not been able to afford the tuition fees and had instead settled on teaching, for which he had no vocation. He had trained for two years at St Patrick's College in Drumcondra and for a year in the Albert National Agricultural Training Institution in Glasnevin. The latter had been set up in the middle of the nineteenth century to train national-schoolteachers working in rural areas on how to give instruction in agricultural methods. James McCabe worked his whole life in the school at Drumkilly, taking only one day off to buy the farm in the neighbouring townland of Corlislea to which he moved with his family upon his retirement. He did not drink, according to his eldest child, because he was secretary of the local temperance society, 'and because it didn't agree with him',[2] did not socialise and seldom relaxed. He was fond of bacon and raw onion, had a weak stomach and had to get up every night to take bicarbonate of soda – towards the end of his life, thanks to a new medicine prescribed by his doctor, which he took daily, his digestion improved. He did not have a sense of humour and never laughed, except when he went to see a play in the Abbey Theatre in Dublin and, according to his son, the 'tears ran down his face';[3] it was his first holiday in years. His one pleasure was smoking a crooked Kapp pipe while reading the newspaper in the evening and, shortly before he died in 1941, he would take a small glass of whiskey in the evenings.

In his seventies, James McCabe was as 'hardy as a wild duck'[4] and could keep up with men forty years younger. He continued to cycle – he had been the first in the district to ride a bicycle 'when the tyre was still solid. But he always mounted by the step on the back wheel. He never adopted the fashion of using the pedal and throwing a leg over the saddle'.[5] His son summed up his punctilious attitude years later:

> Once we began to grow up, he never took a holiday, and he never visited, though he went to an occasional wake out of respect. He brought home the clay pipe, and on the bowl wrote down, in pencil, the name of the person, and the date, of his death. He kept the pipes in a wooden box on a shelf in the room where the potatoes were stored.[6]

James McCabe was as scrupulous in his dealings with his neighbours as he was in the classroom. He never addressed anyone by his Christian name, according to his son, 'the nearest approach to familiarity was to use the initial of the surname', such as 'Good morning, Mr S'.[7] He paid all his bills on time and kept the records for the parish and the temperance society in a model way. But though he 'gave as much attention to backward pupils as he did to his own children' and 'never complained of his lot', his heart wasn't in teaching, 'with all its petty results and top control'.[8]

He used to get literature sent to him about farming and prospecting in Canada. The pictures of 'tall, golden wheat, the height of a man's shoulder and of rolling prairies'[9] must have seemed a dream, but with a large family and a pragmatic frame of mind, it was little more. The young Alex once heard his father say that he wished he had gone to Canada. On another occasion, when he was home from school in Cavan town during the holidays, Alex showed his father some of his Greek and Latin textbooks. 'He glanced at them, thought them a bit "pagan", but said "I wish I had had your chance when I was young."[10] This was one of the few intimate revelations I ever heard him make.' McCabe believed that his father felt a craving to know more about the classical languages and that teachers, 'who had so frequent and intimate contact with the priests', must have felt that 'their culture was on a much lower level'.[11] The eldest son was to fulfil some of the father's ambitions regarding education and travel, if not all his own, by becoming a priest.

James McCabe never joined a teachers' association or attended meetings, and went to school as normal during a strike, even though he risked being boycotted. He was not active in politics, but political discussion was common in the McCabe household and the young Alex heard names such as Arthur Balfour and John Dillon and the Irish Parliamentary Party discussed during adult conversations, as well as 'obscure references to societies that had disappeared'.[12] James McCabe's family had been evicted from their farm and this coloured his political views, according to his son. 'He wasn't a "Rebel", but he had social ideas and ideals,' McCabe wrote of his father in the late 1940s, 'and if he were a young man to-day, he would probably be Labour.' He added that 'he was too old to be convinced by Sinn Féin'.[13]

McCabe's sympathy for his father was of an intellectual, rather than an emotional kind, and, later on, when he was reflecting on his own life, he probably saw something of his father's plight, at least the frustration. There certainly does not seem to have been much warmth between father and son. McCabe described his father as 'a bit odd and sour'[14] and wrote that, in Ireland, there was 'a thick, high wall between a boy and his father' and that parents were 'complete strangers' to their children.[15] This reflection was made in light of his experience in Spain, where 'parents and children are almost "pals", and know all about one another'.[16] He later wrote that this was one of the beautiful features of life in Spain, while at the same time believing Spanish parents to be too indulgent of their children.

McCabe's mother is less present in his diaries, receiving barely a mention. Katie McCabe wore steel-rimmed glasses and was a voracious reader of novels. Her eldest son remembered her discussing the characters and plots of the books that she was always reading. An outstanding memory of his parents was of his mother standing up at night under the small paraffin light that hung on the wall, reading the newspaper or a book. His father would be sitting on a chair alongside, smoking his pipe, and staring into the fire. Sitting in his room in the Irish College in Salamanca years later, McCabe wrote, 'I can see him now folding a piece of paper, lighting it, lighting his pipe, and quenching the lighted piece of paper against the bars of the grate. As I remember it now, the scene was like one from Rembrandt, or an interior by any one of the Flemish painters.'[17]

Everything in the house in Drumkilly was neat and tidy and in its place, though full of odds and ends, the knick-knacks of the Victorian age. The lamp hung on one nail and was never moved. The key to the school, the keys of the farm and the saltbox all had their own nails. In the parlour hung two large pictures, one of Fr Thomas Burke, the nineteenth-century Dominican preacher, the other of a young girl holding an apple. The latter helped to give 'life and colour to the green-distempered, rather dyspeptic walls'.[18] There was a hand mirror and a couple of photograph frames encrusted with seashells. The japanned mantelpiece had two Egyptian heads, 'which gave it an exotic appearance and interest'. On top of the mantelpiece were a couple of vases containing artificial flowers made of wire and coloured paper. McCabe wrote that 'a poor woman, half-tramp, who lived in a broken-down, mud-wall house, rented from a Protestant'[19] had made them. On the parlour window was a row of geraniums sitting in china pots. The earth in the pots was covered under a bed of moss and seashells: 'The moss reminded one of that silly proverb about the rolling stone. It's a good thing for stones to roll and accumulate no moss. As this proverb suggests that people should remain in a rut, or embedded in the earth, and not roll about the world, it can have a pernicious effect. Some of these proverbs – like some of our Irish songs – might have been invented by our worst enemies.'[20]

McCabe would clap the seashells to his ear and hear the 'distant roar of the Irish Sea, or the wild Atlantic Ocean'.[21] One of the bedrooms upstairs contained a depiction of Christ, the Virgin Mary and St John, another of the Crucifixion, a scroll entitled 'What Is Home Without A Mother?', and a bust used to illustrate that pseudo-science phrenology.

The house was full of books on all manner of subjects. The family bible weighed a stone, with the names and dates of birth of all the children entered on the flyleaf. There were two separate editions of Tennyson's poems, one bound in ivory with brass edges, a collection of Pope's poems, 'cheap' editions of Longfellow and Byron, and Ben Jonson's and Shakespeare's complete works. Lew Wallace's *Ben-Hur* was a favourite, as was Dickens's *Dombey and Son*, the first novel read by the young Alex. Alongside the prose and poetry were volumes on agriculture, hygiene, logic, chemistry, hydraulics, electricity and the steam engine, an indication of James McCabe's voracious appetite for self-improvement and education. The house contained a couple of encyclopedias, one of which contained illustrations. The young Alex would pore over the drawings of artillery, comparing them with the guns he had read about in reports from the Balkan Wars, which were rumbling on in the background when he was reaching adolescence. This love of learning and reading in the McCabe household instilled in Alex a lifelong intellectual curiosity.

There were always visitors in the house, though James McCabe was not fond of entertaining and would sit in the corner reading the paper when the neighbours came to hear news or to have a chat, presumably with Katie. He would get up, however, to write or read a letter for them, prepare a will, mend a clock or engrave a coffin breastplate. He also helped his neighbours with applications to purchase their farms, as the ownership of the land throughout Ireland passed from absentee landlord to tenant under the British government's land acts of the late nineteenth and early twentieth century.

Alex received his first schooling from his father in Drumkilly's small national school, a whitewashed rectangular building with porches projecting at right angles. The inside was drab and bare but for a few charts and cards hanging on the wall. Some faded green curtains covered the windows. 'Everything was in its place like the slates in their slots in the top of the desk, but the arrangements were too fixed and rigid'.[22] A card hung on one of the classroom walls with 'Secular Instruction' printed in black letters on one side and 'Religious Instruction' on the other. When catechism class started, McCabe's father would turn the card around so that 'Religious Instruction' was facing out. This was the signal for the Protestant boys to leave the classroom and stand in the porch or yard, depending on the weather and time of year. This formula was laid down in the rules and regulations that governed the British national school system in Ireland. Another was the reading of a lesson containing articles about Christian charity and religious tolerance. This was read to all the boys but did not have much effect, as evidenced on the day a Protestant boy and a Catholic boy had a fight over Home Rule. There was a chart on the wall with the Ten Commandments. McCabe recalled:

> The first Commandment was given in full, and as it sounded unusual, I had some impression that it was the Protestant version, and not the Catholic one we were learning in the Catechism. … When they were out in the porch or yard, the Protestant boys spent the time preparing their lessons. That gave them an advantage over us, but they lost the mental training that we had in the Catechism class.'[23]

It was in his schoolbooks that McCabe first came across Spain, the history and romance, and the names of the rivers – Douro, Guadiana and 'the rushing Guadalquivir' – which sounded poetic to his young ears: 'They seemed to flow across Spain like arrows of song.'[24]

Life at home was strict and the sense of release at escaping through the iron gate at the end of the garden foreshadowed McCabe's later thirst for travel. His peregrinations through the district earned him the nickname 'the Rover'. However, his world still comprised only a few acres of rolling Cavan countryside. Outside of important events, such as fairs or wakes, McCabe and his friends had plenty to amuse them. They played football with a ball made from a stocking or handkerchief stuffed with grass. Occasionally, when a neighbour killed a pig, they would endeavour to get their hands on the bladder. When inflated, this lasted for about an evening. It was not until 1914 that leather footballs went on sale locally. Other pastimes included robbing bees' nests, gathering blackberries, nettles and dandelions, hunting rabbits and hares, and fishing for eels, perch, roach, pike and trout.

During the summer, the McCabe children would help out at their aunt's, making the hay. On one occasion, they were taking a rest from work and comparing the muscles of their arms with one of the servants. 'He had bigger biceps, of course, and we resented it. He used to maintain that his skin was whiter than ours. We resented this still more, because he was a middle-aged man, and, worse still, a servant.'[25] This curious episode, as described by McCabe when he was a young curate some twenty years later, is a telling indication of the family's sense of itself in the social hierarchy.[*]

Farm work and housework in the early 1900s were still carried out using the old methods. There were no threshing machines, and farm implements were lent from house to house. According to McCabe, the houses themselves had 'a bleak, drab, colourless air', and if a house looked 'neat, snug, sheltered and comfortable',[26] it was presumed a Protestant lived there. Inside was the same; furniture was kept to a minimum. Nothing new was bought except for the occasional stool or chair, scythe or reaping hook. One modern invention was the mowing machine, the rattle of which, according to McCabe, was both dynamic and poetic. Four decades later, thousands of miles away in Spain, McCabe wrote:

> the machine was very destructive of an older poetic element – the corn-crake. As the machine went round and round, closing in on the centre, the corn-crake, hidden in the grass, kept running around and away from it. As the blade, like a pair of huge scissors, snipped off the last thin swath, it cut the poor corncrake to pieces. When it was discovered that the corncrake was in danger of disappearing, the men with a poetic heart used to get down off the seat, and beat the crakes out of the grass …[27]

Emigration and superstition hung like a pall over the district. There were few marriages and fewer children. The remains of mud-walled houses

---

[*] In contrast with the current Western preoccupation with tanning, in the early twentieth century those with tans were looked down upon, since they spent their lives outdoors, engaging in manual labour.

were scattered across the landscape. Local people believed them to be haunted – 'the whole district reeked of ghosts'. 'The next townland was very Protestant, and so it was very thickly populated with ghosts. But, being Protestant, they were ghosts of a blacker type and dye, and intimately associated with the Devil or Satan.'[28] The banshee was a frequent visitor and McCabe recalled seeing her coming along the river on the way to a dying woman's house. His description of this event is strangely vivid, a mixture of half-belief and scepticism:

> It was the first and last time I saw the Banshee. She was a poetic creation, sprung from the landscape and the imagination. I never met her outside Ireland. Once or twice I searched for her in a dense blackish-yellow London fog, but she wasn't there. It's difficult to believe in Ghosts. At the same time, it is impossible to rid the imagination of this vast, unseen, invisible, still-surviving World of the Dead.[29]

Then there were the fairies. It was deemed unlucky to plough a fairy fort or to cut down a tree or bush growing beside one. Local legend had it that one man who cut a circle of trees that were growing in a fort on his land had died of consumption shortly afterwards. Another time, a relative of McCabe's told him that there had been an illness in the family and that no one was able to attend to the oat harvest. The family was in danger of losing the crop when, one morning, he had gone outside and found the oats cut and stacked. He had put this down to the intervention of the fairies. In fact, it had been his neighbours who had pitched in to help out. Nevertheless, the relative stuck to his belief that it was the fairies.

There was a general fear of mental illness and people believed that some type of inner demon took possession of epileptics. This was thought to be confirmed by the fact that one of the two cases of epilepsy – described locally as 'falling sickness' – in the district had an attack on the way back from mass, while the other had fits two or three times in the chapel, just at the consecration.

Another local woman was branded a witch. Not only was she a Protestant, her name was Eliza, 'which sounded rare and queer'. According to McCabe:

She was a poor, wild-eyed creature, who always stalked about alone, very threadbare, and though she never spoke to anybody, she was always muttering to herself. And she never seemed to be going anywhere, but always walked at random, without any fixed aim or direction. She was quite harmless, but she inspired a certain degree of terror, because, horrible to relate, she could transform herself into a hare, and used to suck cows.[30]

Physical illnesses and diseases were a scourge. Tuberculosis, typhoid and scarlet fever all took their toll. 'When the "fever coach" came into a district to take a victim away to the Fever Hospital (then in the Workhouse), every family felt the same sense of gloom, as if a hearse had drawn up at their own door. The "fever", especially, was a vivid, black palpable presence all around.'[31]

Childbirth too was dangerous. McCabe recalled the story of a lively girl who had been working as a servant in the house of one of his relations when a tramp had called to the door. She was unmarried and was 'near the spinster milestone and stage'. As she poured a plate of meal into the tramp's bag, she said laughingly, 'I hope that will bring me luck, and that you'll find a good man for me.'[32] She did marry but died alongside her first stillborn child. McCabe's memory of the child's burial haunted him for years:

They buried it at night, and on the way past, called at our house. They took me down with them to hold the lantern. The baby was in a little wooden box of plain timber, and painted. As it hadn't been baptised, it was buried apart, outside the consecrated ground. Two men dug the little grave, while I held the lantern. It was a dark wintry night, and the scene and experience were very gloomy. The men worked in silence, and I had a creepy feeling about the box. I was wondering if this was really a little baby, or if it were only a little animal.[33]

This type of arrangement, where the body was disposed of in a stealthy fashion owing to some crippling stigma, was common. On another occasion, looking out over the graveyard from his bedroom window just as night was beginning to fall, the young McCabe watched a hearse arrive. It was the corpse of a woman who had spent years in a lunatic asylum. She was being buried 'almost secretly' because of the fact that she had 'lost her mind – a social disgrace for the family'. The fresh mound of earth on her grave was 'like a finger-post pointing sharply and directly "To Death", which seemed to be just round the corner'.[34]

But not all was gloomy in Drumkilly. Before 1906, organised entertainment came in the form of social functions, mostly bazaars. These would take place in the school and featured roulette, dice and the wheel of fortune. The stage was a temporary construction consisting of planks laid on big empty barrels. In 1906, the parish hall was built and became the venue for concerts and plays. People from miles around would come to Drumkilly for entertainment because the hall was the only one of its kind in four parishes. The McCabe household served as a cloakroom, dressing room and hotel during these occasions. The 'artistes' and distinguished guests would sit in the front rows. Some of the men wore evening dress or butterfly ties, 'which gave them an "arty" appearance'.[35] The schoolchildren would be dressed all in white. 'The songs were Anglo-Irish, though a good many were English, sentimental and Victorian or Music-hall hits'.[36] There were also piano solos, recitations, step-dancing, ventriloquism, acrobatics and drama. 'One man, a publican and farmer, was only an amateur, but he was a real artist, and his little son, in top hat and swallow-tail coat, swinging his cane, was a "star turn", and used to bring down the house'.[37] All the local clergy attended and sat in pride of place. Some even performed.

One of the most memorable events in McCabe's childhood was when the first moving picture was shown in Drumkilly in 1906. Such was the curiosity that the parish hall was packed to the rafters and the audience struggled to get in through the door and even the windows. The projectionist, from Belfast, drove up the road on a jaunting car from Cavan town and he was regarded as 'a sort of Magician'. Because the key of the parish hall was kept at the McCabes' house, Alex and his siblings felt they had 'proprietary rights'.[38] Alongside the excitement, there was also a distrust of the new technology and parents were advised beforehand not to allow the children to view the film in case they should suffer some form of nervous shock. In 1948, McCabe recalled the scene as the projectionist set up his equipment in advance of the evening showing:

He was an ordinary chap enough, smart, efficient, clean-shaven, and he wore a light overcoat. He took his boxes into the Hall, opened them, and took out the magic contents. He knew where to find things, and he handled them carefully, but with a certain degree of familiarity, and no trace of reverence. He got a couple of coal or bacon-boxes, planted his machine on it, tilted it up at the proper angle, put on something like a black tape-measure – the reel, presumably – fiddled with knobs and things, and threw a few scenes on the white magic screen on the stage.[39]

That night, during the actual performance, a couple of young people fainted and had to be carried out of the hall while watching the image of a huge horse galloping towards the camera.

Life in Drumkilly was governed by social rules and those who transgressed were punished. The priest was the most important man in the townland, and Alex began his day observing the parochial house. He would watch for movement of the blind in the priest's bedroom window so that he knew when he should go down to the church to serve early morning mass as an altar boy. The priest was feared as much as respected, and grown men would shove the pipe they were smoking into their pocket if he approached along the road. 'Protestants, too, observed the same mark of respect, and most Catholics stopped smoking when a Protestant Minister was going past,' McCabe recalled. It was the advent of the car that changed this custom, he wrote, because 'there wasn't time to see who was inside, and people went along the road and smoked more freely'.[40] Yet men still felt uncomfortable smoking in front of the priest, even if he gave them permission to do so. Most women never smoked in public. 'One night, during a Concert, a girl who had taken part was seen by the lynx-eyed smoking a cigarette between the wings,' wrote McCabe. 'She was regarded as a hussy, and a real wench, and ruined her reputation and character for ever.' Still, the anonymous girl's brazen behaviour did not put off everyone, since she 'managed to make a good marriage within a year, which rehabilitated her'.[41] Passing through London and Dublin in 1945 on the way home from Spain, McCabe noticed that 'girls, middle-aged women, and women in [sic] grey hair, walked out of shops and offices, or travelled on buses and trams, puffing their cigarette'.[42] This strange new custom – females smoking in public – was evidence of the liberating effect of wartime conditions on women.

Political agitation was a feature throughout McCabe's childhood. Not only was a great social and economic change occurring with the passing of the British government's land acts, the political situation was tense with the expectation that Ireland would be granted Home Rule. Once, on a cold, frosty winter night, the young McCabe could hear a 'weird, moaning, menacing sound', similar to the booing of a crowd at an eviction or Home Rule meeting. People were blowing bottle-horns to express their hostility to an ex-RIC man who had bought a farm in the neighbourhood. On another occasion, the Protestant owner of a small cottage in the district evicted his Catholic tenant, a carpenter. The United Irish League ordered a boycott. Neighbours did not greet the boycotted man and the shopkeeper did not sell him supplies. Writing in his early thirties and showing an independence of mind perhaps uncommon among the Irish clergy, McCabe described the boycott, as a means of vindicating justice, as 'rather un-Christian and inhuman'.[43]

As was usual at the time, a meeting was held to protest against the eviction, with bands and speeches, banners and flags. For young and old, these lively occasions were brief flashes of colour in otherwise hard, difficult lives. Alex was sick in bed at the time of the aforementioned meeting, but his younger brother, James Charles, managed to steal away from home to witness the pomp and pageantry.

The evicted carpenter's neighbours had built him a temporary wooden hut in which to live and a group of boys were playing football with some of the blocks of wood that were left behind. James Charles was looking in the other direction when a wedge of wood came spinning through the air, hitting him squarely on the forehead. He lost consciousness and a lot of blood and had to be carried home by a couple of RIC constables and a sergeant. The doctor, who was called to the house to stitch the wound, said that he could see the exposed white bone of the skull. James Charles was never the same again, and when he caught influenza a few years later he lost his memory. He died in 1941, and McCabe visited him in the Monaghan county home shortly before his death. James Charles predeceased his father by five months and was the first person to be buried in the 'new' cemetery.

The relationship between Catholic and Protestants in the district 'could never be cordial, but they were correct', according to McCabe.[44] Religious prescripts governed certain formalities, such as attendance at funerals. Neither Catholics nor Protestants entered each other's churches, but would attend at the graveyard. There was as much suspicion as respect between the two religious communities, and the folk memories of pre-Famine sectarian riots between local Orangemen and Ribbonmen survived. A plaque in the Catholic chapel in Drumkilly recalls a curate who was murdered in 1825. Fr Patrick O'Reilly was active in collecting subscriptions for O'Connell's campaign for Catholic Emancipation. 'Great was his Zeal in improving this House of God,' reads the inscription; 'his efforts to rescue his Country from degradation induces a belief that he suffered death by violent hands'.

The Catholic attitude towards Protestants was a mixture of fear and ignorance. 'Some of the Protestants were "white men", but some were really very bigoted, and "black",' McCabe recalled, adding sarcastically that the typical Protestant's sandy "Scotch" appearance, and his hump, helped the notion.'[45] McCabe believed that 'ignorant, fanatic, uncouth, anti-social elements on both sides'[46] were to blame for embittering relations between Catholics and Protestants. He recalled an occasion when a Protestant had died and a Catholic servant boy was about to drop down to say a prayer beside the corpse, only to be given a kick by his Catholic neighbour for daring to pray for a 'dirty Protestant'. McCabe noted that the neighbour doing the kicking was not 'an example of piety, but his doctrine was perfectly sound'.[47] It was also deemed heretical by Catholics to say 'Lord, have mercy on him' when a Protestant died. But McCabe also believed that the wealthy Protestants, 'with their "Ascendancy" notions, and superior social contempt for Catholics, did a lot to poison good relations'.[48]

Political sympathies, of course, ran along religious lines. In the autumn of 1912, the Catholics of the district looked on as local Protestant men and their sons left for Belfast to sign the Ulster Covenant against the introduction of Home Rule. Two years later, bonfires were lit on the tops of hills when it looked as if the Third Home Rule Bill would become law, only for it to be shelved upon the outbreak of the First World War. With both Catholics and Protestants serving in Flanders and the Dardanelles, there was, for a brief moment, common cause between the religions, and the recruiting sergeant was not long in arriving in the district. One young Protestant officer developed shell shock at the front and would wander the district at night raving. Another local man – an ex-soldier who had served in India and was known as John the Point because his family had lived on a dry spit of land in the middle of a marsh – rejoined his old regiment in Portsmouth. John the Point had joined the Irish Volunteers in 1913 and been appointed instructor and drill master because of his military experience. He used to march the volunteers up and down the roads around Drumkilly and give instruction in the parish hall on how to use the few old Italian rifles the unit had in its possession. After first leaving for the war, he had written a few letters to his mother. The McCabes used to read them to her because she was illiterate, but then there was silence and John the Point was never heard from again. Nobody in the parish knew what became of him. McCabe described him as 'a type of the old Irish private in the English Army, in the days when on the maps at school the British Empire was coloured red, when English Dreadnoughts ruled the Seas, and England ruled the World'.[49]

McCabe eagerly followed the events of the war during its first year, and noted that 'it was felt that the Irish Regiments' men were always sent in front to do the dirty work', and that they were employed merely as 'cannon fodder', and got no credit for it. On the other hand, the dreadnought battleships 'appealed to the imagination' and it was felt that Irish security depended on the Royal Navy to prevent a German invasion. The Great War 'created a whole lot of intimate contradictions in the Irish spirit that seem to be inseparable from all Anglo-Irish relations'.[50] And as well as a religious divide in attitudes towards the British armed forces, there was a class element, since 'farmers' sons didn't regard the soldiers' garb or trade as "respectable"'.[51] In other words, it was mostly those Catholic Irishmen with no economic alternative who were forced to join up. Respect for the British army increased when the roll of honour began to be published daily in the newspapers: 'Hundreds of officers from the best English families were fighting and dying for England, and for France and Belgium, too.'[52] These attitudes were soon to change.

The economy of south Cavan benefited from the outbreak of war. In response to the increased demand for linen to make aeroplane wings, many farmers began to cultivate flax again, for which there was a guaranteed price of £60 a ton. But since flax takes a heavy burden on the soil, the result was that the land became sterile for three years. Many years after the war, McCabe could remember the stink of the flax as it lay steeping in the drains. Another downside was the lack of good whiskey. Before the war, whiskey had to be kept in bond for seven years to ripen or mature, but gradually the stocks were exhausted and the period was reduced, leading to a cruder variety of spirit.

McCabe entered St Patrick's College in Cavan town in 1915, with a view to studying for the priesthood. St Patrick's had evolved out of the smaller St Augustine's Seminary, or Kilmore Academy as it was known locally, a diocesan school for Catholic boys which had opened in 1839. Ten years after the British government had passed the Roman Catholic Relief Act, the opening of the Kilmore Academy was evidence in bricks and mortar of the Irish Catholic Church's determination to provide for the educational needs of the diocese. In the 1860s, with student numbers increasing, the bishop of Kilmore decided to build a new college, which would serve as both a minor and a major seminary. Students could complete their course of study for the priesthood at St Patrick's or go on to another seminary. St Patrick's College, designed by the noted Gothic revivalist architect William Hague, opened in 1874. There was accommodation for 100 students in sixty single rooms and three dormitories. As well as student accommodation, classrooms, study hall, chapel refectory and kitchen, there was a dairy and a bakery. The staff at St Patrick's College included a cook, a house steward, a dairymaid, housemaid, matron, houseboys, a gasman and a baker. By 1915, it had ceased to exist as a major seminary and was taking in day students.[53]

Life in St Patrick's was tough. Discipline was enforced through corporal punishment and there was little sympathy for students experiencing homesickness. The future archbishop of Dublin, John Charles McQuaid, who left St Patrick's in 1910, confessed to being miserable during his time in the college.[54] McCabe did not seem to have been unduly unhappy, though he longed to get out into the world and felt constrained during the four years he spent in St Patrick's. Perhaps he recognised this period as the first step on the road to independence. He was certainly cut off from Drumkilly. In his diaries, he wrote that he and his fellow students knew little of what was happening on the front lines during the last three years of the war, and it was a week after they were over that they heard about the events of Easter 1916. They did, however, get caught up in the growing nationalist ferment.

Writing in the 1940s, McCabe characterised political and cultural attitudes in the years before the First World War as essentially Victorian. He wrote that there was 'a genuine respect for the Throne, or at least, a personal respect for Victoria and Edward the Seventh'.[55] The executions of the leaders of the 1916 Rising and the vigorous opposition to the British government's attempt to extend conscription to Ireland in 1918 changed all that. In June 1918, at the height of the Conscription Crisis, Arthur Griffith, the Sinn Féin candidate, beat the Irish Parliamentary Party candidate, John F. O'Hanlon, in the East Cavan by-election. The young McCabe found himself getting into arguments with some of his peers who believed that the son of a teacher could not be anything but a 'West Briton'. Yet he was well able to defend himself, once giving a classmate a black eye during a 'stand-up fight'.[56]

The growing nationalist feeling was mirrored in St Patrick's. The boys would sing *The Soldier's Song*, *The Foggy Dew*, *Wrap The Green Flag Around Me Boys* and *A Nation Once Again* and practised céilí dancing on wet days. This contrasted with the English songs that had been popular before the war.

The most tangible expression of this new nationalist sentiment was the creation of a Volunteer unit. Wearing caps made of cardboard and carrying dummy rifles or hurleys, the students drilled and marched around the walks of the college. A picture of the College Volunteers taken in 1918 shows the seventeen-year-old McCabe – before his political convictions were fully coherent – wearing his cap cocked at a jaunty angle and holding a dummy rifle. The formation of football, hurling and handball teams at St Patrick's reflected the Gaelic cultural revival.

In 1918, McCabe obtained passes in English, Greek, Latin, Irish, Arithmetic with Algebra, Geometry and Mechanics in his Intermediate Certificate, the equivalent of today's Leaving Certificate. The following year he passed the Matriculation Examination of the National University of Ireland in Latin, Greek, Irish, English and Mathematics. As was common for the elder sons of the burgeoning Irish Catholic middle class, however, it had been decided that McCabe would study for the priesthood. He had contemplated joining the Dominicans at one stage, but he was encouraged to take one of the scholarship places at the Irish College in Salamanca.

The idea of seeing foreign fields appealed to McCabe – 'how I longed to get on a boat'[57] – and Salamanca represented a chance to escape. In an essay about his schooldays, John McGahern wrote that in the late 1940s, when a relieving kick from defence was made by his local football team, the spectators on the sidelines would shout 'Salamanca!' For McGahern, the word 'Salamanca' stood 'as a symbol of the outer limits of the North Roscommon imagination, which is no mean leap'.[58] The same must have been equally true for McCabe in south Cavan in 1919.

In the autumn of that year, McCabe passed the Irish College's entrance examination, which was held in Holy Cross College on the Clonliffe Road in Dublin. While anxious to see the world, the young clerical student still found it difficult to leave the familiar landscape of home. The night before he was due to travel to Dublin to catch the mail boat, he walked across the road to the school in Drumkilly and stood at the gate: 'One felt that he was part of it, and that the gate and the piers and oneself were being pulled down, then up and dragged away.'[59]

McCabe travelled to Spain via London and Paris with two other students bound for Salamanca, McGinley from Donegal and O'Donovan from west Cork. They were a naïve group, it being the first time they had left Ireland. McCabe had only twice been in Dublin, and one of those times had been to sit the Salamanca examination, yet he seemed the most adventurous of the three boys. At Westland Row Station, however, waiting for the boat train to Kingstown, McCabe 'felt a bit depressed. We were all three tired, inexperienced, and a bit helpless. None of us knew French, and we really wondered if we'd even get there.'[60]

The crossing to Holyhead was a rough start to their journey. Most of the passengers on board were seasick and the three students went below to seek shelter from the violence of the storm that had engulfed them. 'Down below, the bunks were full of soldiers,' McCabe recalled, 'and as the boat heaved from one side to another, a little avalanche of empty Porter bottles rolled and rattled across the floor, struck against the timber of the bunks, and rolled and rattled back again.'[61] Soon the three students were also throwing up.

At Holyhead, they caught the train to London. As they travelled by horse-drawn cab to Waterloo Station, where they deposited their luggage, McCabe was favourably impressed with the city. He forgot a bag of books in the cab and when he left the station, he found the driver waiting for him. 'This little act of honesty gave me an initial prejudice in favour of English character and the English people,' he wrote.[62] McCabe was sorry to be leaving London that night.

Arriving in Paris less than a year after the end of the war, McCabe noticed that 'all the people were dressed in black, and they looked sad and silent and sombre'.[63] The three young Irishmen, used only to seeing the occasional car in their rural districts at home, were shocked by the traffic. A couple of policemen holding white batons stopped the cars as they crossed the road by the Quai d'Orsay railway station. 'For some reason, or, perhaps, without any, we concluded that the occupants were Germans,' McCabe recalled.[64]

On the train to Irún, they shared a carriage with a Spanish woman, a French man and a group of Belgians on their way to the Congo. 'At first, we took if for granted that nobody spoke English except ourselves … and cracked jokes at their expense,' McCabe wrote later. 'We felt pretty ashamed afterwards, when the Frenchman made some remark in perfect English, and when the Spanish lady, in perfect English also, explained who she was. After that, we spoke in Gaelic and confounded the lot of them.'[65] The train was late arriving in Irún and the three students were tired. 'With all the foreigners around,' McCabe added, 'I didn't sleep a wink. It seemed to be a bit risky.'[66]

They arrived in Spain to blazing sunshine, 'peculiarly white, such as we had never seen before'. The country seemed 'alien' and 'exotic' and 'the ox-carts trudging and rumbling along the streets were very novel and picturesque'.[67] The town smelled of wine, though McCabe did not sample any, having taken the Pioneer pledge to abstain from alcohol.

The last stage of their journey took them from Irún to Salamanca. When they arrived at the station, they took a horse-drawn coach into the *plaza mayor*. McCabe had 'such exaggerated notions of the size of the College that I thought we had arrived, not in the centre of town, but in the middle of the College Square'. Finally, they arrived at the Irish College and the porter showed McCabe up to his 'bare, dark' room.

As McCabe remembered it, 'the journey – and life itself – had come to an end'. Later on, when McCabe and his travelling companions started classes, and saw 'the unshaven professors, and students wearing green mouldy soutanes, it struck us that this was this most antediluvian place in the world'.[68]

# Chapter 2

# THE SALAMANCA STUDENT

The city of Salamanca stands high on the *meseta*, the plateau that covers much of northern Spain, in the modern-day region of Castile and León. In the winter it is bitterly cold, while the summers are often unbearably hot, with little rain and frequent droughts. This part of Spain is traditionally rural and conservative, yet Salamanca has also been at the heart of the country's academic life for over 800 years; the first university in Spain – and one of the oldest in Europe – was founded in Salamanca in 1218.

Salamanca is renowned for its architecture. The city boasts some of the most beautiful examples of the Spanish plateresque style, while the eighteenth-century baroque *plaza mayor* is arguably the finest of its kind in Spain – in 1988, the historic centre of Salamanca was declared a UNESCO heritage site. Most of the finest buildings in Salamanca are built from sandstone, quarried from a site close to the nearby village of Villamayor. The stone is soft and white when it comes out of the ground but acquires a sunburnt appearance when exposed to oxygen, and in the evening sun, the city takes on a pleasant reddish hue.

The building that housed the Irish College is now owned by the University of Salamanca and is used as a residence for visiting academics and students. The Irish College or, as it was grandiloquently named upon its creation, Real Colegio de San Patricio de Nobles Irlandeses (St Patrick's Royal College for Irish Noblemen) was founded in 1592 by Fr Thomas White, at a time when the laws penalising the practice of the Catholic faith in Ireland meant that colleges for the training of Irish priests were springing up across Spain, France, Italy, the Netherlands and Belgium.

White was from a wealthy Catholic family in Clonmel, County Tipperary, which had been dispossessed of its lands in the Elizabethan expropriations of the late sixteenth century. While studying for the priesthood in Valladolid, White found that many of his fellow students from Ireland were living in abject poverty. Though there was an English college in Valladolid, the rector was not disposed to allow Irish students to live and study there. So White decided to set up a dedicated college for Irish students and petitioned the king of Spain, the Habsburg monarch Philip II, to sanction the establishment of such an institution. Philip agreed, provided that the college was in Salamanca and under the care of the Jesuits.

Aside from their basic function of training Irishmen for the priesthood, the Irish colleges in Spain – others were subsequently founded in Seville, Santiago de Compostela, Alcalá de Henares and Madrid – became a crucial ideological instrument of the Spanish monarchy during the Counter-Reformation. The monarchy's prestige was enhanced by its role as the protector of exiled Irish clergy, while its patronage of the Irish colleges and the wider Irish Church gave it great influence. For their part, the Irish were anxious to please their patrons by recognising the role of the Spanish king as the leader of the fight against the Protestant English.[1] Despite a generous royal endowment, White had also to use his own funds to open the college in Salamanca. There was a Spanish rector and an Irish vice-rector, and the Jesuits governed the Irish College until the order was expelled from Spain in 1767. Subsequently, the Irish hierarchy chose the rectors of the college from the ranks of the secular clergy. Underpinning the relationship between the Irish Church and their royal protectors in Spain was the idea that the Irish were descended from Spaniards: the Milesian myth. This idea resurfaced in Irish and Spanish propaganda during the Spanish Civil War, when the Irish Brigade under General Eoin O'Duffy went to Spain to fight on the nationalist side.

The Irish Brigade and the men who fought on the other side in the civil war, that of the republican government, were not the first Irish soldiers to come to Spain. The Gaelic lords who fled Ireland after their defeat by the English crown forces included many who settled in Spain, including Donal Cam O'Sullivan Beare, whose portrait hung for many years in the Irish College in Salamanca. Many of these exiles entered Spanish service, and Irish regiments fought for the Spanish Habsburgs in Flanders during the sixteenth and seventeenth centuries. Their descendants became officers in Spain's armed forces in the seventeenth, eighteenth and nineteenth centuries and served in Europe and the Americas.

General Leopoldo O'Donnell, the Duke of Tetuán, a descendant of the O'Donnells of Tyrconnell who defied England's Queen Elizabeth I during Ireland's Nine Years' War, became prime minister of Spain for a brief period in the middle of the nineteenth century, after making a *pronunciamento* (one of Spain's habitual bloodless coups) against the government. He earned his title for defeating Rif tribesmen at Tétouan in Morocco in 1860. His grandnephew, Juan O'Donnell, the third Duke of Tetuán and minister of war under the dictator Miguel Primo de Rivera, was a good friend of the Irish College in Salamanca. Juan's children, the fourth Duke, also Juan O'Donnell, and his sister, Blanca, who inherited her brother's title upon his death, were acquaintances of McCabe in Salamanca. They were all proud of their Irish heritage and Blanca later acted as a mediator between the nationalist authorities and the Irish Brigade.

Along with the Dominican church of San Esteban, the church of the Espíritu Santo and the Casa de las Conchas, the Irish College was one of the finest buildings in Salamanca to survive the ravages of the Napoleonic era. Behind a simple façade, the two-storeyed cloister, made up of sixty-four arches, surrounded a patio with a well at the centre, 'a poem in stone', as described by McCabe. Its grand chapel contained a reredos from 1529 and over its doorway was a relief depicting St James conquering the Moors. It was a pleasant place to find retreat from the burning Castilian sun during the high summer but provided little warmth in the freezing cold winter months. The building was begun in 1521 at the instigation of Archbishop Alonso Fonseca, a pre-eminent churchman of that era, and was originally a college for Galician students studying at the university. It was a major or constituent part of the University of Salamanca until the Spanish monarch Charles III suppressed the colleges in the eighteenth century. The Irish College moved into the building in 1820 after its previous accommodation in Salamanca had been destroyed by French troops during the Peninsular War. A decade later, the staff and students were forced to leave when the major colleges were restored. For the next ten years, the students lived in Aldearrubia, a few miles outside Salamanca, where the college then owned a summer villa. But by 1838, following a petition to the Spanish queen, supported by the British embassy, the Fonseca building was restored to the Irish College.

By the beginning of the twentieth century, the Irish College was under the trusteeship of the Irish archbishops and on the brink of closure. The repeal of the penal laws and the foundation of Maynooth College in 1795 had reduced the importance of the continental colleges. Discussing the matter with his bishop, a young priest from the Irish diocese of Achonry, Michael O'Doherty, expressed his concern at the prospect. Bishop John Lyster agreed but remarked that no one was willing to take up the position of rector, whereupon O'Doherty, then a professor in St Nathy's, the diocesan college, offered himself for the job. He was appointed in June and served as rector of the Irish College in Salamanca until he became the bishop of Zamboanga in the Philippines in 1911. Five years later, O'Doherty became archbishop of Manila, a position he held until his death in 1949.

Michael O'Doherty was credited with modernising the Irish College during his tenure as rector. A former student, Mgr Richard Glennon, described him as 'an able administrator and a determined character'.[2] He reorganised the Irish College's finances and built individual rooms for the students. Michael O'Doherty's brother, Denis, succeeded him as rector in 1912. Although he, too, had certain administrative and educational talents, he was not as popular as Michael with the students or with Salamancan society.

The Irish College enjoyed great prestige in Salamanca and Ireland, and its superiors were invited to the most important academic, civil, ecclesiastical and military functions. The king of Spain and his family made a point of visiting the college whenever they were in the city, and the ordinary citizens regarded the Irish clerical students as the symbol of an unbroken link between the city and Ireland that stretched back over three centuries. Many former students became bishops and archbishops, one even became mayor of New York City.[3] To be a 'Salamanca student' was a source of undoubted pride.

Before the establishment of an Irish legation in Spain, the Irish College acted as an unofficial Irish embassy. In the early 1920s, Denis O'Doherty was in contact with diplomatic representatives of Dáil Éireann about propaganda work in Spain, including Seán T. O'Kelly and George Gavan Duffy – in Paris since the 1919 peace conference to seek recognition of a sovereign Ireland – the London-based Art O'Brien and Robert Brennan.[4]

At the end of 1921, O'Doherty put Brennan in touch with the Duke of Tetuán. Brennan was organising the Irish Race Convention in Paris, which was to take place the following January. At a meeting in Madrid, he asked the duke to preside at the convention. Though Tetuán told Brennan that it would be impossible to preside at the convention without the permission of the Spanish government, he promised that he would attend in a personal capacity. Brennan wrote to O'Doherty that he was left with 'no doubt in my mind as to his pride in the [Irish] race and in the fight we are making. The interview lasted over an hour and he was keen on hearing details regarding the struggle etc.'[5] The Irish Race Convention took place in January 1922 with both Tetuán and O'Doherty in attendance. The split over the Anglo-Irish Treaty dominated proceedings and was reflected in the composition of the Irish delegation. There was little communication between the anti-Treaty nominees, led by Éamon de Valera, and the pro-Treaty side, led by Eoin MacNeill.

In February 1922, Gavan Duffy, the newly appointed minister for foreign affairs in the provisional government, wrote to O'Doherty asking him to help the new envoy to Madrid, Osmond Grattan Esmonde. 'I know that I can always count upon your good help, although I do not suppose you can do much for the new delegate until he learns the language,' wrote Gavan Duffy. 'We are very hard put to it to find adequate linguists for the different countries'.[6]

O'Doherty was not known for his diplomatic skills and was given to delivering himself of lectures in Salamanca about the iniquities of the English. He came close to provoking a diplomatic incident in June 1921 when he refused to see the British ambassador, Esmé Howard. The diplomat, a member of the British delegation to the Paris Peace Conference, had turned up at the door of the Irish College to pay a courtesy call but O'Doherty had refused to meet him. O'Doherty sent Howard a note telling him that he could not receive a representative of a government whose conduct had earned the contempt of global world opinion, to which Howard had replied that he regretted the fact that the rector 'should close his doors on a fellow Catholic'. Howard wrote to the British Foreign Secretary, Earl Curzon, about the incident and outlined what he thought were the three ways he could have dealt with O'Doherty's note:

firstly, to ignore it altogether, secondly, to reply in a controversial tone, and thirdly, to give the reverend gentleman a lesson in common politeness in which it appeared to me (I trust without presumption or rash judgement on my part) he was somewhat lacking. I chose the third course ...[7]

The celebrated Basque philosopher and writer, and erstwhile rector of the University of Salamanca, Miguel de Unamuno, told Howard that 'the moving passion of the Rector [of the Irish College] appeared to be the hatred of everything English' but that 'outside some clerical circles, he exercised very little [influence]'.[8]

The Irish students were normally aged eighteen or nineteen when they arrived in Salamanca to begin their six-year course. They studied philosophy and theology in the diocesan seminary alongside their Spanish peers, and since the classes were in Latin – and there was a difference in the Castilian and Irish pronunciation – it was often difficult for the Irish students to understand the lecturers. Classes in sacred liturgy, pastoral theology, sacred eloquence, church music, declamation, English, Irish, French and a supplemental class in moral theology were taught by the rector and vice-rector, and the students also learnt Spanish – mostly to help them understand their Spanish lecturers' pronunciation. The Irish clerical students were a familiar sight in Salamanca as they walked through the city's narrow streets from the college, past the Casa de las Conchas, with its famous façade covered in stone shells, towards the Clerecía – the former headquarters of the Jesuits in Salamanca, which was home to the diocesan seminary. They were instantly recognisable by the violet shamrocks sewn onto their soutanes above their hearts.

The Irish students found it hard to adjust to life in Spain. Problems with the language, the diet and the climate all contributed towards a feeling of homesickness. They were also subjected to the moods of the irascible rector, whose difficult personality was to provoke occasional outbreaks of revolution. Denis O'Doherty tended to take umbrage easily and he was obsessed with discipline, keeping detailed notes on the failings of the students. Trivial misdemeanours, such as smoking, failing to sweep one's room or talking after lights out, tended to take on a disproportionate significance. This made for a tense atmosphere between students and rector, which was not helped by the fact that O'Doherty routinely opened the students' letters and jotted down in his notebooks the most egregious passages.

Nineteen-year-old Alex McCabe arrived in Salamanca in the autumn of 1919. In Paris, the Great Powers were thrashing out the future of Europe, while in Ireland the IRA was carrying out sporadic attacks on RIC men and raids for arms on police barracks. Spain was also going through a period of considerable change. In 1898, the Spanish military had experienced a humiliating defeat at the hands of the United States, which had led to the loss of Cuba and the Philippines. This in turn had led to malaise at home. In July 1909, during the *Semana Trágica* (Tragic Week) in Barcelona, the army and the workers – most of them members of anarchist and socialist trade unions – had faced each other in a series of violent confrontations, precipitated by the conservative prime minister Antonio Maura calling up reservists to serve in Spanish Morocco in its colonial war against local Berber tribes. The workers responded by calling a general strike. Over 100 people were killed as soldiers fired on demonstrators, and anti-clerical sentiment led to religious buildings being attacked and set on fire.

The First World War had brought something of a respite to the country's ills, as demand for Spanish exports soared, but the postwar slump heightened social unrest. In 1921, Berber tribesman from the Rif region of Morocco, led by Abd el-Krim, defeated the Spanish army at the Battle of Annual, in which thousands of colonial troops were killed. It was a demoralising loss for the country and led to a political crisis as the Berbers advanced through Spanish-held territory with little or no opposition. King Alfonso XIII was widely blamed for the disaster and deputies in the Cortes (the Spanish parliament) criticised the army. The Spanish monarch was said to have gone behind the back of his minister for war and encouraged the commander-in-chief to launch an attack so that he could announce a victory on the feast of St James.* But the king was to hang on, when the army, resentful of criticism, overthrew the parliament. In 1923, Miguel Primo de Rivera, the captain-general of

---

* The patron saint of Spain is often depicted in paintings and sculptures in the country's churches beheading Moors on the battlefield in his incarnation as Santiago Matamoros or Saint James the Moor-slayer.

Catalonia, who had led the coup, became dictator. A humorous, hard-living character, who enjoyed drinking and womanising, Primo de Rivera kept odd hours, spending much of the night carousing and rising late, yet he was initially successful, spending money on public works and bringing an end to the colonial wars in Morocco.

Life in Salamanca still moved to the rhythms of the nineteenth century. Some streets were cobbled with flint but others were little more than mud tracks. Mule-drawn *domicilios*, or 'house-to-house' four-wheeled coaches, ferried passengers around the city. McCabe remembered them 'tearing along at full gallop, as if they had taken fright at something and were running away. They used to fly around corners at breakneck speed, and it was a marvel how the whole apparatus of mules and coach would double round a right-angled corner, to get from one narrow street into another.'[9] Unlike his fellow students, McCabe picked up the rudiments of Spanish quickly, and soon grew to master the language. He was a careful – if prejudiced – student of the country's habits and traditions and must have found Salamanca an intriguing place, even if he was initially disappointed by the Irish College's frugal comforts and his musty companions.

Miguel de Unamuno was among the city's best-known residents and perhaps the country's most famous writer and intellectual. He was a philosopher, poet, playwright, essayist and novelist, and a distinguished academic, though his political views often got him into trouble with the authorities. He had been a strident opponent of the monarchy in the nineteenth century before softening his views in the early part of the twentieth. Appointed rector of the University of Salamanca in 1901, he had been relieved of his duties in 1914 for espousing the Allied cause in the war. In the early 1920s, when McCabe was a student, Unamuno would greet the Irish seminarians on the street. In 1924, Primo de Rivera forced Unamuno into exile in the Canary Islands for his harsh criticism of the regime. In 1930, after Primo fell from power and on the eve of the Second Republic, Unamuno was welcomed back to Salamanca and became university rector again. Critical of the Second Republic, he initially welcomed the attempt to overthrow it in July 1936 but quickly changed his mind after witnessing Franco's repression in the rearguard and was publicly critical of the nationalists in a famous incident in October 1936, shortly before his death.

When McCabe arrived in Salamanca, Unamuno was to be seen at his regular spot in the famous Café Novelty in the *plaza mayor*. Founded in 1905, the Novelty was a Salamancan institution. Customers entered the round salon, with its coloured glass ceiling, through a revolving brass door. In the early 1920s there was also a restaurant, a dance pavilion and a billiards room. One night, the Spanish monarch King Alfonso XIII ate there incognito in a private dining room. Politics divided the clientele of the Novelty, who would while away hours enjoying their *tertulia* – the daily discussion of arts and current affairs beloved of the educated Spanish male. Academics, lawyers, doctors and those of a liberal disposition sat to the left of the door as one entered. Merchants, factory owners, stockbreeders and rightists sat on the right. Unamuno sat outside on the terrace, as befitted his own ambiguous politics.

During the summers, the superiors and students of the Irish College would escape from the stifling heat of Salamanca to the seaside. From 1913, they holidayed in the north of Spain, and in 1920 the college bought a villa in the small Asturian village of Pendueles, about halfway between Gijón and Santander along the northern coast of Spain.[10] The temperate climate and proximity to the sea made it a more pleasant place to spend the summer than the Castilian plain surrounding Aldearrubia, where the Irish College had previously owned a retreat. Most of the students would have preferred to return home for the holidays, but O'Doherty insisted that they stay in Spain. They were allowed to return to Ireland for the summer only every third year.

McCabe was a capable student. In 1923, the parish priest in Crosserlough, Fr Hugh Brady, was able to report to the rector that McCabe, on a visit back home, 'gave valuable assistance at the teaching of Catechism, frequented the Sacraments and conducted himself in every way becoming an ecclesiastical student'.[11] In September 1923, the week after Primo de Rivera's military coup had overthrown the Spanish government, McCabe travelled to Santander with a fellow student to be ordained a subdeacon – then the first stage in the process of becoming a priest – in the city's cathedral. They were completing the final hours of their six-day retreat and had to remain silent and meditate as they travelled north by train. Around them the rest of the passengers were still excited by the political revolution. The two clerical students spent their last night before taking orders in a hotel in Santander, kept awake by the shouts of the customers in the café on the ground floor. The next morning, they took the 'big step' on the road to ordination. 'I was a bit nervous, and the Bishop, I remember, had as grim a face as any Spanish Inquisitor is supposed to have had.'[12] McCabe became a deacon the next year.

In 1925, McCabe was ordained a priest in the chapel of Salamanca's diocesan seminary. Upon receiving holy orders, he was given a temporary appointment in the diocese of Brentwood in England. This was a common practice at the time for priests ordained for the diocese of Kilmore, because there were not enough vocations in Brentwood and there was a surplus of ordained priests in Kilmore. London's East End was to prove a sharp contrast to sleepy Salamanca.

# Chapter 3

# THE EAST END CURATE

The diocese of Brentwood was carved out of the archdiocese of Westminster in 1917 to cater for the rapidly growing Catholic population of east London and Essex. In 1919, the first Irish-ordained priests arrived 'on loan' in Brentwood. Over the next decade, thirty-nine of the fifty-three Irish-ordained priests whose applications for a temporary position in the diocese of Brentwood were accepted during the period 1919 to 1939 came from Kilmore. Since the nature of their appointments was temporary and they were subject to recall by their own bishop at short notice, the Irish curates were shifted around the dioceses as need arose. Most of the Irish-ordained priests served in the urban parishes of east London, including the large council estates at Dagenham and Becontree where Henry Ford had built his car assembly lines and to where many Irish families had emigrated in search of work.

McCabe's first port of call was Walthamstow, but he was there only a week before he was transferred to Canning Town, a deprived part of the East End of London on the north side of the River Thames. The area had developed following the opening of the Royal Victoria Dock in 1855. Traditionally, it was home to the poorest dock workers, who were dependent on casual labour to feed themselves and their families. In November 1925, a chapel-of-ease was built at Wilberforce Street to cater for the growing Catholic population in the parish. The first two Sunday masses were attended by approximately 600 people. According to McCabe, this 'tin' church had been built to cater to the poor people who 'suffered from sort of "inferiority complex", and felt that they could not dress properly to attend St Margaret's [the parish church], which was only across the road'.[1]

There was endemic poverty amid the Victorian-era slums of Canning Town and many of the 8,000 or so Catholics who lived in the parish suffered from malnutrition and disease. McCabe was soon to become familiar with the awful effects of cancer and tuberculosis. But amid the misery and squalor, he found much to admire. In December 1925, three months after arriving in Canning Town, in a letter to O'Doherty, he wrote that 'the people are very generous, very grateful, and, for the most part, very good'. It helped that many of his parishioners were Irish and McCabe found the atmosphere of his new parish 'very congenial'. He noted:

a lot of that wretched poverty amongst Irish people over here that you might also call heroic it is so voluntary, and along with it, as often happens elsewhere, a lack of the religious spirit. But we have hundreds of people – Irish or otherwise – whose lives are models, and one feels, especially when he sees the efforts of young people in the midst of their difficulties, that it would be mean not to help them and think well of them.[2]

McCabe expressed pleasure in working among the poor people in his parish and showed a laudable tolerance for the vices to which they turned to escape their hard lives. 'I am past the stage when I can be scandalised,' he wrote. 'Perhaps I never arrived at it; so you need have no worry on that score.'[3] In comparison, he had little time for some of the more self-important middle-class Catholics.

Most of the working-class men in the parish worked on the docks, the Beckton Gas Works – then one of the largest of its kind in the world – or the sugar and chemical factories in Silvertown. On Saturday nights, they would let off steam in the local pubs, 'but there was no rowdiness, and in the streets, one rarely saw cases of extreme intoxication'.[4] The women would go to the pub to fill jugs or tankards with beer or stout for consumption at home. On Monday mornings, the pawn-shops were busy, as was the curate, who was 'on audience' for the hard-luck cases who would arrive at the door of the presbytery.

McCabe thought his parishioners were genuinely happy despite their hardships. 'Some of the people led heroic lives, and even the poorest had the spirit of sublime charity, he wrote. 'When they came to die, or were down and out, they all helped one another, no matter what church they went to – even when they didn't go to church at all.' He believed that the people, 'even the toughest types', had a great respect for the priest. 'Of course, they were all largely of Irish descent, and though they might be lapsed for a couple of generations, they still, in spite of religious indifference, retained an ancestral respect for the priest. In the two years that I spent in the East End, I was never insulted even once, not even by a young rough.'[5]

The curates in Canning Town lived together in the presbytery beside the parish church on the Barking Road. It was a busy trading area with a large Jewish community. The intersection with Beckton Road was a favourite spot for labour meetings and preachers. In 1926, during the General Strike, the road was filled with thousands of workmen. The 'terrific, terrifying mob' left a great impression on McCabe but the protests passed off relatively peacefully – although a private car was thrown over a bridge and a furniture van trying to break the strike was jostled and its occupants beaten up. 'One felt', McCabe wrote, 'that if the right man had appeared and the right word were spoken, this dense compact mass would explode like a huge bomb, and blow down half the East End.'[6] After the strike ended, the rector of the parish, Fr J.J. Deady, insisted that the curates carry out the weekly collection, despite the fact that most of the men had no work. The curates, wrote McCabe, 'were a bit ashamed and apologetic. We asked for very little, and we got less.'[7]

McCabe confessed to being 'fed up' with his superior.[8] He and his fellow curates felt Deady overworked them. This problem with authority was a weakness McCabe was never able to shake. It stemmed from a strong stubborn streak and an intellectual confidence bordering on arrogance.

McCabe's room in the presbytery overlooked the Barking Road, which was busy day and night with traffic to and from the nearby docks or the port at Tilbury, making it difficult for him to sleep and wake up in the morning. He said mass in the parish church at 6.30 every morning, then he went to say mass at the Franciscan convent on Bethell Avenue. He had his breakfast in the convent after mass, and after eating would enjoy a few of the cigarettes that were left on the table by the reverend mother every morning, together with a copy of the *Daily Mail*. He would then return to the presbytery before heading back to the convent in the afternoons to give benediction.

On Saturdays, the priests were available all day in the parish church to hear confessions, though often there were very few to be heard. But during Lent and Advent, the priests of the parish would hear confessions 'solidly' from 10 in the morning until 8 or 9 at night. Those who were not on 'stand-by' for confessions on Saturdays had to make a house-to-house 'penny collection'. On Sundays, there were five masses in the parish church, a mass and benediction at the convent, a mass at the chapel-at-ease on Wilberforce Street, as well as another house-to-house collection in the afternoon. Then, there were the rounds of visits to the sick and the elderly, baptisms, weddings and funerals.

The priests dreaded mixed marriages, though they were common, because of the added paperwork involved. After the Catholic ceremony in the church, the registrar would perform the civil ceremony in the sacristy and would invite the priest to participate. 'We young-blooded curates were inclined to object to this, and to object on principle, to take any part in the ceremony,' McCabe wrote later. 'Gradually, we learned to have a little common-sense and politeness, and to leave theological scruples in the text-books.' Many of those getting married were from extremely poor backgrounds. 'Some of the contracting partners came from filthy dens in the back-streets, but they generally managed to dress magnificently for the occasion, have a car or taxi adorned with white ribbons, and plenty of rice and confetti to scatter around at the church door after the ceremony.' They may have been dressed magnificently, but many of the non-Catholic men who turned up for the weddings were to feel the sting of McCabe's tongue if they forgot to take off their hats. 'I had great satisfaction in telling them on one or two occasions that the church isn't a cinema, and that people didn't wear their hats in church.'[9]

More awkward for the curates was the question of marriages that had not been performed in a Catholic church after the *ne temere* papal decree came into effect in 1908. *Ne temere* had been designed to legislate for clandestine marriage and invalidated Catholic marriages that had not taken place in a church. This put the priests in Canning Town in the tricky position of having to knock on the doors of those parishioners who had been married in a register office but not in a church and tell them that they were living in concubinage. Generally these were mixed couples, and more often than not it was the wife who was Catholic. It was unsurprising that the priest's visit was not received with great warmth on these occasions. 'Curiously enough, the women – who should be more devout and scrupulous – were often more obstinate and reluctant than the non-Catholic husband,' McCabe wrote. 'It was a difficult, delicate business to have to go into a home, and tell the people that their children – usually a whole nestful – were all bastards.'[10]

One thorny case was that of a man dying from tuberculosis who had been married in a Protestant church but had left his wife and was living with a woman who was caring for him. The problem was not that he had been married before, since this was an invalid marriage in the eyes of the Catholic Church, but that he thought he might have been baptised a Catholic. In which case, his having been married in a Protestant church would have contracted a censure and complicated matters. 'At the time, he was in bed, a mere coughing skeleton, dying of TB. He was anxious to be instructed, baptised and married to the woman, who was really looking after him, and was the only help he had.' In the end, having found no evidence of Catholic baptism, it was decided that he was not a Catholic. McCabe got the necessary faculties from the bishop and the marriage took place in the 'evil-smelling hole of a room, where the poor devil – and extremely nice devil – lay coughing and spitting between dirty, yellow sheets.'[11]

McCabe explored London in his free time. During his first weeks in the city he browsed the bookshops in Holborn, pottered down the Embankment and visited Westminster Abbey. He got to know most of the old churches and went on day trips to Oxford and Cambridge. He attended concerts – including one by John McCormack – art exhibitions and sporting events. In February 1927 he watched Ireland being beaten by England at Twickenham in the Five Nations Championship. In 1928, he heard G.K. Chesterton debate in Essex Hall and 'had the "cheek" and audacity to get up, not in order to say something, but to have it to say, or remember, that I had spoken in Chesterton's presence'.[12]

McCabe enjoyed his two years in Canning Town. He got on well with the other young curates in the parish and in neighbouring parishes and believed that working among the poor people of the slums 'never disappoints, disillusions, or ends in ingratitude'. 'Some young priests can't stand the shock of leaving college and coming into contact with all this rough humanity, but students should be compelled to go through this experience in order to give them a good training, and plenty of common-sense.'[13] This common sense, instilled in McCabe from an early age at home, was to remain with him for the rest of his life.

In 1927, McCabe was transferred to the neighbouring parish of Upton Park. It was not as poor as Canning Town, his duties were lighter and he found his new parish priest a more amenable sort. The church where he served, Our Lady of Compassion, stood on Green Street in the shadow of Upton Park, West Ham United's then stadium. The priests had a free pass into the ground but McCabe was able to attend only one match. It was known locally as the Boleyn Church because of its association with Henry VIII's second wife. Henry was believed to have courted Anne Boleyn in Green Street House, which stood beside the church until it was demolished in 1955.* The lands along Green Street upon which the stadium was developed originally belonged to the Catholic Church.

McCabe was not long in Upton Park: he was transferred that same year to the Essex fishing port and seaside resort of Leigh-on-Sea, overlooking the mudflats of the Thames Estuary beside Southend. His new parish priest was Francis Walter Gilbert, a scion of a wealthy Catholic family from Hampshire. Two years previously, Gilbert had built a new church and presbytery in Leigh, a fact that he was not shy of mentioning to his new curate. McCabe was soon at odds with his superior. Before a month was out, the two men had a row because McCabe had been tapping his foot on the floor unconsciously while Gilbert was preaching:

> In the end, I happened to look up, and he turned round his swollen face, and asked me, or signed to me, to stop. I told him after Mass, that I wanted to 'apologize', and that he might have waited to speak to me until he came in – because I was not going to be insulted before the congregation. I was in fighting mood, and we went into the dining-room and had some words. I told him that I did not want to be dictated to, like a school-boy, or to learn manners in a

---

* West Ham's stadium was officially known as the Boleyn Ground.

presbytery. He threatens 'to kick me out' if I don't do everything he tells me. I nearly struck him, and when I saw his half-closed Oriental eyes, protruding lips, and bulging greasy face, I wanted to put my fist through it, or to send him sprawling over the floor.[14]

This combativeness and fierce independence of mind were to be features of McCabe's relationships with his superiors throughout his life.

Despite the row, or perhaps because of it – 'after that, we understood each other, and he understood me better'[15] – McCabe enjoyed Gilbert's company, found him well-informed, active and practical. The parish priest was full of local historical lore, especially the Catholic history of Essex, though when listening to his superior's digressions, McCabe noted that Gilbert was always shy of recognising Irish names, a distinguishing mark, perhaps, of his venerable English Catholic ancestry and that caste's neurosis about being lumped together with the mere Catholic Irish.

The bracing sea air of the Essex coast was in marked contrast to the fetid conditions in London's East End slums. McCabe indulged his pleasure in walking, along the promenade, around the port, through the neat park and down the residential roads – full of middle-class homes with tidy gardens – and farther afield into the semi-rural lanes on the outskirts of Leigh and Southend, passing commuters, fishermen, sailors and housewives. Often a dense fog would lie on the river and all that could be made of the ships toing and froing from the capital were the horns booming over the marshes. Sometimes the remains of a wreck would wash ashore. When he was not on his perambulations, life was a round of masses, baptisms, catechism classes and church bazaars, enlivened by regular games of cards.

In January 1929, McCabe returned to Ireland to serve as curate in Drumlane parish, outside Belturbet in County Cavan. He was not keen about the move. Waiting for his train at Euston station in London he pondered his future, 'which has very few attractions. It may be a great privilege to get away from "pagan England" and back to "Catholic Ireland", but I wonder.'[16] Arriving back in Dublin early in the morning, he noticed 'a hard-faced chap in black felt "caubeen"* smoking a clay-

---

* Irish beret. From the Irish cáibín.

pipe, and carrying an ash-plant' driving three pigs down the centre of O'Connell Street. 'This is Ireland all right, but it makes one feel hot-faced and ashamed. When there are so many back-streets, people should not be allowed to drive pigs along O'Connell St at any hour, even in the early morning.'[17]

From Dublin, McCabe travelled directly to Cavan town to see the bishop of Kilmore, Patrick Finegan, who was pacing up and down the room when he was shown in. McCabe found the interview enervating: 'People in authority cannot expand, or be good, entertaining conversationalists. Even when they sit, they must stand on their dignity. And when they are talking, why do Bishops keep on fiddling with the Pastoral ring?'[18]

McCabe was unhappy in his new situation and quickly realised that he was not suited to pastoral work in a rural Irish parish. To make matters more difficult, his parish priest, Charles Magee, was ill and needed constant care. Much had changed since McCabe had left home and he was cynical of his countrymen's attempts to forge a new Irish Ireland:

> The Free State, with its own Customs, has broken us off from England, and deprived us of good cheap bargains. Even the extreme patriots realize and regret this. Now we have to pay dearly for the experiment in infant Irish manufacture. It's part of the price that citizens have to pay for having a Government of our own. ... I knew half-a-dozen people at home who got their blankets, serges, and curtains direct from the English factory, paid for them when they arrived, and had scarcely any need to go to the local draper, except for odds and ends. Most of the business people, therefore, had sound economic motives for backing Sinn Féin.[19]

McCabe was scornful of the 'loud patriots' who insisted on playing Irish games. He believed that 'a lot of our patriotism in Ireland is pure mercenary cant'[20] and regarded 'most of this rebel stuff as the green biliousness of frustrated cranks.'[21]

Dismissive of Ireland's native politicians, McCabe was an admirer of two leading lights of the British cabinet, Lord Birkenhead and Winston Churchill, both signatories of the 1921 Anglo-Irish Treaty. Birkenhead, a trenchant opponent of Home Rule, was 'the cleverest statesman, and one of the cleverest men in England'. McCabe admired how he tore his parliamentary opponents into 'little pieces like paper'. Churchill was 'breezier' and not so 'sarcastic and nasty' as Birkenhead, but had 'more imagination, good humour and humanity'.[22]

Despite his Anglophilia, McCabe acknowledged, nevertheless, that as a Catholic Irishman he was incapable of shaking off certain attitudes. A visit to a proud ex-British army man who had his home in Cavan decorated with 'British flags and tokens' made the 'pro-English' McCabe 'feel the difference between the Irishman and Saxon'. The imperial paraphernalia in the man's house 'seem to flaunt one in the face'.[23] Paying a visit to a sick man, he met a woman in the house called Miss Crawford. 'When I heard that she was a Protestant, I was more or less on my guard. I never had any prejudices against Protestants, but it is difficult to be at home with them, even in a social way'. As always, he wished to analyse his own sectarian thoughts and emotional reactions. 'This subtle but steel wall that divides the minds of people who profess different creeds or political principles is very curious.'[24]

Elsewhere, McCabe described relations between Catholics and Protestants in his home parish as 'excellent'. Like many of his co-religionists, he most likely did not see a contradiction in the fact that he felt uncomfortable in the company of non-Catholics. This paradoxical attitude can be found in his description of watching the Orange Order marching down the main street of Cavan town on the Twelfth of July. McCabe was in the company of some fellow priests, enjoying a drink at the bar of the Farnham Hotel when from down the main street they heard the shrill blast of the flutes and the mighty 'clud' of the malacca cane against the Lambeg drum's taut goatskin. They all assembled outside the door to watch the march go past:

They probably thought that we were scowling at them, but they should have heard some of John Heany's jokes. I'm very tolerant and as Protestants don't attend football matches, or sports of any kind, the 'Walk' is the only day's outing they have in the course of the year, and they should be allowed to have it in the Free State. And, after all, in the Siege of Derry, they defied one English King, and, at the battle of the Boyne, they beat him. Nevertheless, and trying to be as reasonable and tolerant as possible, the Orange Walk still retains something of the old spirit, brazen, truculent and defiant, and if the small boys began to fling stones at it, it shouldn't surprise the leaders and organisers. It would be a good test of the spirit of the celebration if the Free State Government insisted on them carrying a few Irish flags. Until they do this, the famous 'Walk' will always be a sectarian display.[25]

McCabe spent his free time walking or cycling around the lakes and hills of north Cavan or his home parish, taking pleasure in observing nature. These walks in the fresh air were a tonic from the daily routine of a young curate's life: the visits to the sick and the elderly, the baptisms and funerals. Yet in the familiar landscapes of his boyhood were catalysts for bouts of melancholia. Sprinkled throughout the empty countryside were the ruins of houses that had been lived in when McCabe was a boy, including that of his maternal grandmother, a short distance away in Kilderry. He wrote later: 'In some places, new and better-built houses have taken their place, but on the whole, houses disappear and the population goes on decreasing. This process of decay is due to emigration, sterility, starvation and disease, and it will result in a smaller agricultural population owning larger farms.'[26] The sight of the broken stones lying in heaps amid the overgrown grass that once was the family homestead depressed the young priest during a visit in late February 1930. His disillusionment with his native land had not deserted him later that evening, as he recalled standing on the hill overlooking a lake:

> From here, I used to see the train moving along, tiny in the distance, leaving a trail of smoke behind, and moving slowly up to Dublin, 80 miles away. It crawled past the bog, and went over the hills and far away into the great big world, and how I longed to go with it. … Now, my grandfather and grandmother are dead, my three aunts are dead, my uncle is dead, the crows' nests are dead, and the place is a ruin. Just beside them, there used to be another house, and it is still there. The old pair are alive, the three middle-aged sons are alive, the middle-aged daughter is alive, but they, too, are practically dead. There's a lot of 'dry rot' in Irish life, and all this district round about, without any children, seems to be sapless.[27]

This morbid tendency was ever present. Attending an auction of books that had belonged to deceased priests, McCabe spotted a pile that had been owned by his former parish priest, an erudite man whom he had respected and admired. They were selling for a penny or twopence apiece. For McCabe, it was akin to seeing the 'man's corpse thrown aside into some neglected corner, because one realises that Hugo's books were a substantial part of the man himself'. He added, 'If a cultured man leaves all his ideas behind him in a disorderly little heap like this, the lesson is that a man should leave something more permanent behind him than books, and take something more permanent with him.'[28]

In September 1930, McCabe went on a trip to Switzerland, Austria and Germany, which included a visit to the Bavarian town of Oberammergau to see the famous Passion Play, which he had first witnessed as a six-year-old boy on the flickering screen in the parish hall in Drumkilly. On his return, McCabe received a letter from Denis O'Doherty, asking McCabe to call on him in Dublin. The following day, McCabe travelled to the capital by train. O'Doherty told McCabe that the vice-rector was resigning and that he wished to offer him the post. McCabe was surprised and begged for time to consider. After having supper with the rector, he returned to his hotel. Walking down O'Connell Street that night, McCabe mulled over the proposition in the company of the 'white and ghostly' monuments.[29]

McCabe returned to Drumlane the next day. Though he longed to escape the watery pastures of north Cavan, he was unsure whether to accept the offer: he suspected that living with the rector would be difficult; on the other hand, there was the attraction of learning more about Spain, decent holidays with time to travel, and the opportunity to escape his current situation. It was the chance to get away, rather than the lure of Spain, that made up his mind. 'I haven't settled down in Ireland, I hate the climate, I hate Staghall,* and as I'm not a full curate, and have no house of my own, I have no roots to hold me.'[30] It bucketed down with rain the next day, which helped McCabe cast off any lingering doubts as he went down to the post office to wire the rector and to let him know that he had decided to accept his offer.

---

* The curacy where he served mass.

With his decision made, McCabe was anxious to leave for Spain. But first he had to wait for the bishop to give his assent to the appointment before it went before the archbishops, the trustees of the Irish College, at their October meeting in Maynooth. As he counted down the days, the health of the parish priest was worsening and he would often wake McCabe in the middle of the night, asking him to anoint him. Five days later, the bishop approved McCabe's appointment. At the October meeting of the hierarchy at Maynooth, the archbishops confirmed the appointment and McCabe began planning his return to Salamanca.

# Chapter 4
# THE SPANISH CAULDRON

Salamanca was much changed compared to the city McCabe first knew as a nineteen-year-old clerical student in 1919. Then there had been no mechanised transport at the railway station. Now, eleven years later, there were plenty of cars and the road network in Spain was among the best in Europe, thanks to the considerable expenditure of the military dictatorship that had governed the country for six years.

Primo de Rivera had done his best to modernise Spain, and had had some success, yet his efforts had managed to alienate the army, the landowning aristocracy and the northern industrialists in the process. Without the support of the most conservative elements in the country, his regime was doomed to failure. By the late 1920s, and with the onset of economic depression, Primo de Rivera's popularity was on the wane. When McCabe arrived in Salamanca on 1 November 1930, the country was in political turmoil. Primo de Rivera had been forced to resign at the beginning of the year and had died a couple of months later in Paris. During the summer, a coalition of republicans and socialists had signed a pact to bring about the downfall of the monarchy. Hanging on by his fingernails, the king appointed another general, Dámaso Berenguer, as his prime minister.

A few weeks after McCabe arrived in Spain, two army officers launched a failed revolt in the Aragonese garrison town of Jaca, in the foothills of the Pyrenees. They demanded an end to the monarchy and the establishment of a republic. King Alfonso's insistence that the two officers should be executed further destabilised his regime. A few days later, there was another revolt against the monarchy by members of the armed forces. An air force captain, Ramón Franco, the brother of the future Spanish dictator, and General Gonzalo Queipo de Llano dropped pamphlets on the Royal Palace in Madrid calling for the establishment of a republic, before continuing their flight into exile in Portugal. 'There's a certain amount of Comic Opera in all this,' McCabe wrote in his diary shortly after his arrival back in the country, 'but Spain is beginning to seethe.'[1]

Although the country's political life was in chaos, McCabe had a pleasant time during his first few weeks back in Spain rediscovering old haunts and paying courtesy calls to the ecclesiastical authorities and clerical colleagues. These included visits to the bishop of Salamanca, Francisco Frutos Valiente, and the vicar-general, Pedro Salcedo, two good friends of the Irish College.

At the beginning of November 1930, McCabe went on a road trip with Ricardo Estrada, the Marqués de Canillejas. Ricardo's father, the Conde de la Vega del Sella, was a famous archaeologist and palaeontologist. When the superiors and students of the Irish College had first started holidaying in Asturias, the count had welcomed them into his home at Nueva, close to Pendueles. The young Ricardo, or Dick, as McCabe knew him, was visiting the family estates outside Salamanca.

The party travelled along the newly built motorway, one of the many engineering projects completed under Primo de Rivera's dictatorship. Most of the land in this part of Castile formed large estates and belonged to members of the (often absentee) aristocracy. The marqués drew £1,000 a year from his estate and the family owned several. McCabe described the scenes they passed in his diary:

> The new winter wheat is just up, and gives a green spring note to the autumn landscape. Farther on, the grass is grey and coarse, and then we run through groves of evergreen oak-trees. The plains out here are very silent and solitary. Occasionally, we see a village or a flock of sheep, but these rare signs of life only emphasise the loneliness.[2]

When they arrived at the modern complex that formed the administrative centre of the estate, there were hundreds of black pigs – from which the best quality *jamón* is made – feeding on grain and offal in a yard:

> Then we went into the office, Dick sat pontifically in the high chair, and Eloy – a charcoal contractor, very like Sancho Panzo – came

in. He offered 1.25 a fanega (43 kilos) for the green oak, and Dick and himself talked and haggled over it for an hour. It takes a lot of haggling over pence, before a young gentleman can afford to spend £1,000 a year.[3]

Back at the college, McCabe quickly realised that living with the rector was going to be difficult. O'Doherty was petty, irritable and prone to harbouring grudges. McCabe's predecessor had clashed frequently with him – 'they couldn't agree on fundamentals, they couldn't agree on trifles'[4] – which had led to the former's resignation. McCabe had been through many quarrels with his superiors as a curate and did not think it was a good idea to put two priests in the same house: 'We clerics spend three or four hours every day for six or seven years, spinning out metaphysical arguments, objecting, counter-objecting, and learning to be disputatious. This must make us uncivil and a bit uncivilized for the ordinary, intimate relations of life.'[5]

Now McCabe was in the same position as his predecessor. He suspected that part of the reason his elder colleague was so crabby was because he had been passed over for a bishopric. There was also considerable tension between the rector and the clerical students. The students had written to Cardinal MacRory, the archbishop of Armagh, at the beginning of 1930, objecting to the fact that they were obliged to spend their summers in the villa in Asturias and seeking permission to return home for the holidays that year. MacRory referred the matter to the standing committee of the hierarchy that April. The bishops resolved that the matter be left in the hands of the rector, with a suggestion 'that he might be generous in granting vacations in Ireland to individuals, as far as the interests of discipline will permit.'[6]

The rector was incensed by the students' action and sought to punish the ringleaders. McCabe was caught in the middle. As a student he had seen the same tensions pervade the college. Though he attached much of the blame to the rector, McCabe believed that many of the students were not cut out for ecclesiastical life, and were deliberately trying to cause difficulties:

It is a pity that the wrong type of boy cannot be eliminated before he enters an ecclesiastical college, or, at least, before he begins to study Theology. This would be fairer to the Church, and, of course, much fairer to the student, himself. An ecclesiastical student that 'cuts' late in his course [gives up studying to become a priest close to ordination] is almost as useless for any career as for manual work and, of course he is more or less branded for life. The rustic folk regard him as practically an apostate.[7]

The student who had led the 'rebellion' against the practice of spending the summer in Spain had been reprimanded by his bishop, which added to the bad feeling in the college. The latter had been prepared to petition Rome to have him dispensed from his obligations and his rank of sub-deacon.

Aside from their discontent with the rector's authoritarian style, the students also suffered from the cold weather. The Irish College was freezing in winter and many of the students, and the housekeeper, were struck down with the flu. The doctor prescribed leeches, which the local barber applied to the helpless patients. The patients and housekeeper recovered. After a few months in Salamanca, McCabe had mixed feelings. In March 1931, he wrote:

Feeling better, and in fine form. One has as many moods as the weather. Sometimes, I am in love with the old place, and sometimes, I think that it's a private lunatic asylum, and I wonder how anybody can retain his sanity in it. There's something always wrong, and whoever, or whatever it is, there seems to be a radical, and, perhaps, a mental defect, somewhere all right. ... This soft Spanish sky, with its thousands of stars, is a great consolation. The starlight here is not so cold and frozen as it is in the Northern skies, and in this deep dry transparent atmosphere, the large stars sparkle like diamonds.[8]

Long walks were a release from the claustrophobia. McCabe rediscovered the streets of Salamanca during those early months, from the glorious architectural jewels of the historic city centre to the filth of the tanneries, home to the city's gypsy population. During one walk through the latter district, McCabe noticed some peculiar skins hanging out to dry on the wall of a tannery. They were from the wolves that would come down from the mountains and attack flocks grazing on the outskirts of the city during the harsh winters.

In January 1931, raucous student demonstrations and a university strike designed to bring down the monarchy, which was led by some of the most renowned intellectual figures in Spain, including the writers José Ortega y Gasset and Antonio Machado, caused unrest in the hallowed halls of Salamanca. The following month, the king and his new prime minister, Admiral Juan Bautista Aznar, decided to test public opinion by calling local and municipal elections for April. Conservative Salamanca feared the worst. One of the traditions of the Irish College was to host a banquet marking St Patrick's Day, to which Salamanca's municipal and ecclesiastical authorities were invited. Among the guests on 17 March 1931 were the bishop of Salamanca, Frutos Valiente, the vicar-general, Salcedo, and the rector of the University of Salamanca, Unamuno. The civil governor, 'a small peevish little man from Malaga', who had just been appointed, was also invited. He 'knows nothing about Salamanca' and 'less of course about St Patrick', wrote McCabe that evening, 'and he sat there in a maze, wondering what all this banquet is about, and why he's at it'.[9] Such was the mood of despondency and the underlying political tension in the country, the rector decided that there would be no speeches at the banquet and 'everybody seemed to sit under a black pall'. McCabe added that:

> The Bishop, who is usually as fluent as a barrel with the tap open, and can talk about everything, was quite dumb to-day. Benuela [Professor of Mathematics at the University of Salamanca], who was opposite me, seemed to be in mystical contemplation, and ate in silence, but he kept eating all the time. These mystics have good appetites. The Rector of the University [Unamuno] did all the talking. He is very highly strung, and he ate practically nothing, but smoked cigarette after cigarette, and talked about the strikes, and the student riots that took place recently in the University. He, as Rector, has been in the news quite a lot recently, and it is thought that if the students keep up their agitation against the Monarchy, he will have to resign in a protest against all this anarchy. But in spite of his volubility, the Rector of the University was strained, everybody was strained, and the dinner was a 'frost'.[10]

The king's position was increasingly precarious and the elections, held on 12 April, were regarded as a referendum on the monarchy. McCabe noted how apathetic the monarchists seemed in the run-up to the poll, while the republicans, including the workers, were busy electioneering. The results showed large majorities for the liberal republicans and socialists in most of the provincial capitals. 'The result has taken the country – or, at least, the pious, timid folk – by surprise, and it is felt that the old regime is in a crisis,' McCabe wrote the day after the poll.[11] It was a shock to conservatives who had been persuaded by the right-wing press that the king's position was secure. The Catholic newspaper *El Debate* had argued in a leader published a few days before the poll that the people were still loyal to the monarchy.

The results of the election are still contested in Spain, with sections of the right arguing that they were distorted to bring down the monarchy. This was a view shared by McCabe upon publication of the full results two days after the poll. 'Numerically, and including all the small urban towns, the vote is in favour of the Monarchy, but public opinion – rigged, of course, by the republicans – regards the majorities in the large towns, which are all against the King, as decisive,' he wrote. 'It is said that Alfonso slipped out of the Palace alone last night and drove to the Royal Pantheon in the Escorial to pray at his mother's tomb.'[12]

On the evening of 14 April, the college porter told McCabe that the official portraits of the king and queen had been torn from the walls of the town hall and the republic had been declared in Salamanca. Later that evening, two of the Irish clerical students reported that they had seen a 'strange new flag' – the republican tricolour, composed of three horizontal stripes of red, yellow and purple – being hoisted in the *plaza mayor*, to the delight of the crowd. 'I can hear all the Church bells ringing,' wrote McCabe that evening, 'though the Church authorities must be full of grief and self-pity, the rockets begin to go up, and the crowds – even the children – are pouring through the streets shouting, yelling and singing the anti-clerical song:

Si los curas y frailes supieran
la paliza que les van a dar,
Bajarían [*sic*] al Coro cantando
Libertad, libertad, libertad.

[If the priests and monks knew
the beating they're going to get,
they'd form a chorus and sing
Liberty, liberty, liberty.][13]

These unofficial lyrics were sung to the tune of *El Himno de Riego*, the
national anthem of the short-lived First Republic in the 1870s. The hymn
was also to become the anthem of the Second Republic.

King Alfonso was already preparing to leave Madrid, for what
would turn out to be permanent exile, as McCabe discussed the volatile
political situation with O'Doherty in his room in the Irish College. In
this 'tense and electric' atmosphere, they were afraid that the college
would be attacked by an anti-clerical mob, so they cleaned and loaded
two revolvers in case there was need to defend themselves. 'We've seen
the long-threatened fall of the Spanish Monarchy, and though it's been
a bloodless Revolution so far, the blood might start to flow before to-
morrow morning,' McCabe wrote.[14] In May, it looked as if his fears were
to be realised. At the beginning of that month, Cardinal Pedro Segura
y Sáenz, the archbishop of Toledo and primate of Spain, addressed
the faithful in a pastoral letter. Segura was a staunch conservative and
monarchist who believed in a confessional state:

> If we remain 'quiet and idle', if we allow ourselves to give way to
> 'apathy and timidity'; if we leave open the way to those who are
> attempting to destroy religion, or if we expect the benevolence of our
> enemies to secure the triumph of our ideals, we shall have no right to
> lament when bitter reality shows us that we had victory in our hands,
> yet knew not how to fight like intrepid warriors prepared to succumb
> gloriously.[15]

A few days later, a group of monarchist army officers meeting in a house
on the Calle Alcalá in the centre of Madrid enraged a crowd on the street
outside by playing the Royal March on a gramophone and shouting
monarchist slogans. The mob set fire to the officers' cars on the street
outside and set alight the offices of *A.B.C.*, the rightist newspaper. The
following day, the mob turned its wrath on the Catholic Church. Several

hundred churches, monasteries and convents throughout Spain were burnt to the ground. 'They've been doing this periodically for about a hundred years,' was McCabe's laconic response.[16]

In Salamanca, the ecclesiastical authorities closed the seminary when parents demanded that their children return home. Some of the nuns and novices living in the city also went home or took shelter with friends. The Irish College remained open and exams went ahead as usual, but with the future uncertain.

The new provisional government, led by Niceto Alcalá-Zamora, was a coalition of republicans – both conservatives and leftists – and socialists, and progressive elements within the government would spend the next two years trying to implement much-needed reforms. The government immediately sought to help rural workers who were living in near-feudal conditions by introducing an eight-hour day and measures to prevent evictions, arbitrary rent increases and the use of blackleg labour to break strikes. Its efforts pleased few. The right was fearful that the newly proclaimed Second Republic would start to undermine its privileged place in society, especially when socialist ministers began introducing agrarian reforms. Rightist anti-government organisations collected funds for a campaign of opposition to the republic. They used all means at their disposal to attack the new regime, employing black propaganda and playing on a fear of the mob to drive moderates into their arms. Meanwhile, the left was impatient at the slow pace of reform. Over the next two years, as they realised the impossibility of the republican government driving through reforms against the will of a conservative bloc, comprising aristocratic landowners, industrialists, bankers, the army and the Catholic Church, many on the left drifted towards revolution.

In June 1931, McCabe returned to Ireland for a holiday, travelling leisurely overland through France. On the train to San Sebastián, he overheard 'two gentlemen in the first class carriage, and so, men of Conservative views'[17] discussing the political situation. They believed that the republic was going to be around for a while, but that the monarchy would be restored in thirty years. In fact, it was forty-four years before Juan Carlos I succeeded Franco as head of state, marking the beginning of Spain's transition from dictatorship to democracy. In San Sebastián,

McCabe noted that the beaches were not as busy as they had been in the past. The local business people, 'who are Basques, very Catholic, and not very Republican', believed they were facing ruin because of the 'mass emigration' of the aristocracy.[18] 'They're getting a lot of cheap vulgar French people from over the border, who can't afford to go to Biarritz, or be seen there.'[19] At the customs post at Irún on the French border, new currency measures had been introduced to prevent the flight of capital out of the country.

In Hendaye, just across the border in France – where in 1940, during the Second World War, Franco met Hitler to discuss the possibility of Spain joining the Axis powers – McCabe watched Spanish aristocrats pay homage to the exiled Cardinal Segura, who was staying in the Hotel Midi, opposite the railway station. 'The landlady, who wears black-rimmed glasses, and has a pleasant smiling face,' he wrote, 'seems to be satisfied to the point of inundation to see this constant stream of Spanish nobility suddenly invade her house, which, too, has been suddenly transformed from a plain Railway Hotel into an Archiepiscopal Residence.'[20] In late May, after the new government had pronounced a decree proclaiming religious freedom in Spain, the cardinal had travelled to Rome. There, he had publicly denounced the Spanish government, embarrassing the Vatican, before returning secretly to Spain across the Pyrenees. On being apprehended, he was escorted under guard across the French border, becoming a monarchist hero for his defiance. McCabe noted the incongruity of a monarchist cardinal being protected by republican France.

McCabe's next stop on the way home was Lyon. At his hotel, he shared a table at dinner with a French priest who put him off his food but gave him an opportunity to indulge his talent for acerbic pen portraits:

He's a notary or ecclesiastical scrivener of some sort. We spoke a mixture of French and Latin. He keeps looking round furtively and suspiciously at the other tables, he's very solemn, secretive and significant, and much more gloomy than any undertaker. I suppose it's the job he's got that stamps him like that, or it may be his natural character, which eventually got him a dusty morose sort of job. In any case, this necrological confrère, with his 'Memento Mori' looks, didn't help one's appetite at supper, and the good wine of Burgundy tasted a bit like corpse.[21]

There followed a rumination on the type of priest produced by different nations:

I have my own ideas about Latin methods, and about ecclesiastical Seminaries on the Continent, and I much prefer the breezy Irish or American type of priest, and the way in which he's produced. Every nation produces its own peculiar ideal types, and the Latin ideals are different from ours. That's why it's difficult for Italians to rule a world-wide Church, and it would be much better if the Cardinals at Rome were an international body. As time goes on, it will be increasingly difficult for the large Catholic body to be content with a small Italian head, and if the Church had been more widely represented at Rome in the 16th Century, the Reformation might not have happened.[22]

In Dublin, McCabe unsuccessfully sought a meeting with the minister for external affairs, Patrick McGilligan, to update him on the political situation in Spain. Instead, he met the secretary of the department, Joe Walshe, to discuss what course the college might take, given that the Spanish government had begun nationalising ecclesiastical property. Despite the wave of church burnings in May, McCabe was bullish and told Walshe that the rector had no intention of closing the college, even though the Spanish seminaries were shut. He added that the college was in touch with the British embassy in the case of trouble and asked Walshe what flag should be hoisted if violence did break out. Walshe advised putting up the Irish tricolour.[23]

McCabe and Walshe discussed the hostility of the Church to republicanism in Latin countries in continental Europe and the fact that the Jesuits in Spain and Portugal preached that republicanism was a mortal sin. Walshe did not have a high opinion of the work the foreign colleges were doing on the Continent and believed it would be better if the students were educated at home. 'In Foreign Affairs, yet anti-Foreign', McCabe wrote about Walshe.[24] Walshe's was a viewpoint shared in Irish clerical circles.

Before returning to Salamanca that autumn, McCabe visited his brother in the county asylum in Monaghan town. James Charles had never recovered from the blow to the head he had received as a boy, and McCabe described the meeting with his brother as the 'saddest and most sickening experience I've ever had'.[25]

The Irish students returned to Salamanca for the new term in the autumn of 1931, just as the Spanish government was facing new threats from the left and right. The anarchists of the Confederación Nacional del Trabajo (CNT) union had called a general strike, which undermined the government's promise to maintain order. The conservative interior minister, Miguel Maura, ordered the civil guard – hated by rural and urban workers alike as the oppressive instrument of the rich and powerful – to crush it. Meanwhile, the right was appalled at the new constitution, which came into force at the end of 1931, establishing freedom of speech and freedom of association, permitting divorce and curtailing the special status of the Spanish aristocracy, and, most significantly, abolishing state support for the Church.

McCabe observed attitudes towards the new government as he prepared to spend Christmas travelling in Andalusia and Morocco. In Madrid, while waiting for the train to Granada, he ate dinner in Atocha station. He wrote:

As it was early, they prepared a 'quick' supper for me at the Restaurant, and I washed it down with a half-bottle of 'Marqués de Riscal', which, even in a Republic, is a fine aristocratic claret, with a genuine Rioja flavour. ... The waiter shuffled about slowly, and wasn't in a hurry. He doesn't think that the Republic has been of much benefit to Madrid. When the Court and aristocracy flourished, there was much more life, and far more money went around. Now that the aristocracy and wealthy Royalists have left Spain, half the big houses and flats in Madrid are empty, the owners can't get tenants for them, or rents out of them, and the Republic can't collect taxes on them, so that public revenue is down.[26]

McCabe had loved the idea of seeing new places ever since he had pored over pictures of sultry foreign climes in his earliest school readers. 'Travel is a frightful lust,' he mused. 'One is never satisfied with what one has seen, and there are so many hundreds of famous places to see.'[27] He was especially curious to see Granada, capital of the great Moorish kingdom and home of the fabled Alhambra. Yet both Granada and the Alhambra disappointed. The cathedral, a 'large bald Renaissance church', has 'no artistic or historical interest'.[28] McCabe shared Victor Hugo's resentment towards Renaissance architecture for having dispensed with the Gothic:

> When I go into a Renaissance Cathedral, I always feel like walking out in disgust. This may be pettishness, but, really, Christendom invented Gothic. It is original and splendid, and a style that Christians can call their own. On the other hand, a Christian Church in modern, antique Classical style, is an anachronism and a contradiction. It is a relief to go into the Gothic Royal Chapel alongside.[29]

After Granada, McCabe set off for Gibraltar, where he stayed a few days with the bishop of Gibraltar, Richard Fitzgerald, who had been vice-rector of the Irish College in Salamanca when McCabe was a student. McCabe arrived in Algeciras just after midnight on 1 January 1932. Across the bay, 'lamps all over the high dark Rock seemed to be a fairy network of twinkling lights suspended from the sky'.[30] This tiny piece of the British Empire, marking the crossroads between Europe and Africa, the Atlantic and the Mediterranean, left a deep impression on the Anglophile McCabe. Sitting on Europa Point, the southernmost tip of Gibraltar, he watched the ships pass through the straits and contemplated the might of the Empire. Like most other boys of the Edwardian era, McCabe had grown up on stories of imperial derring-do, and had even toyed with the idea of running away and joining the French foreign legion.

McCabe admired men of action. He perceived the world in terms of those who achieved great things and those who sat at home talking about them, while doing nothing. Hence his admiration for those Irishmen who, with no prospects at home, had, throughout history, left their native land to fight for Britain.

In Salamanca, he was following in the footsteps of generations of Irish priests who had trained on the Continent to lead their people against their English oppressors. Yet, in many respects, he found Catholic Spain,

Ireland's ally for hundreds of years, a barbaric, uncivilised country and Protestant Britain an enlightened, progressive force for good in the world. McCabe compared favourably the regular, ordered society of Britain with the chaotic, unpredictable nature of life in Spain. As a curate in the East End of London and in Leigh-on-Sea, watching the slow-moving ships coming up and down the Thames carrying their exotic cargoes from the four corners of the globe, he saw at first hand the efficiency of British imperial administration. London, the crossroads of the world, had thrilled the young priest. There is little sense in McCabe's diaries from the early 1930s of a great power on the wane. Instead, there is a positive contrast with the lethargy and lack of will that he regarded as characteristic of Ireland and Spain.

An Irishman could admire the British Empire and still be a patriot, McCabe believed. After all, had not the British built their empire on the backs of Irish soldiers and sailors? For McCabe, it was fascinating 'to try to explain the expansion and power of England, which no educated person – unless it be a spite-ridden Irishwoman – can deny. Even Mary Mac Sweeney [sic]* who hates to see it, and hates to admit it, must admit it.'[31] McCabe was scornful of the nationalist reading of Irish history, with its long lists of grievances, and was inclined, instead, to blame the Irish themselves for their problems, rather than foreign conquerors. He believed that the insular nature of the Irish compounded their problems, a nature that did not exist on the neighbouring island. Despite this criticism of his compatriots, McCabe did not reject the Irish part of his identity, no more so than when he was abroad. During his trip to Gibraltar in the winter of 1931–2, he reflected:

> Sitting here, looking out over the Mediterranean, how proud one would be to see a great trans-Atlantic liner go past, flying the Irish flag, or to see an Irish battleship, bristling with great guns, ride into the harbour down below, and to feel that Irish ships are on all the

---

* Mary MacSwiney was the sister of Terence MacSwiney, the Lord Mayor of Cork who died on hunger strike in October 1920. She was elected Sinn Féin TD for Cork Borough in 1921 and was vehemently opposed to the Anglo-Irish Treaty; she broke with Éamon de Valera over the latter's decision in 1926 to abandon Sinn Féin's policy of abstention and enter the Dáil.

seven seas, and that we are a great Empire and rule the world. We protest against Empire, because we haven't got one ourselves, and the feeling hurts. But I can understand the patriotic pride of the Englishman – who, it must be admitted doesn't swagger – and all honour to our neighbours from the other little island, who have built up a World Empire of 400,000,000 inhabitants. They're a great people …[32]

According to McCabe, there was no reason why the Irish,

> should not be a sea-faring folk, like the English, Germans or Dutch, or if we cannot compare with them, then like the Norwegians, who are a small peasant people like ourselves. We explain everything by saying that the English kept us down. We believe this, and there we lie, grumbling and grousing and perfectly content. By train, every point in Ireland is only about three hours from the sea, but we seem to regard it as our enemy. This may be due to the tragedies of Emigration. The Atlantic has been a sort of Styx over which people have to pass from Ireland to America. We don't regard the Atlantic as our own, and the sea a place of adventure, romance and fortune, too. It is rather our enemy, the wide channel over which we pass from poverty to exile, and this spirit is reflected in Gaelic and Anglo-Irish literature, where the 'salt ocean' is generally regarded as the symbol of bitterness and sorrow.[33]

This perceived lack of moral fibre prevented the Irish people from realising their potential, McCabe believed, and he attributed the reason for this to the romanticism of the Gaelic tradition. In fact, he was quite hostile to attempts to revive Gaelic culture at home. He believed that English should be a worldwide language, and did not wish to see it replaced at home by the Irish language; 'this little schismatic language will never make its way in the great wide world, or help Irishmen get anywhere'. McCabe thought there was something missing from the Irish character which had prevented the nation from achieving greatness, and he was scornful of what he perceived as the tendency in the Gaelic tradition – and the Anglo-Irish writers who had tried to resurrect it – to bemoan the wrongs inflicted on the country by others. He described them as 'wretched poets, with all their unmanly alcoholic sobbing' who 'might be almost propagandists, specially paid, to ruin the character and manhood of the Irish people'. 'This type of "patriotic" literature is so insidious,' he wrote, 'and we are so thoroughly "doped" with it, that anybody, venturing to protest against it, would probably, or most certainly, be regarded as a traitor.'[34] In his diaries, he advocated burning half the canon of popular Irish songs, because the sentiment of both the music and the lyrics was bad for the soul and the nation, and this 'Granny-wailing' was a 'bug' in the brain.

McCabe also expressed his contempt for those 'neo-Patriots' in Cumann na nGaedheal and Fianna Fáil, which had replaced John Redmond's Irish Parliamentary Party – to which McCabe would have been more instinctively inclined, and who now formed the government and opposition of the Free State. A diary entry from 1931 sums up how he felt about national progress in the first decade of the Irish state:

> Arthur Griffith, the father of Sinn Féin, had sound realistic views on what Ireland needs, but the little beggarly breed that came after him, trying to make a hungry living out of his movement and writings, have done as much for the spirit of our manhood as the wailing of the 'banshees'. Alongside them, we have had a few 'toughs' who think that they are heroes solving every problem, if they can shoot their innocent neighbours with a six-chamber revolver.[35]

From Gibraltar, McCabe travelled to Morocco, which did not leave much of an impression. 'The "glamour" of Africa is a mere mirage,' he wrote.[36] His thoughts on Morocco and Africa were based on typically European attitudes: superior, racist and imperialist; his fundamental belief in the civilising colonial project of the white man was not yet shaken. While strolling over a piece of waste ground in Morocco, he came across an old steamroller made in Darlington in the north-east of England:

> The Men from the North, with their funny but efficient machines, will eventually drive the Devil out of Africa. Moralists say that the modern Machine will kill the Soul. This is nonsense. The Machine

is one of the healthiest and noblest things that the Mind has ever created. Compare it, for instance, with the dark, bloodthirsty superstitions and customs that the African Mind has produced. The superiority of Europe is due to Philosophy, Law and the notion and recognition of Merit, and to Religion based on these. But it also owes its superiority to the Instrument and to the Machine, whereas the repulsive prostration of Africa is largely due to the primitive Traditional Mind, which believes that all these ingenious works of men are inventions of the Devil. Nobody, least of all a moralist, would maintain that Africa or Asia is saner and healthier than Europe.[37]

McCabe stood on a hill overlooking the Moroccan city of Tétouan, to the east of Tangier, the capital of Spanish Morocco, and where one of the most famous battles in Spanish colonial history had been fought. Yet it was the achievements of two other colonial powers that impressed him, as he contemplated the '"Dark" Continent' stretching thousands of miles through the desert, across the Equator to the Cape of Good Hope:

> It is amazing – and consoling – to reflect that this vast area belongs to the White Man – or rather, to two White Men – the Englishman and the Frenchman. It may be their 'Burden', but the natives help to carry it, and the two White Men divide all the earnings. It must make an English or French schoolboy very proud to learn that his country owns huge estates and broad fat acres everywhere in the world.[38]

Tétouan did not live up to the exotic locale imagined from the old Victorian school maps but the idea of reaching into the continent's heart bore a romantic appeal: 'the mountains on the horizon lure one on towards the Illusion. One would like to penetrate into it, go right across it, see the lions, and have a miraculous escape from the cannibals.'[39]

Returning to Spain, McCabe stopped in Seville. Andalusia was a hotbed of anti-clericalism and anarchism, as rural workers, frustrated by the government's slow pace of reform, felt the fervour of revolution. This poverty-stricken region of the country had long been the preserve of the large feudal landowners or *latifundistas*, who employed landless labourers, or *braceros*, to work their vast estates. In his classic account of the roots of the Spanish Civil War, *The Spanish Labyrinth*, the English author Gerald Brenan described the average *pueblo* in the province of Seville:

> A few wretched shops selling only the bare necessities of life: one or two petty industries – soap-making, weaving of esparto mats, potteries, oil-distilleries that between them employ some couple of hundred men: the ancestral houses of the absentee landowners, dilapidated and falling into ruin.[40]

Three-quarters of the population of these towns were landless workers who were hired by the day, the month or the season, but who would typically spend half the year unemployed and were often close to starvation. Most of the best land in the province was given over to bull-breeding or shooting, rather than growing crops. According to Brenan:

> Such a lack of self-interest in rich landowners living in Madrid or Seville may appear extraordinary, but the average aristocrat simply took the advice of his steward and did not bother his head about estates where he knew no one by sight and which he regarded very much as if they were in some distant colony.[41]

In the spring of 1932, these owners were refusing to plant crops, contravening the agrarian reforms introduced by the government. In Seville, McCabe could hear shots being fired in the street outside his hotel. Many Catholics, who had initially welcomed the arrival of the republic, were being driven into the arms of the right. They were upset by the removal of crucifixes and religious statues from public buildings and the implementation of taxes on Catholic ceremonies. The right exploited these measures at every opportunity. In the summer of 1932, disaffected army officers, angered at the government's efforts to reform the military, launched an abortive coup under General José Sanjurjo.

In June, O'Doherty, McCabe and the students returned home for the Eucharistic Congress in Dublin. They travelled by bus from Salamanca to Gijón, where some Spanish priests joined the group, on the first stage of their journey. One of the Spanish priests suggested raising a congress flag.

McCabe overruled him, believing that the proposal was 'sheer madness'. He wrote:

> the Socialist workmen boast that the dish they like best is 'eating Curas [priests]'. As foreigners travelling without a flag, they would not molest us in the slightest. But when passing through the Mining area, for example, if we were flaunting a big flag on the bonnet of the car, and the workmen also saw two 'shovel hats' inside, they would come at us like cannibals.[42]

The staff and students of the Irish College and their Spanish guests embarked for Ireland at Gijón aboard a German steamer and arrived in Cobh some forty hours later. The journey was smooth except for a group of Communists 'who tried to kick up trouble'. According to McCabe, the ringleader was a Russian professor who, alongside a group of 'lower-class Communists', had been expelled from 'some South American country' and was trying to organise a 'cell' down below in steerage. The group had been refused entry to the United States and Spain. The ship was full of Catholic priests, nuns and laity, some from the United States, on their way to the Eucharistic Congress. The priests would say mass for the pilgrims in the ship's oratory every morning. McCabe wrote:

> As the Communists would not be allowed to stage a manifestation on board, they decided to organize a counter-manifestation against the Catholics. They began to assemble outside the Oratory during Mass every morning, and to demonstrate and obstruct by talking aloud, shouting and whistling. Three of the leading agitators were put into chains, and there was no further disturbance above or below decks.[43]

The German crew was obviously well versed in how to deal with political undesirables. While the passengers waited to be taken by tender off the ship at Cobh, the captain radioed the Irish customs officials, telling them to be on their guard. Once on board, the inspectors scrutinised the Communists' papers, refused them entry to Ireland and shipped them off to the next port of call, Rotterdam. McCabe speculated that their final destination would be the Soviet Union.

As the rest of the passengers left the ship on the tender, the band on board struck up the Irish national anthem. McCabe was glad to be home on that June evening 'when Ireland is really beautiful, and merits all the poetic praise that its beauty has inspired',[44] but within a few short days, spent in Cork, he was bemoaning the state of his native land: 'If there weren't whiskey in Ireland, life would be as gloomy as the "Wearing of the Green".'[45]

The Eucharistic Congress was the great triumphalist set-piece of the young Irish state and civic authorities across the country were determined to have their towns and villages looking at their best for the arrival of their visitors. It was an opportunity for the newly elected Fianna Fáil government to show off its Catholic credentials, having been portrayed by opponents during the 1932 general election as gunmen and 'Reds'. Despite his erratic mood, McCabe was impressed by the work that had gone into the preparations for the congress and got caught up in the national sense of pride:

> All Ireland seems to be covered with flags and bunting for the Congress, and there is not a single house, even the poorest, that has not been washed and painted. The country never had such a nation-wide 'lustrum' or Spring-cleaning in its history. There is an enormous wave of piety and enthusiasm everywhere, and rich and poor, Catholic and Protestant, have responded to a great occasion, and in a wonderful spirit of patriotism.[46]

Because he had spent most of his adult life outside the country, visiting home infrequently, McCabe found a striking contrast between this great national celebration and the political divisions of the past:

> Ten years ago, when the Civil War was raging bitterly, I went to Glasnevin Cemetery one Sunday morning, just before going back to Spain at the end of the summer holidays. We saw the grave of Arthur Griffith, and close by, the two large open plots where the Free Staters, on the one hand, and the Irregulars, on the other, were being buried. One plot was almost alongside the other plot (Harry Boland was buried in one, Mick Collins in the other), and at each,

there was a group of family mourners, and political sympathisers. One could see that they were deadly, bloodthirsty rivals, hating each other, with a badly suppressed instinct to start shooting and killing there on the spot, no matter how sad and sacred a spot it was. These open graves and these two groups were like trenches dividing the two political parties, and the whole Irish nation. At night we could hear the sniping in the centre of the city. One felt and feared that Ireland was 'split' for, at least, another generation.[47]

McCabe perceived a profound contrast between Ireland – where the great bulk of the population, men, women and children, were uniform in their religious observances and attitudes – and Spain, where anti-clericalism and church-burnings were common, and even those who professed themselves Catholic had an ambivalent attitude to religious observance. In Spain, the Catholic Church was an obstacle to national unity; in Ireland, it was the guiding national institution.

The arrival at Dún Laoghaire of the papal legate, Cardinal Lorenzo Lauri, was one of the set pieces of the congress. McCabe watched from opposite Trinity College, one of the historic bastions of ascendancy Protestantism in Ireland, as the cardinal made his way into Dublin in a baroque Catholic procession. It was a triumphant moment for Irish Catholic nationalism, and the Trinity students, perched high on the roof of their redoubt, were determined to upset proceedings by flashing mirrors onto the crowd. 'In a more ferocious age,' McCabe wrote, '[the crowd] would probably have stormed Trinity college and made a wreck of it, to avenge this mockery and insult against their religious convictions.'[48]

Most of the crowd where McCabe was standing missed the papal legate on his way to the pro-cathedral in Marlborough Street, because instead of travelling via Westmoreland Street as had been expected, the procession made its way up D'Olier Street. They were treated instead to the sight of the lord mayor of Dublin, Alfie Byrne, 'a dignified little figure with a sharp face, and sharp, smart moustache.'[49] The wags dusted off their witticisms as the lord mayor's highly ornamented eighteenth-century coach became separated from the rest of the procession. McCabe remarked drily on one vignette: 'The Lord Mayor is very popular with the poor, and when some of the old Dublin women in the midst of the crowd saw him, they began to exclaim affectionately, "Ah, good Lord, sure it's Alfie." On great State occasions, it's sometimes awkward to be popular with the apple-selling public.'[50] The crowds thronged the streets around the pro-cathedral as a *te deum* was sung.

The week-long congress was a success, the biggest occasion of its kind to be held in the country up to that point. But there were some disappointments, not least that few Spaniards had made the trip, despite the efforts of the Irish organisers:

> In the end, the congress secretary in Dublin gave the Spaniards up as hopeless, and asked the rector to undertake the propaganda work, and to organise the expedition from Spain. The Bishop of Salamanca might have gone, if he had not been dragged so much. In the beginning, he was quite enthusiastic, but by continual reminders and constant forcing, he grew obstinate in his refusal to go.[51]

The congress was also the scene of a disagreement between McCabe and O'Doherty. The moribund union of former students of the Irish College had organised a dinner in Clerys department store to give it a new lease of life and to mark the congress. Though no formal invitations had been issued, the rector had been informally invited, though many of the former students still held a grudge against him and had wished to exclude him because he had not been a student of the college himself. In the end the rector had not shown up, and McCabe, instead, made a speech in Spanish. 'It was all meant to be a "good-will" affair without any malice or offence for anybody,' McCabe wrote. 'The Rector expected to get a printed invitation, to see his "enemies" eliminated, and to be asked to preside.'[52] Instead, the rector came to believe that McCabe had 'supported faction' and he would not forget it. 'I get sick of this feminine vanity and dignified cant of the Union of Salamanca,' wrote McCabe, 'and of my connection with it', adding that the 'whole thing was as vulgar as a case in the Petty Session Court, and no two rustic farmers, quarrelling over the trespass of a goat, with their rustic wives, children and neighbours to give evidence, could be more absurd and contemptible'.[53]

The relationship between Denis O'Doherty and McCabe was worsening, owing principally to the former's domineering ways but also partly to the latter's stubborn streak. Just over two years after making the decision to return to Salamanca, McCabe was expressing himself 'pretty sick of the whole life'.[54] Back in Spain, life, which meant O'Doherty, was becoming more 'petty, peevish, irritating and exasperating than ever'. O'Doherty would make jibes at the amount of food McCabe would put away at the dinner table, calling him a scavenger for having second helpings. And McCabe would throw a remark back at O'Doherty. McCabe compared the Irish College to a lunatic asylum: 'even the students, who are young, and should be healthy and sane, seem to be getting neurotic. Half-a-dozen get attacks of scruples, and give a lot of trouble'.[55] One student was perpetually complaining about his sight and his glasses. Eventually, his sight became so bad – or, perhaps, his religious imagination so fevered – that he began to see communion particles on the seat every morning during mass. The tensions between O'Doherty and the students were still simmering away, and he had taken to opening the letters they sent home for evidence of treason.

'I made a bad mistake to come back here at all,' wrote McCabe. 'When I was a student, there was a bad spirit amongst the older men. As soon as the rector was appointed, he fell foul of the students almost immediately, and they disliked him just as much as they liked his brother, who preceded him. That bad spirit died down during our time, but it seems to have revived in recent years'.[56] The fallout continued over the students' 'memorial' to the Irish archbishops, in which they had expressed their desire to spend their summer holidays in Ireland. 'The culprits are still in the house, and as they have to purge their rebellion. We are in the castor oil period,' wrote McCabe. 'Castor oil may be good for young people, but it's poor nourishment and tastes bad, and when a good strong dose is mixed up with everything, the discipline, the amusements and recreation, and the sermons, of course – all this lubricant makes the students pretty sick.' McCabe felt that it was he who was expected to administer O'Doherty's medicine but that, 'all things considered, I haven't much stomach for it'.[57] The same bad feeling towards the rector existed among some of the notables in Salamanca. Many of them had been very fond of the former rector, Michael O'Doherty, but were less warmly inclined towards his brother, and they had no problem admitting as much to McCabe.

Outside the walls of the Irish College, the right was denouncing the Second Republic with ever more vitriol. A new coalition of parties, the Confederación de Derechas Autónomas (CEDA), led by the Salamancan lawyer José María Gil-Robles – the head of the Catholic organisation Acción Popular – directed the charge. The CEDA saw itself as defending Christian Spain from the Marxist hordes. The left believed the CEDA was the thin edge of the fascist wedge and fell into disarray about how best to respond, with the hardliners preaching revolution. Every day, from his room in the Irish College, McCabe could hear children from the poorer districts of Salamanca singing anti-clerical songs, 'as sweetly and as fervently as if they were hymns to Our Lady'.[58] Meanwhile, the Spanish Church remained aloof from the everyday concerns of the working class, preferring instead to intrigue with aristocrats, officers and industrialists. McCabe mused:

> One often wonders why the Spanish Church does not take a more active part in the social problems and the social movements of the present day, just as the Irish priests played a big part in the land agitation of the century. Of course, the Irish landlords were Protestants, which isn't true in Spain ... the Spanish Church wraps itself up in the liturgical dignity, remains as tranquil and lifeless as a mummy and does nothing.[59]

McCabe remained in Salamanca throughout Christmas 1932 and Easter 1933, and this lack of a break took its toll, especially since one of the principal reasons that he had agreed to fill the position of vice-rector was the prospect of travelling in his spare time. 'I feel that I'm off my hinges, that everybody in the house is off his hinges, and I don't feel that I'm solely responsible for all that,' he wrote in early 1933.[60] But relief was to come. In the spring, McCabe visited the United States for a holiday. Before he departed, he was starkly reminded of the troubled state of Spain when, the morning he left Salamanca, a small bomb exploded outside the door of the Jesuit church. Then, while en route to Algeciras, from where he was to embark, he saw two civil guards standing on the platform in a town just outside Madrid. They were guarding a bomb that looked like a 'huge iron pot', which had been placed on the line by 'Communists' [in fact, it was probably the work of anarchist militias].[61]

McCabe spent the long voyage across the Atlantic watching his fellow passengers and noting their frailties in his diary. Among his fellow passengers were two Irish-American spinster sisters who had been to the Eucharistic Congress in Dublin and had then spent a year travelling in Europe. 'These sisters were very good and pious, and so, didn't indulge in such profanity as playing deck games on board like the other mundane folk,' he wrote. 'Their only hobby seemed to be to collect gossip and scandal about the passengers, getting awfully shocked (which is a magnificent satisfaction) and retailing the stuff hot.'[62] The sisters had a companion who had lost a fortune in the Wall Street Crash and was 'hurrying home to collect whatever remnant may be left'. McCabe remarked mordantly of this unpleasant-sounding trio:

> There is a new type of pious Catholic in the modern world who has arrived at such a high degree of spiritual perfection that he (generally she) can afford to be supremely and profoundly uncharitable about their neighbours and their lives. ... All these three ladies are agreed that they want to get back to America where the male acts the part of a gentleman towards a lady and get right away from the Latin male, who is rather canine in his approach to strange females.[63]

Aside from these snooty Americans, there was a mix of Old Europeans – 'Greeks – a nice, simple, friendly crowd – Italians, Austrians, Germans and Jews' – on their way to the New World.

> The last three groups kept arguing about Hitler and the new movement in Germany, and when we were about four days out, they were all so bitter and hostile towards one another, that the stewards had to change the places at table to avoid a major row. Our boat seemed to be a piece of Central Europe, adrift in the Atlantic, and packed full of the jabbering natives that live in these parts.'[64]

McCabe was travelling second class and, since there was not much room on deck, it was not possible to walk right round the ship. Most of the American tourists returning from Europe were in first class, which occupied half the room on board and meant the rest of the ship was quite cramped. The description of life on board during that trip could have been a metaphor for the global political situation, with the Americans – though in the same boat as the Europeans – remaining aloof, detached and isolated. McCabe, an Irish Catholic priest, travelling in second class, was, of course, a strictly neutral observer:

> Then there was a big crowd of Germans in Tourist Class, which is even more cramped. These Germans came into our section, and used to spend the greater part of the day in our Bar, lounge and writing-room. And, of course, with all their political talk, they helped to make the atmosphere more ugly.
>
> The Second Class passengers object to this German 'invasion', and the communication with Tourist Class had to be closed and locked, in order to keep them out, and in their own place. The German seems to have as much respect for a fence, as a hungry cow has.[65]

McCabe's initial view of New York was that it was 'cementy and ugly in appearance' and 'it makes a bad violent impression on one coming from the clear blue skies and the old, golden, stone-wrought towns of Spain'.[66] One of his first trips was to the Polo Grounds in upper Manhattan to see the All-Ireland champions, Kerry – who had won their fourth Sam Maguire cup in a row against Mayo the previous September – take on New York.* 'This New York football venue might have been Croke Park, and it was homely to hear all the Irish accents around about, but the play was rough and ugly, and the match, which ended in a draw, was not up to All-Ireland standard.' McCabe was not impressed by the GAA in New York and was taken aback by the factionalism within the Irish community. 'I was amazed to discover the rivalry and bad feeling that exists in Irish sport in New York, and amongst the Irish people there generally. There is the narrowest provincial feeling between people from

---

* Later that year, McCabe's native county of Cavan won the first of their five All-Irelands against Galway at Croke Park, foiling Kerry's bid for a five-in-a-row at home in Breffni Park along the way. Cavan also had a strong connection with the Polo Grounds. In 1947, Cavan beat Kerry 2-11 to 2-7 in the New York stadium, in the only All-Ireland final to be held outside Ireland. The match was held in the United States to mark the centenary of the Great Famine.

the North and South, and the Southerners do not like the "Far Downs", as they call the Northerners.' To make matters worse, during the dance in honour of the Kerry team, there was some sort of dispute, 'though they did not use sticks, as on previous occasions', wrote McCabe. 'GAA "sport" which is so narrow-minded, fanatical and rancid at home is pretty factious and tribal in New York City.'[67]

While McCabe may not have shared his countrymen's enthusiasm for their native games, he shared the racial prejudices many Irish emigrants displayed towards African-Americans, and was obviously shocked by the number of black people he saw while in New York. Abhorrent to modern ears and eyes, especially in the context of what was to follow in Europe, these attitudes towards non-white races were common, especially among the Irish Catholic clergy.

McCabe arrived in the United States at the height of the Great Depression, and Americans were suffering:

> On the whole, the colossal prosperity of the past ten years seems to have been largely a gamble with fake paper credit, and now that the game is up, people are beginning to discover that it was all a colossal swindle, a new South Sea bubble, in which 120,000,000 Americans went for a joy-ride, and which was great fun until the bubble-balloon burst.[68]

McCabe believed that it was a 'bad system that offers no security to the ordinary people, who can be robbed overnight of their hard-earned, hard-kept life savings. This lack of security and honesty in a natural system is far worse than having a half-dozen gangsters in the public streets. They seem to be only violent symptoms of a silent disease that eats up the whole system.'[69]

Though the financial crash had sent a 'wave of indignation' all over the United States, the average American retained a cheerful demeanour, an approach to life that greatly impressed McCabe. He did not notice too many manifestations of the Depression, except for the notorious Bowery slums. 'As usual, the working classes are showing a fine spirit of solidarity with one another in their misfortunes. It reminds me of the spirit of the East End during the General Strike in 1926.'[70] While McCabe may not have seen much evidence of hardship in New York, he did not venture into the south-central states of the Dust Bowl, such as Kansas, New Mexico, Oklahoma and Texas, where small farmers and their families were struggling to survive, in much the same way as the landless labourers of Spain were desperately trying to keep body and soul together.

Whereas Americans in Europe were regarded as loud and vulgar, among themselves, according to McCabe, they were 'quiet, simple, cheery, hospitable and off-hand in their generosity'. They were not so 'cautious, suspicious, warped and crooked-minded' as Europeans, though he could not get his head around their humour, which he regarded as infantile.[71] Yet he also felt the 'stale monotony' of the United States compared with the 'rich variety' of the Old World:

> One hungers, even during a short visit, which should be all novelty, for the extraordinary patchwork variety, interest and excellence of Europe, where there are races, languages, customs, noble buildings, royal palaces, picture galleries, museums, dramas, operas, histories, and politics, even, to keep the mind interested for a thousand years. In America, too, all the colourful tradition and Romance of great History is lacking.[72]

Still, American politics and history fascinated McCabe, especially the role that the Irish had played in building the country. In his diary, he noted the voting patterns for Herbert Hoover and Al Smith in the 1928 presidential election, and listed the Irish-American representatives at federal and state level, as well Irish-American heads of congressional committees, rear admirals, brigadier generals, civil servants, diplomats and district attorneys. In fact, McCabe was surprised at how few Irish names figured among these ranks and was also struck by what he regarded as the average Irish-American's weak grasp of history:

> It would be a good thing if the Irishmen that settle in America learned, as well, something about the History of America, about the part that Irishmen have played, and also, about the part they haven't played, in American public life. It is a defect of Irishmen that they have no vision of the world, or even, of the American nation, as a

whole. They are not exactly sectarian, but they are interested only in segments. Very often, they are quite parochial in outlook. Like the people at home, they are content to live in the parish, or on the parish, and to let the world sail by. A good many of them don't understand American politics, and what they are all about. I have asked a dozen educated Irish-Americans to explain the difference between Republicans and Democrats, and they couldn't do it.[73]

There was much about America that impressed McCabe. His hunger for the culture and traditions of Europe notwithstanding, McCabe admired American modernity. He believed that the recently completed Empire State Building, with its gleaming 'flat steel ribs' embedded in the surface, was the greatest thing that man had built since the first great Gothic cathedral and a sign of mankind's material progress. McCabe thought that architecture represented the ideas, methods, tastes and fashions of men in material form, and that the skyscraper was practical, efficient and modern:

We are living through a period of change. Within a short decade, we have had new experiments and changes in Ireland, England, Spain, on the map of Europe, and in life everywhere. And if we could distinguish between the little things that mark the passing of an age, and the monuments that make it permanent, we might pick out the sky-scraper as one of the permanent marks of the Twentieth Century. For better or worse, the leisurely ages of carved stone have disappeared. This reflects, too, the social and economic character of our century, as distinct from those that went before. The rebellious working masses, intent on leading their own lives, and enjoying their own leisure, have no longer the ideals, the craft, the time or the patience (or submission) that they lovingly spent on the old classic buildings.[74]

McCabe was torn between the rich, layered history of Europe and the simple stability that the United States offered. The United States was a 'solid' and 'sane pleasant place to live in', compared with Europe and its 'Communists, Socialists, Fascists, Hitlerites, Royalists and all the other political and social fauna'. 'America is new, whereas Europe is a composite or compost of old, dead, decaying things.'[75] During his visit, McCabe stayed with an Irishwoman whom he knew from home and her American husband, an estate agent. The woman, from 'a very humble home', had received only a primary education before emigrating to the United States, yet she and her husband had their own home, car and an income of 'about £1,500'. McCabe reflected that this woman would have 'lived hungry and died in poverty' if she had stayed at home. 'Ireland is a depressing place,' he wrote baldly.[76]

The longer McCabe was away from Ireland, the less disposed he was to return home, especially after his trip to the United States. During the same visit in 1933, he wrote that he 'should like to live here for a couple of years, see the whole country, the plains, the rivers and the mountains, walk every morning in a garden, tramp across the American fields, and be familiar with some stretch of road'. He confessed to never feeling so lonely as when his ship was on the Hudson River watching the skyscrapers of New York recede. 'The first time I left home was bad enough, but it lasted for only a couple of hours,' he wrote of his departure from the United States. 'This time it lasted for three days, which is curious, because I'm used to change, and to leaving folk behind, and it never affects me.'[77] McCabe mused on this nostalgia as he steamed home to Ireland:

> The man that goes aboard a ship, and sails away, leaving the coast behind, not only feels the separation, but in a dim way, the sadness of the ocean, of the Earth, of life itself – and the 'lachrimae rerum', and all the tears of things. The old Greek and Roman poetry is full of this, and Homer and Virgil, typical Mediterranean folk, haunted by a love of the sea, must have sailed on many a ship, and felt that life too is like a ship, sailing along over a wide deep ocean of sadness.[78]

Despite his contempt for the nostalgic laments of the emigrant in the Irish popular tradition, McCabe was not immune to bouts of melancholy, perhaps aware that, like the protagonists in the tales of Homer and Virgil, who were the playthings of the gods, his fate was not his own to decide but that of a higher power – in his case, not the gods but the Irish hierarchy. 'People were very homely and kind,' he wrote of the trip, 'and I'd prefer America to life in a small college in Salamanca, where I feel completely de-centred.'[79] In later years, when the Irish bishops were debating the future of the Irish College in Salamanca, McCabe expressed a desire to the bishop of Galway, Michael Browne, that he be given an appointment in California. The request was not entertained. 'If I could become a millionaire, I'd buy a yacht first thing, and see this old globe of ours properly,' McCabe wrote in 1933.[80]

His melancholia intensified when he arrived in Ireland for a brief visit before returning to Spain. The people at home seemed to him 'sadder, duller and more dull-witted' every time he returned. 'The lonely fields have the air of cemeteries,' he added. 'How sluggish the people are in their gait and manner, as compared with Americans or with Latin people. The most of them walk along as if the earth were a magnet and they had iron in their shoes.'[81] As if pointing to his own situation, he compared the Irish who had emigrated to the US and returned with those who had stayed behind:

> The Americans stick out their heads, and laugh and talk without any restraint. They seem to forget that this country is a funeral, and that it's rude to laugh like this, in the presence of the mourning population. When they have been at home for a few months, their manner will have changed, and they will realise, like so many other emigrants that return, that they should not have left Ireland, or that they should not have returned to it.

McCabe attributed this lethargy to a lack of young people, but no doubt it was also due to the harsh times and lack of economic opportunities. Even the weather got him down when he returned: 'And there's the rain again, blotting out the landscape, soaking everything.'[82]

McCabe returned to Spain and the villa in Pendueles in the summer of 1933 to find the rector in peevish form. 'It's not pleasant to be back in this little lunatic asylum, but after a refreshing change, I can stand it for some time longer.' McCabe admitted that part of the problem with their relationship was his own fault. 'I may be obstinate and even peculiar in some of my views. I certainly have a temper, and can explode easily enough.'[83] After one particular row over a game of bridge, McCabe told O'Doherty that he wanted to discuss their relationship. He said that he needed to be given more space to carry out his duties – a request he had made of O'Doherty when he was first appointed vice-rector – or otherwise he would lose interest in his work. After their talk, the remaining weeks in Pendueles passed quietly and McCabe and the rector seemed to get on reasonably well.

Pendueles and Buelna, a village about half a mile away, formed a community of roughly five hundred inhabitants. Each had its own church and tavern, but there was only one priest, one doctor and one civil guard barracks to serve both villages. In Pendueles, there was a bowling green, a public fountain, a large cement *lavadero* – an outside sink for washing clothes – and a public telephone. The palace of the Countess of Cortina dominated the village, surrounded by a garden with palm trees and a fountain. The palace comprised two distinct parts: the bottom half was built of stone, while the top part was all glass, and it was guarded by a high iron railing that ran all the way along the main road through the village. The countess also owned a deer-park on the hill behind the palace. The count of the Valley of Pendueles was the richest man in the village, but O'Doherty and McCabe were in a dispute with him over the water supply at the villa and they were not on speaking terms.

The Irish College's summer villa, the *casona de verines*, located along the main road to the east of Pendueles, remains one of the finest buildings in the village, and is also known as the *casa de los irlandeses* after the clerical students who once holidayed there. Standing a five-minute walk from the seashore, it is now owned by the University of Salamanca. The villa was built in the *indiana* or colonial style by a returned emigrant from the Americas and was surrounded by a fine garden. During the summer, the Irish students would sometimes have classes outside under the shade of a chestnut tree. There was also a secluded orchard surrounded by a high wall, where McCabe, during the 1920s, spent time meditating and studying as he prepared for his ordination.

The local mason lived behind the house and the principals of the Irish College had squabbled with him over the question of the water supply, as they had with a local engineer. McCabe described the latter as the *cacique* or political boss of the village. According to McCabe, he was 'very Radical and a bit anti-clerical, and when he has a public job in hands [*sic*], he gives employment to workmen who hold strong Leftish views like himself'.[84]

The local school was next door to the summer villa. There was a two-storey residence for the schoolmaster and the schoolmistress in the centre, with one-storey classrooms at either end for the boys and girls. At the front was a yard with a clay floor. A row of plane trees on either side provided shade for the teachers and children during break-time and the pupils would sometimes steal pears from a tree growing in the summer villa's orchard next door. The schoolmaster, 'a low stocky figure with a short bull neck, and a gruff voice and manner',[85] would assist in the sanctuary of the church and would sing the chant during mass.

Up the main road in Pendueles was the casino. Traditionally a meeting place for the gentry, it had been closed when Primo de Rivera banned public gambling. Farther along was the railway station, which was built high over the road. The railway master, a republican, lived above the offices and waiting room and McCabe would pass the time of day with him when he was out for a stroll. There were a couple of large semi-detached houses farther up the road. In the early 1920s, a viscount and his family spent the summers in one of them, until his wife was killed in a motor accident. He and his seven small daughters did not return afterwards. Dr Marina, the village doctor, lived in the other semi-detached house. He was a thin, small man, about five foot tall, 'with a piping voice, and an occasional squeal when he's talking. In ordinary conversation about the most trivial things, he always has a serious face, as if he were in the consulting room, or examining a bad internal wound. Though he seems to suffer from worms and to live on medicine, himself, he is as healthy as a fish'.[86] Another doctor, Dr Morales, who ran a nursing home in Santander, spent the holidays in a large detached house next door. At the sweep in the main road in the village was the cemetery, which was walled all around and from which projected a couple of large mausoleums holding the remains of the ancestors of the district's wealthy families.

A lane between the cemetery and the butcher's house led up to the Romanesque church. In the summer, the men would sit on the hewn stones that had been left outside in the chapel yard for a building project that had never been completed. The parish priest wore a black, velvet 'fez-shaped cap' and a soutane. 'He has no teeth, but he talks like a whirlwind, spluttering all the time. During the summer, he takes a long swim every day, fishes in the sea, and he can climb over the mountain like a goat. He is a rough diamond, very self-willed, but exceedingly active and zealous.'[87] He would say the first mass in Buelna and the second in Pendueles.

Along the road to Buelna, which was east of Pendueles, was the house of the Villar family, who were good friends of the Irish College. There were 'three or four well-built, middle-class houses,'[88] a couple of shops and a tobacconist's in Buelna. Little Miguel, a hunchback, lived with his family in a house high above the road. The Barballas, cousins of the Villars, were one of the best-known families in the village and staunch monarchists. The mother of the family was from Andalusia. 'The children take after her,' wrote McCabe, 'and have a lively Southern temperament, whereas the Villars are serious and stolid. It is a delight to hear the Barballas speak Spanish. The speech is very refined and they mix it up with fantastic ejaculations, to make it vivid.'[89]

Since he had first come to Pendueles as a student, McCabe had sensed a hardening in the relationship between the classes in this small part of Asturias. 'Formerly, there was a wonderful social spirit in this little village, and when we first came here in 1920, this valley seemed to be a little Arcadia. There were few motor-cars, and no motor buses then. We found the people more expansive and sociable than the folk down in Castille [sic], and not unlike the Irish people.' McCabe remembered all social classes attending the local feasts and getting on well together. 'They all enjoyed life, and were merry and spontaneous.' Whereas the villagers would work hard, the 'leisured aristocrats and middle-classes idled away their time, and did nothing. They spent two or three months on one of the beaches up here in the North, and spent the rest of the year in Madrid. They had a glorious time all the year round.'[90]

McCabe believed that in the early 1920s there had been a 'good understanding' between rich and poor and 'neither was intolerant of the other'. The poor people would go to the beach on Sundays, the only day they did not work, and sat apart from the señoritos, the wealthy sons of the aristocratic class. The poorer class did not bathe, leaving that pastime to the young gentlemen. 'But there was no snobbery on one side or hatred on the other. Every village and town for 15 miles around had its own annual "fiesta" in the summer, with High Mass, a special preacher, a procession in the morning, and a dance in the bowling green all night.' There was a weekly round of feasts from June to September, with each village devoted to a different saint. The young people would try to attend as many as possible. 'A young aristocrat had no scruple about dancing with a middle-class, or even a servant, girl.'[91] But all this had changed. Distrust, suspicion and petty jealousies governed relations between the classes in Pendueles in 1933.

McCabe laid the blame at the door of the republican government: 'Since the fall of the Monarchy and the coming of the Republic, the social spirit of the villages has changed. Rich and poor tend to keep apart and to be naturally hostile.'[92] Two incidents in Pendueles were evidence of this new attitude. That summer, some of the *señoritos* got together to build a tennis court down by the beach, with a shed for storing the equipment and taking shelter during a shower. 'These lazy, leisurely young people, working hard, in order to indulge in Sport later on, gave the young republicans in the village a real pain in the head.' So they noted the work as it went on and reported it to the urban authorities in nearby Llanes. The inspector arrived to assess the 'wretched shed – four poles, with a few boards and sods on top', fined those responsible for building it without permission and levied a tax. 'Spain, at present, is full of informers and "denouncers", and they love to use authority and the law, in order to persecute their political opponents, and to wreak some personal petty revenge.'[93]

More ominously, on the way back from the beach one day, McCabe arrived at the road at the same time as a man in an 'immaculate white suit'. The leader of the Spanish right in the period, José María Gil-Robles, had been addressing a gathering at Covadonga, the site of one of Spain's most important Catholic shrines. Situated in the foothills of the Picos de Europa, the stunning mountain range covering much of southern Asturias, Covadonga was where the Christians had achieved their first victory against the Moors in the eighth century and begun the *Reconquista*. It was thus a highly symbolic choice for the Spanish right to hold a rally there. Cars full of rightists were passing along the road on their way back from the meeting, and the road had been scattered with tacks to puncture the tyres of the cars of the rightists as they drove past.

'Two or three of the passengers put out their arms and held them stiffly over the edge of the car, in a sort of Fascist salute,' McCabe wrote.

> This set my immaculate friend wild. He's evidently not a Fascist or a follower of Gil-Robles. He actually danced on the road, shook his fist after the flying cars, and called them 'sin vergüenzas' [scoundrels] and 'sons of putas' [sons of whores]. He flung various other tit-bits of obscene abuse after them, before he realised that they were well out of hearing.[94]

McCabe's memories of those Arcadian summers in Asturias in the 1920s were coloured by his distaste for the regime that had come to power in 1931. His natural conservatism led him to sympathise with its opponents. He thought that, unlike other countries, the Spanish aristocracy had not 'made a parade of luxurious, dissolute living':

> The chief charge that Republicans make against the old regime is that it was backward in several ways. It might be said, too, that the wealthy people in Spain were also 'backward' in the art of living. They didn't spend money lavishly on luxuries or comforts, even, and, in general, there were no glaring disequalities [sic] between wealth and misery.[95]

He did concede that this feeling between the classes might have existed before 1931, but that it had not manifested itself:

> The poor people and the working classes feel that they are the authorities in the new regime, and they are most zealous to make the wealthy people obey the new Republican laws. Employees have to give higher wages and better conditions to workers and servants, and though some of the laws would be reasonable enough in another country, there is a certain degree of penal and class persecution in the way they are applied here.[96]

This paranoia was typical of the right in Spain in 1933. Moderates who believed that reform was necessary were now afraid of change and being driven into the arms of the extremist parties: 'The Conservatives don't want the new modern legislation, and their traditional feelings, as well as their economic interests, are wounded. The Republicans, with a certain degree of vindictive triumph, rub in the new legislation all the more vigorously, even though they must know that it's as painful as salt in a wound.'[97] McCabe noted presciently that a revolution was required to drive through reforms in Spain 'and it provokes a counter-revolution to put an end to all this novelty'. He lamented the absence of what he regarded as the old days of social harmony and regretted the fact of a new class-consciousness. 'As the Republic has separated Church and State, and is more lay or anti-clerical than clerical in tone, and as the fervent Catholics are mostly Monarchist in sympathy and loyalty, rival politics have spoiled even the religious feasts, which used to be so popular.' The village church, which had been a common meeting place for those of all political persuasions, came to be regarded as the stronghold of the monarchists and it was 'difficult for a good Catholic and sincere Republican to enter, without becoming suspect to both parties'.[98] In economic terms, nothing much had changed in Pendueles:

> Those that have the money still have it, and those that hadn't haven't. As politics is largely a scramble for power between different sets of gamesters – or gangsters – a Revolution benefits one set at the expense of another. But the people that do the rough work of the world, that dig and plough or wash and milk, go on as they were, in pretty much the same relative conditions.[99]

McCabe was prone to his dispiriting moods, and perhaps the simmering political atmosphere did not help. Sometimes he would bask in the beauty of tranquil Asturias. At other times the simple lives of the villagers enervated him and brought out a latent misanthropy. During one particular episode, he wrote:

> If the minds of men were in proportion and tune with the majesty and immensity of the universe, human life would be different, sublime, perhaps. As it is, 99% of all human beings exercise just enough intelligence to attend to their physical and economic needs, and to gossip about their friends and neighbours. If a community of

rabbits, living in their warren, could only think and talk a little, they would be, remaining rabbits, almost on a level with human beings.[100]

This gloom extended to the age in which he was living: 'One of the things lacking in modern life and arts is dignity and repose. Everything, life, architecture, locomotion, dress and conversation are becoming more standardized and violent every day.'[101] Daily scenes engaged his artistic sensibility, as when he witnessed Spanish workmen talking German politics over thimblefuls of brandy and glasses of red wine in a remote tavern in Asturias in 1933. 'In a Dutch picture, there would be heavier-drinking,' he wrote. 'Then, too, the picture of an old Master would be much finer than the reality. This scene is too vulgar and lacks artistic tone. The hard uniform electric light, though more efficient, cannot compare with the lights and shadows cast by the candles of the old days.'[102] For McCabe, the very fact that in the Asturian mountains these illiterate men were talking about foreign politics heralded something strange and terrible:

> The Radio opens up wonderful possibilities of education, and, in the end, it ought to bring nations together. But it has come too suddenly, before people have got the groundwork of education necessary to be in touch with the whole world and to understand it all. The workmen here are evidently following what is happening in Germany, and it shows the spirit of class solidarity and international sympathy that European workmen everywhere have to-day.[103]

The butcher and Alejandro Villar came together to say goodbye to McCabe and the students as they prepared to return to Salamanca at the end of the summer. The butcher was a republican; Villar was a monarchist. 'There is a good deal of political antipathy between the two of them, and the parting with both was a bit strained and tense.'[104] The small world of these aristocrats, professionals, shopkeepers and workers was to be turned upside down over the next decade; some of them would end up paying with their lives for their political views.

Back in Salamanca, much of McCabe's time was taken up with administration. The Irish College was not only a seat of learning but also a household that had to be fed and heated. In the wine cellar were six large casks, each with a capacity of six hundred litres of wine, though only two were generally in use. There were also five smaller sherry casks and three or four glass jugs protected with wicker. Olive oil was kept in a six-foot high tin vessel. Next to the cellar was the meat-house, the meat itself was stored in an old safe. Beside the meat-house were the wash-house, the pantry – where the chickpeas, beans, potatoes and apples were stored – and the coal cellar. On the other side of the building were the lavatories, lumber-room, gymnasium and boiler room.

As an example of the daily domestic chores with which he was entrusted, shortly after he returned from Pendueles McCabe ordered 574 kilos of *garbanzos*, or chickpeas, for the season. The Irish College owned about 660 acres of land and so was mostly self-sufficient. These supplies were kept in the *paneras* or store-rooms. There was one opposite the college chapel, which was where the wheat was kept until it was profitable to sell – after 1936 all the wheat was bought by the state at a fixed price.

Soon after returning to Salamanca that autumn, McCabe discovered that some of the wine in the cellar had turned sour because the barrels had not been corked properly. The wine merchant sent someone around to clean them. 'He scalded them with hot water, put lighted sulphur tapers into the tap-holes, and then plugged them tightly. After three or four days, the barrels were clean and sweet again. As might be expected, in Spain they know all about making wine and storing it, which is just as important.'[105]

Another chore was managing the domestic staff. In the autumn, the *ama*, or housekeeper, an elderly, pious woman, contracted pneumonia after going on a pilgrimage to Ávila to celebrate the feast of St Teresa. She was transferred to the provincial hospital next door to the college before eventually succumbing to her illness. The new housekeeper, the porter – an ex-civil guard – and the cook were constantly at each other's throats. The housekeeper was paid 100 pesetas a month, or about £30 a year, and her keep. Her responsibilities included grocery shopping, supervising the cooking, and laundry for the superiors and students. She had a cook, a maid and a boy to carry out the work. The washerwomen who did the college laundry would scrub the priests' shirts and trousers on wooden boards beside the Tormes River that flowed through Salamanca. McCabe suspected the housekeeper of pilfering or skimming off the top:

> It seems that all the servants that handle money and buy in the market and shops for their employers indulge in 'la sisa' [petty theft]. That is, they extract some quantities for themselves or mark down a higher price, and keep the difference for themselves. This pilfering is a recognised custom and it's not regarded as dishonest, but as secret compensation for the low wages that they are paid.[106]

The rector was in poor health, suffering from a variety of complaints including uric acid, acute rheumatism and chronic throat trouble. That winter he caught a cold and started to complain of heart palpitations. 'The house-doctor, Señor Ganedo, who is a timid, very gentle sort of man, was called in, even though the Rector hasn't the slightest faith in him. After a couple of visits, the rector began to stare sceptically at him, and to ask him snappy questions.' The doctor gave up coming to see the rector, telling McCabe he thought it was futile. 'There were a couple of students ill at the time, and when the Doctor called to see them, he merely and barely asked how the Rector was.'[107] O'Doherty travelled to Cannes to recuperate at the end of the year, leaving McCabe in charge of the college.

Period postcard, which belonged to McCabe, depicting Salamanca. (Courtesy of the National Library of Ireland.)

62 SALAMANCA. PATIO DEL COLEGIO DE IRLANDESES

Period postcard, which belonged to McCabe, depicting the patio, galleries and tower of the Irish College. (Courtesy of the National Library of Ireland.)

The Salamanca students pictured on holiday with the rector, Denis O'Doherty (back row, sixth from left), and vice-rector, Richard Fitzgerald (back row, fourth from left), in Salinas, Asturias, in 1916. (Reproduced by permission of the Librarian, Maynooth University, from the collections of St Patrick's College, Maynooth.)

Members of Óglaigh na hÉireann, or the College Volunteers, as they were also known, in St Patrick's College, Cavan, in 1917. McCabe is back row, fourth from the left. (Courtesy of the National Library of Ireland.)

The Duke of Tetuán (third from left) with the rector, Denis O'Doherty (far right), and vice-rector, Richard Fitzgerald (second from right), in the Irish College, 1922. (Courtesy of the National Library of Ireland.)

King Alfonso XIII of Spain and the Infanta Beatriz, his elder daughter, with the rector, Denis O'Doherty, during a visit to the Irish College in spring 1928. (Reproduced by permission of the Librarian, Maynooth University, from the collections of St Patrick's College, Maynooth.)

The rector, Denis O'Doherty (front row, third from left), and vice-rector, McCabe (front row, third from right), with students in the Irish College, *c.*1934. (Courtesy of the National Library of Ireland.)

Eoin O'Duffy (seated centre, in leather coat) with Irish Brigade volunteers aboard the SS *Avoceta* en route from Liverpool to Lisbon, November 1936. (P13/95, Stradling Collection © Image courtesy of Special Collections and Archives, Glucksman Library. Copyright of the University of Limerick.)

Members of the Irish Brigade outside the ruined church in Ciempozuelos with liturgical objects and vestments, 1937. (P13/64, Stradling Collection © Image courtesy of Special Collections and Archives, Glucksman Library. Copyright of the University of Limerick.)

Eoin O'Duffy (marked with an X) distributing shamrock to members of the Irish Brigade outside the church in Ciempozuelos, March 1937. (P13/65, Stradling Collection © Image courtesy of Special Collections and Archives, Glucksman Library. Copyright of the University of Limerick.)

Irish Brigade volunteers training in the trenches at Ciempozuelos, spring 1937. (P13/69, Stradling Collection © Image courtesy of Special Collections and Archives, Glucksman Library. Copyright of the University of Limerick.)

Members of the Irish Brigade posing in front of cannons at Ciempozuelos, spring 1937. (P13/70, Stradling Collection © Image courtesy of Special Collections and Archives, Glucksman Library. Copyright of the University of Limerick.)

Irish Brigade volunteer James Roche buying a looted bottle of wine from *regulares* at La Marañosa, spring 1937. (P13/71, Stradling Collection © Image courtesy of Special Collections and Archives, Glucksman Library. Copyright of the University of Limerick.)

Fr Joseph Mulrean celebrating mass in front of members of the Irish Brigade at La Marañosa, spring 1937. (P13/73, Stradling Collection © Image courtesy of Special Collections and Archives, Glucksman Library. Copyright of the University of Limerick.)

Fr Joseph Mulrean (left) with members of the Irish Brigade, including James Roche with looted bottle of wine (second from left), at La Marañosa, spring 1937. (P13/74, Stradling Collection © Image courtesy of Special Collections and Archives, Glucksman Library. Copyright of the University of Limerick.)

Fr Joseph Mulrean (third from left) with members of the Irish Brigade outside a bunker at Ciempozuelos, spring 1937. (P13/77, Stradling Collection © Image courtesy of Special Collections and Archives, Glucksman Library. Copyright of the University of Limerick.)

# Chapter 5

# THE ROAD TO REVOLUTION

In November 1933, following national elections, Alejandro Lerroux, the leader of the Radical Party, formed a new government with the support of the right-wing CEDA coalition, ushering in the period in modern Spanish history that became known as the *bienio negro*, or the black two years. This new coalition was of a very different political hue from that of the previous republican government.

The new prime minister had enjoyed a colourful career. From Córdoba, Lerroux had started out as a journalist in the 1890s and first become famous for his campaign against the torture of anarchist prisoners. He had earned a huge following in the slums of Barcelona, because of his fiery rhetoric, which urged his followers to engage in church-burning and other acts of violence against priests and religious. Lerroux tapped into the profound anti-clericalism of migrant workers from the impoverished south of Spain. For them, the Church was the defender of the brutally unjust rural social order from which they had fled. Many of the radical members, who had entered into coalition with the republicans and socalists in 1931, were more interested in the financial benefits of wielding power than the task of reforming the country.

The CEDA, led by the Salamancan lawyer Gil-Robles, had won the most seats in the Cortes, but the president, Niceto Alcalá Zamora, a confirmed republican, had refused to appoint Gil-Robles as prime minister. Instead, he had chosen Lerroux, who governed with the support of the CEDA deputies. The CEDA were anxious to roll back the reforms of the first two years of the Second Republic, and they played upon middle-class fears of socialism, anarchism and communism to present themselves as the party that would hold back the revolutionary mob. In

fact, the CEDA's militia, the Juventudes de Acción Popular (JAP), which
had started out as the party's youth wing, was increasingly involved in
street violence. They were joined by members of the Falange Española
de las Juntas de Ofensiva Nacional-Sindicalista, an organisation made up
of different fascist groups under the leadership of José Antonio Primo de
Rivera, the son of the dictator who had governed Spain in the 1920s.

At the beginning of 1934, McCabe escaped the college by walking
through Salamanca and the surrounding countryside. He enjoyed being
away from the rector:

> Now that I am alone and can walk leisurely, I am taking in all the
> points of the compass by turn, and re-visiting the old haunts and
> places of interest. It's much more pleasant than having to listen to
> grammatical and phonetical criticism, or finding out the points
> that we shall give the students in our next sermon on humility and
> obedience.[1]

McCabe did not believe that walks should be taken up with 'skeleton
sermons' and 'pedantic points of grammar'. 'Since I left College, I have
always walked alone, and always enjoyed walking. On a walk, in a sermon,
on a journey, or in anything, I hate to be tied to anybody's strings, or
taken on a lead.'[2] He resolved to refuse to accept a position in the future
where he could not enjoy his walks alone. 'One should avoid, as much
as possible, living contact with the minds of his fellow-men, because the
human mind, though it's generally as small as a gnat, is a most irritating
insect.'[3]

During these walks in and around Salamanca, McCabe would pass
the washerwomen busy at work beside the River Tormes. They would
kneel on wooden boxes to protect their knees from the frozen ground and
work the clothes on wooden boards or large stones. 'As we learned to our
cost when we were students, these washerwomen ruin linen.'[4] He would
also pass the political graffiti and posters that were still plastered across
many of the city's most historic buildings from the previous November's
elections.

Many of the wealthy families in Salamanca kept a large car. 'They
drive out for a mile or two every day, stop at the same point in the road,

sit in the car, or get out and stand around outside, take the fresh air for about a quarter of an hour, get in, drive back, and sit over the charcoal brazier for the rest of the day.' This car was 'mainly for show' and many of the families who owned one did not wish to pay for petrol. There may also have been another reason: 'The Spanish workmen are learning the Gospel of greed and grudge, and they glare furiously at these "bloated aristocrats" – though they may be only small middle-class people rolling around in their four-wheeled luxury.'[5]

When he was not out walking, McCabe spent his free time reading or writing. The morning newspapers from Madrid would arrive in Salamanca at 2pm. The rector took *El Debate*, the Catholic newspaper that supported the CEDA. McCabe took *El Sol*. In the early 1930s, it was a liberal republican newspaper, though many of its contributors would later become leading lights in the Falange. Readers of *El Sol* were 'severely frowned at by the Conservative classes, but it's well-written, and gives better literary articles that any other Spanish papers, even the Monarchist "A.B.C."'[6]

There was also plenty of reading matter in the college library. It contained centuries-old volumes and McCabe despaired that 'there is so much to read' and that it would be impossible to get through everything 'even if there were forty-eight hours in the day'.[7]

One cold night in January, McCabe went up to the library to have a look at the silhouette of the town:

> Through the window, I can see thousands of lights, the dark towers, and the huge mass of the Clerecía, which seems to be half the town. … There's no electric light in the library, and it gives one a weird creepy pleasant feeling to be alone in here. On the brick floor, there are a few cannonballs of the type used to shell the town during the Peninsular War. I stuck my toe against one of them, and it rolled along the floor with a hollow rumbling sound that filled the whole library.

Half of the library had been destroyed during the war. 'One might almost expect one of Napoleon's soldiers, wearing a cocked hat, to jump suddenly out of a corner, present his musket, and shout in French, "Who goes there?" … But this library is over four hundred years old, and there are more ancient ghosts in it than those of Napoleon's soldiers.' He continued:

> Looking over at the shelves, I can see dimly all the large folio tomes of Philosophy and Theology, bound in old white calf. A book is an author's spirit, and here are all these 16th-century spirits, wrapped in their white shrouds, waiting for the Cathedral clock to strike midnight, when they will come forth from the calf-bound volumes that imprison them, hide in the dark corners of the library, and meditate again on this old world of ours. There is a less respectful way of looking at these old volumes. They are a little better than the dry brains of learned men pressed into paper.[8]

The patio and the cloistered galleries that surrounded it also provided the perfect place for quiet reflection. 'From one season to another and from one day to another, the appearance of the Patio was always changing. Besides being a work of architecture and of art, the Patio is a marvellous combination of stone, sky, sunlight, moonlight, silence and Peace.'[9]

As the new government rolled back the hard-won agricultural reforms of the previous two years, the landowners began reasserting their authority in the countryside. Workers belonging to trade unions were denied employment. Civil guards fired at workers during demonstrations and strikes. Many of the students at the University of Salamanca became interested in fascism and joined the Falange. Gil-Robles of the CEDA was making ever more aggressive speeches. With the socialist opposition becoming radicalised and anarchist protests taking place throughout the country, the JAP militia began to view Gil-Robles as the supreme leader who would rescue Spain from the Marxist hordes. They began marching through the streets, shouting *Jefe! Jefe! Jefe!*[*] In February, the porter told McCabe there was going to be a revolution the following Saturday. 'This is an amusing country,' he wrote. 'They announce a revolution as if it were a football match, but it always arrives late like the trains. And they seem to regard a Revolution as a pleasant little affair like a pic-nic.'[10]

---

[*] *Jefe* was the Spanish equivalent of the German *führer* or Italian *duce*.

Safe from the cold winter and the revolutionary fever outside, McCabe was quite content within the walls of the college:

> My stove is drawing well, the coal is pretty good, and, at night, with tobacco and a book, I feel quite comfortable in my little cubby-hole. I have a writing table, a stiff-backed armchair, and a small plain bookcase with open shelves. There's no carpet on the wooden floor, and I haven't a picture on the walls, a photograph, an ornament of any kind. It's really a bare cell, and I shouldn't let an Irish Professor see it. But it is in a bare hole like this, that one can study best, and be really happy.[11]

The anti-clerical mood among the workers was coming to a head. 'There are three popular terms of contempt here,' McCabe noted, '"cura" [priest] for a man, "puta" [whore] for a woman, and "Portugués" [Portuguese] for a foreigner, when the people don't like him.'[12] The bookstall in the railway station sold a satirical magazine published in Valencia called *La Traca* full of anti-clerical humour. Priests, monks and nuns were presented as lascivious, aggressive caricatures in the illustrations within. Periodically censored, *La Traca* had been published in one form or the other since the late nineteenth century, its anti-monarchism and anti-clericalism proving extremely popular. It became more political during the Second Republic, allying itself with the Popular Front and enjoying huge sales. The editor and many of the cartoonists were shot at the end of the civil war. McCabe was disgusted by the magazine's contents, though he still bought a copy. 'The like of it would not be exposed for public sale at a provincial station in the Free State, or even Belfast, I fancy,' he harrumphed.[13]

McCabe believed that the Spanish Church bore some responsibility for these attitudes. 'At present, when talking to most priests about the situation, one expects them to sit down suddenly and start to cry. They see that the country is drifting, that they are losing the people, and yet they are as helpless to prevent themselves from going under as a new-born baby in a bucket of water.'[14] Some confessed to McCabe that they wished they could speak another language, so that they could leave Spain, such were their fears for the future and the distrust and suspicion between left and right. 'There is an intense degree of social incivility and hatred here at present,' wrote McCabe after he had witnessed an old lady sneering at 'a respectable-looking man' and his wife out for a walk.[15] McCabe was contemptuous of the Spanish clergy's passivity and the absence of a more 'muscular' spirit. Much of this weakness he attributed to the Spanish seminaries. The contrast between Irish and Spanish Catholicism was profound, he believed, not least in the way the clergy was trained.

McCabe visited Madrid in the spring of 1934 to interview a candidate for college housekeeper and her former mistress. He met the latter in an apartment opposite El Retiro (the park in the centre of Madrid). 'It had a stuffy horsehair, anti-macassar, badly ventilated Victorian air, with a jumble of too much furniture, and too many family photographs and knick-knacks, like an Old Curiosity Shop.'[16] His impression of Madrid on this visit was that the city was rather provincial and French: 'It hasn't the genuine character and flavour of an old Spanish town. On the surface, it seems to be modern and cosmopolitan. It used to have a tone of aristocratic distinction about it during the Monarchy, and the people were very lively, friendly and simple.'[17] His interview with the prospective housekeeper took place in a poor district of the city, covered with drying laundry. Local residents directed him to the woman's dwelling: 'Even though a wet towel or shirt brushes across one's face, there is no greater pleasure in life than to go into the homes of the poor, to find them friendly, and to be one of themselves. Visits like this a few times a month would be good for the soul.'[18]

McCabe went on holiday to Greece and Turkey that spring. On his way back to Salamanca from Gibraltar, he stopped in Toledo. In his hotel, he saw an elderly man wearing clerical garb on the other side of the dining room. He was wearing a ring with a large precious stone. Presuming him to be a Catholic bishop, McCabe went over to introduce himself: 'I very nearly bent down and kissed the ring. God forgive me! He turned out to be a Mr McConville, a Protestant minister from Antrim.' The minister had been attending a Protestant conference in Madrid. 'Though he's from the "Black" North, he's a nice man to talk to, and though he has an air of a lay, non-Conformist preacher, he's quite cultured and refined. He knows his Spain, too.'[19] The two clerics did not discuss religion. 'It's rather funny how educated non-Catholics appreciate Catholicism as Art, but condemn the Religion – and the Art – as superstition.'[20] McCabe hurried back to

Salamanca because he wished to return before May Day and what he feared would be violent demonstrations against the government.

Throughout the summer Spain continued to seethe. In September, Gil-Robles addressed members of the JAP at another mass rally in Covadonga. At the end of the month, he said that the CEDA could no longer support the minority government of Ricardo Samper, another radical who had replaced Lerroux as prime minister the previous April. Three CEDA ministers joined a new coalition in early October, and Lerroux was reinstalled as prime minister. With the CEDA gaining in political strength, the left began to fear a fascist coup, the overthrow of the republic and the declaration of a dictatorship. The UGT, the socialist trade union, called a general strike. In response, the government proclaimed martial law and brought in the army to run services. In Barcelona, the Generalitat, the semi-autonomous Catalan government, declared an independent Catalonia within a federal republic of Spain. The army was called in to restore the authority of the central government in Madrid.

Most of these confrontations between the workers and the military passed off with little or no bloodshed, except in Asturias. There, the miners, organised by the UGT, the anarchist CGT union and the communists, formed a revolutionary front and began to arm themselves, though they had few weapons except the explosives that they used to dynamite the rock in the mines. Faced with this overt challenge to the government's authority, the minister of war authorised General Francisco Franco, a co-founder of its battle-hardened foreign legion, to use all means necessary to put down the rebellion. The repression was bloody. Franco employed the brutal methods that he had honed fighting the Rif tribesmen in Spain's bloody colonial wars in North Africa. In the way that he dealt with the Asturias uprising, Franco showed a ruthless streak towards his fellow countrymen that was to find its full expression during the civil war. Two battalions of legionaries and two battalions of *regulares* – Moroccan mercenaries – were dispatched to Asturias from North Africa. Franco bombed and shelled the miners' villages and towns without discrimination, killing women and children. When the principal Asturian towns of Gijón and Oviedo fell, and the rebellion had been quelled, Franco began to carry out summary executions of anyone he deemed culpable.

McCabe and the students had returned to Salamanca from their summer holidays in Asturias just before the rebellion. 'Before we left, there was a certain degree of tenseness in the air, and lorry-drivers gave the Communistic salute as they raced past.'[21] In conservative Salamanca, there was little trouble. McCabe was alone with the students, though he remained calm. 'I felt my responsibility for the students, and we were prepared for anything'.[22] There were fears that the Asturian miners would march south to take the nearby city of Valladolid, through which most of the train routes passed, and then Salamanca. After a couple of nervous days, news came through that the rebellion was over. Though the miners in Asturias had little chance of success against the superior firepower of the Spanish foreign legion, right-wing Spain had had a fright:

> We were much safer in Salamanca but I was a little bit preoccupied. If the trouble became serious, we should have put up a flag, and if the workmen tried to storm the College, I had decided to close the heavy front doors and get the students out by the back. Or, as the windows of the Medical Faculty are on a level with the back garden of the College, I had decided that we could break through them, pass through the Faculty, and get out into the street, without being noticed.[23]

This shows how seriously McCabe took the threat of rebellion in Salamanca.

Despite the fears of a workers' uprising, McCabe noted that 'the workers never molested us, interfered with us, or took any notice of us. In fact, they always respected us and were friendly, because we never took any part or interest in public life, and because they regarded the British Isles as the classic home where workers received good treatment and more justice than in Spain.'[24] However, events in Asturias increased fears among the Salamancan middle classes of a workers' revolution. Many of them now threw in their lot with the CEDA and awaited the overthrow of the Second Republic by a fascist or military coup.

The monarchist newspaper *A.B.C.* had a picture of a Moroccan sniper picking off targets from the tower of Oviedo Cathedral during the confrontation with the workers. McCabe thought it 'a bit funny to have a Moor defending a Spanish Cathedral against Spaniards'. He added: 'However, they are excellent soldiers, and can be relied on to fight against Spaniards, when a fellow Spaniard couldn't be trusted. Over half of the Spanish Army are Communists, and as they sympathise with the workers, they couldn't be relied on to shoot down fellow-Spaniards of their own condition and class.'[25] When it came to fighting a civil war a couple of years later, Franco used his Moroccan troops to strike terror into enemy soldiers and the civilian population, encouraging them to rape, loot and murder at will.

The rector returned from Ireland in November. Though O'Doherty looked thinner and paler than usual, he was in good form and surprised McCabe by telling him that he was going to resign and take a parish in Ireland. It was not only his failing health that had led to the decision, McCabe suspected, but the increasingly fraught political situation in Spain. The rector was 'an Aristocrat in outlook and tastes', according to McCabe, who was loyal to the Spanish monarchy and could not get accustomed to the republic.[26] The uprising in Asturias had been the final straw and it had frightened him. O'Doherty had already begun to put arrangements in place for his return to Ireland, hoping to replace the parish priest of Boyle in County Roscommon who had died in November. Boyle was regarded as one of the best parishes in the rector's native diocese of Elphin, and the bishop had offered it to O'Doherty.

It was an unpleasant shock for McCabe, who had already decided to offer his resignation the following year, after he had completed five years as vice-rector. He did not see his future in Spain, had become disillusioned by life in the college, and had begun saving some money so that he could return to Ireland. But he also knew that it would be difficult to find a replacement: 'I'm quite sure that there isn't one Irish priest out of twenty that would live here as Vice-Rector for more than two years!'[27]

O'Doherty told McCabe that he wished to retain his old title, because he was afraid the Spanish authorities would try to take over the Irish College if they discovered that he had returned to Ireland, even if a new rector was appointed. He told McCabe to tell no one that he was preparing to return for good. McCabe was not impressed. At the beginning of December, and contrary to his wish of hiding the fact that he was returning to Ireland, the rector decided to hold a farewell lunch. He and McCabe were on their way down to extend an invitation to one of their guests, when they came across Miguel de Unamuno. The philosopher had been a friend of the previous rector, 'but on account of [Unamuno's] political postures during the Dictatorship and the Republic, the Rector had practically broken off relations with him'.[28] The meeting was a cordial one, however, and Unamuno took the Irish priests into his confidence, explaining how the death of his wife had been 'a great mental crisis for him'. The farewell lunch was a 'quiet affair, because the Rector wanted to keep his departure a secret from the students'.[29]

The following evening, Unamuno came to the Irish College for tea. 'Fortunately, Don Felipe Alcántara, Provincial of the Salesians, turned up by accident a few minutes beforehand, and this helped to break the ice, because the Rector didn't feel that he could warm up to Unamuno'.[30] Unamuno had written a pamphlet that had condemned the military's summary executions that had followed the suppression of the uprising in Asturias. The authorities had banned the pamphlet but it had been circulating clandestinely in Salamanca. Over tea, Unamuno expounded on the subject. He told his companions that executions, rather than suppressing revolt, served only to promote it. 'This was sound patriotic doctrine in Ireland after the 1916 Rebellion,' McCabe wrote later, 'and Unamuno, though not a Separatist, was a good, rebellious Basque.'[31] McCabe recalled in his diary the occasion when O'Doherty had 'literally closed the door against the British Ambassador' but noted that he was not 'sufficiently "Rebel" to be with Unamuno against King Alfonso'. Unamuno discussed his problematic relationship with different governments in Madrid, saying that 'his policy was not to do anything that they forced him to do. After tea, Padre Alcántara left, but Don Miguel [Unamuno] came upstairs, and sat in the Blue Room and talked for over an hour.' When he was leaving, Unamuno said that he would return frequently now that he had come back to visit the Irish College. 'I remarked to the Rector that he enjoyed the stay, and talked a lot. "Yes, he did to you." This was one of the Rector's little jealousies. But the Rector kept looking hard at Don Miguel, and staring him out of countenance and he must have found me receptive. Beside, Don Miguel always likes to lecture to young audiences.'[32]

Two days after Unamuno's visit, in the early hours of a Sunday morning, and just a few days before he was due to return home to

Ireland for good, the rector complained of a pain. The doctor diagnosed appendicitis and peritonitis. O'Doherty's inflamed abdomen meant that an operation was impossible. On the Tuesday, the situation was grave enough for McCabe to send for the college's confessor, Padre Celso, from the Augustinian convent in Salamanca. However, Celso was afraid to tell the rector that his life was in danger and decided not to perform the last rites. The following Saturday, while McCabe was resting in his room, one of the students, who had stayed with the rector throughout the night, knocked on the door. When McCabe arrived in his room, he found O'Doherty prostrate and his eyes dull:

> I asked him if he'd like to see Padre Celso. He answered something incoherent, but I could catch the words 'a general Absolution'. I had the oils at hand, and while I was anointing him, he had a haemorrhage and, perhaps, a heart attack. The legs kicked and spread out, the head fell down over the shoulder, and he never moved afterwards.[33]

The rector had been due to take possession of his new parish in Ireland that very day. McCabe sent for Francisco Ramos, the college administrator, while the porter and his wife laid out the corpse. On the Sunday, the body reposed in the college's Blue Room. Members of the cathedral chapter, the university and the seminary, as well as prominent lay people, came in all morning to pay their respects. That evening, the students carried the remains down to the college chapel. The following day, the vicar-capitular, Pedro Salcedo, presided over requiem mass. Afterwards, the students carried the remains to the cemetery. Except for a couple of Spanish friends of the college, only McCabe and the students were in attendance. 'It was a grey Irish day, and the burial was very simple. The Rector was always very fond of counting several Bishops on his list of friends. The diocese of Salamanca is vacant, and it struck me as remarkable that there wasn't a single Bishop, Canon or ecclesiastic at his burial.'[34]

The gravediggers dug the grave about an inch too short in a few spots at one end. 'Instead of taking a spade and framing the surface properly like Christians, or rational animals, at least, they wanted to force the coffin down by pushing and stamping on the lid. I nearly lost my temper with them. They bury a man here as if he were a dead mule.'[35] The next day, two municipal officials arrived to spray the rector's room. They sealed up the doors before they left.

The rector was buried in the college's plot in the cemetery. Later, during the Second World War, his brother, Michael O'Doherty, the archbishop of Manila, himself a former rector of the Irish College, asked McCabe to purchase a private plot, reinter his brother's remains and erect a monument to his memory. He composed the inscription in Spanish and paid for all the expenses. It was just after All Saints Day, when the Spanish remember their deceased relatives by bringing flowers to their graves. This second funeral, with only McCabe, himself then rector of the Irish College, and his vice-rector, John O'Hara, in attendance, was a grisly business:

> I ordered a new coffin, and late one November evening we opened the grave. There was nothing left but the skeleton, and a few black pieces of sodden, grave-eaten vestments (it was the best set we had in the Sacristy). We gathered up all the remains (on this occasion, a word full of vivid meaning) placed them in the new coffin, and closed the lid. … In November, this Cemetery, with its well-kept graves, lighted lamps, and beautiful flowers has a strange sad attraction of its own, and I like to walk here. But this was a gruesome evening, and the best sermon ever I've had on the vanity of life.[36]

The weeks and months following the rector's death were difficult. McCabe had wished to leave Spain, but the rector's sudden death had put him in charge of the college, with no other suitable candidate to replace him.

In April 1935, the archbishop of Dublin, Edward Byrne – the most senior Irish prelate, in the absence of Cardinal MacRory, who was attending a congress in Australia – referred to the likelihood of McCabe being offered the position of rector on a permanent basis. McCabe was torn. On the one hand, he felt responsible for maintaining the Irish College in Salamanca, an institution dating back more than three centuries. There was no one better attuned to the political and cultural climate in Spain and this had an undoubted appeal to his intellectual vanity. On the other hand, he was tired of Spain and had already decided to leave.

Mulling over his future, McCabe recalled one evening when he and the late rector had been out for a walk close to the cemetery. They had looked through the side gate, where, in one corner, the heretics, freemasons and prostitutes were buried. There had previously been a wall surrounding this portion of the cemetery but it had been torn down during the republic:

> We were saying that it wouldn't be nice to die in Spain. Well, died he did, at the end of 23 years. The thought of meeting the same fate freezes my blood. I thought this thing over in all its aspects, until I had a pain in the head. I shouldn't like to clear out of the old ship, if she were in danger of sinking. Of course, I know half-a-dozen men who would regard it as a glittering appointment and like to have it. They know nothing about the life, or the changes in Spain, or of what the future may have in store.[37]

On 25 June 1935, McCabe was formally appointed rector. He read the news in one of the Irish newspapers a few days later while he was taking a break from packing his late predecessor's possessions in order to send them to his brother in Manila.

> It was extremely hot, I was all dusty and tired, and for the moment, I believe that the news irritated me more than anything else. I'm stuck into the hole for better or worse, and that's the end of it. So I finished the packing, and took a good resolution – to leave no letters, paper, or dusty rubbish behind me when I die.[38]

For a man who liked to be on the move, it had been a frustrating year. He had not been able to leave Salamanca since the previous summer and could not get away until a vice-rector was appointed. His one trip, in early June, had been to the Aragonese town of Alba by taxi with the leader of Fine Gael and former head of the Irish government, W.T. Cosgrave, who had visited the Irish College with his two brothers-in-law, both of them priests.

Meanwhile, Spain was moving towards the precipice. In March 1935, Gil-Robles, striving to take control of the government, pressed for the execution of the leaders of the 1934 rebellion in Asturias. Instead, the president, Alcalá Zamora, commuted the death sentences on the advice of the prime minister, Alejandro Lerroux. The CEDA ministers resigned in protest. Unable to govern on his own, Lerroux formed a new coalition, with five CEDA ministers, including, for the first time, Gil-Robles himself, who demanded to be made minister of war, and Cándido Casanueva y Gorjón, another native of the province of Salamanca, who became the new minister of justice. The new coalition drew up a programme designed to reverse many of the reforms made by the republican-socialist government in the first two years of the Second Republic.

The right was eagerly awaiting the overthrow of the republic that summer. It seemed only a matter of time before Gil-Robles would be leading the country. The leaders of the left, meanwhile, were on trial for their alleged involvement in the previous autumn's convulsions. Gil-Robles' speeches became ever more bloodthirsty. At the end of June, the municipal authorities in Salamanca held a ceremony to honour Gil-Robles and Casanueva, the native-born sons who had become ministers in the new government. The festivities included a military parade, a march-past and a reception in the town hall. The organising committee requested the use of the college patio for an open-air banquet. Over 1,000 guests were invited and the patio turned out to be too small, or, perhaps, given his future machinations to prevent unwelcome visitors, McCabe pulled a diplomatic stroke to block the reception from being held there. He did, however, attend the festivities as a guest.

As well as the two new Salamancan ministers, Lerroux and the new minister of the interior, Manuel Portela Valladares, were in attendance. Shaking hands with the Spanish prime minister, McCabe recalled Lerroux's anti-clerical past when he had invited his followers in Barcelona 'to enter the convents with the precocious advice to "lift the veils of the inmates". It takes a Latin to coin a nice, innocent-looking, very obscene phrase. Now he is a fine clean-looking old man of seventy, with a strong, middle-aged figure, a genial face, pince-nez, and a fraternal smile.'[39] Despite the rightward tilt of the government, many in the conservative Salamancan crowd were hostile to the republic and the presence of the radicals. 'The extreme "Apostolic" crowd never forgave Gil-Robles for this alliance with Satan,' McCabe noted, speculating that having gone through the formalities, this same crowd went home and 'probably washed their hands, or had a bath, to get rid of all this filth and infection'.[40] However, Gil-Robles impressed McCabe. He had a 'round babyish face, and the flabby figure of a porpoise, and his enemies make the most of this in their personal allusions and caricatures. But I noticed and liked his handshake. His hand is as large and hard as that of a ploughman or oarsman, and he grips tight from the heart. This is the first time that I've seen Gil-Robles, and I like him. There's plenty of iron underneath the fat.'[41]

Despite sporadic violence throughout Spain, the students spent a peaceful time in Asturias that summer. Rural unrest was affecting the college's income, and some tenants were in arrears, but the college administrator had managed to collect most of the rents. McCabe was able to report to the Irish bishops that there was a 'healthy spiritual atmosphere' in the Irish College after his first year in charge.[42]

He was helped in his endeavours by the arrival of the new vice-rector, John O'Hara, a former student of the college from County Sligo. O'Hara had attended St Nathy's College in County Roscommon before studying for the priesthood in Salamanca. The president of St Nathy's had recommended the student O'Hara to Denis O'Doherty as 'a very quiet boy, attentive to his religious duties and devoted to his studies'.[43] After ordination in 1931, O'Hara became dean of studies at St Nathy's.

The physical health of the students was good too, after one of the warmest and wettest winters in Salamanca in years. Unfortunately, though, the rains had caused substantial damage to the outer roof of the college: many of the old wooden beams were rotten and in danger of crashing through the inner roof, and the bare wiring, which had not been replaced for thirty years, was also highly dangerous.

At the beginning of 1936, the president of the republic, Alcalá Zamora, dissolved the Cortes and a general election was called for February. The president had refused to invite Gil-Robles to form a government, partly out of his own political convictions, partly out of spite. The political right in Salamanca was confident of success. 'Ponte las botas, que los Reyes te echan'* was a piece of monarchist graffiti seen around the city. This was a play on Alcalá Zamora's nickname, 'botas',

---

\*   'Put on your boots, because the King and Queen are going to throw you out.'

and a reference to the Día de los Reyes, the Feast of the Epiphany, which was held around this time.[44]

There was a sense of foreboding in Spain in the run-up to the election, which seemed to mirror McCabe's mood. On one of his walks,

> it began to sleet out of black heavy clouds in the North-West. I took refuge in the Cemetery, strolled up and down the covered walk, and had a look at the long rows of tombs in the wall. There are three or four tiers from top to bottom. It seems unnatural to bury people in a thick high boundary wall, and not in the Earth, which, in addition, is a great disinfectant. There were several groups of black[-clad] females around. Only one was weeping. All the others were chattering like jackdaws. I got tired of all this babble and of the smell of death, and decided to get a good drenching just to have a clean bath in the fresh open air, and to enjoy the sensation of being alive.[45]

McCabe bought a radio for 600 pesetas in the New Year. On the night of 20 January, he tuned in to discover that the English stations had gone silent out of respect for the king, George V, who was dying. At 11.45pm, the announcement came that the king was dead. McCabe was impressed by the fact that he was hundreds of miles from London listening to the coverage of the king's last moments on earth. 'When one is living in Spain, where there is so much rebellion and violence and where even the highest authority is the victim of vulgar indecent jokes, if not of assassins, this reverence that the English people feel for the person and sacred office of the King fills one with admiration.'[46]

In Spain, the build-up to the election continued. Placards for the CEDA went up around Salamanca. In the centre of Madrid, the soft, flabby features of Gil-Robles, whose supporters were attempting to create a cult of personality along the lines of Hitler or Mussolini, stared down from a gigantic billboard in the Puerta del Sol. The left had organised itself into the Popular Front, comprising the socialists, left-wing republicans and communists. Rumours of revolution were rife. The college administrator, Francisco Ramos, told McCabe that he had been made aware of the fact that the left was preparing a coup. Propagandists warned of the dire consequences of fascism or Marxism triumphing should the other side gain power.

Polling day was 16 February. 'It rained most of the time, and this helped to keep down the political fever,' wrote McCabe. 'In Salamanca, [the election] passed off as quietly as a funeral. … We got the first results on Radio. They seem to indicate a victory for the Right and Centre parties.'[47] But by the next day, things had changed and it looked as if the Popular Front was going to take power. 'I had a walk around the Plaza. Everything is quiet but there are several groups of workmen around, looking very expectant and determined.'[48]

On 20 February, the final result showed that the Popular Front had won 34.3 per cent of the vote to the National Front's 33.2 per cent. Those on the right began preparing to achieve by force what they had lost through democratic means. The new government faced an impossible situation. The socialists were split between a revolutionary wing headed by their leader, Francisco Largo Caballero, dubbed the Spanish Lenin, and the moderates, led by Indalecio Prieto and Julián Besteiro. The last two had argued in favour of joining the Popular Front despite Largo Caballero's reservations about participating in an electoral pact with the communists. But Largo Caballero refused to let the party join the government, which meant that it was unstable before it had even got off the ground. Instead, it fell to Manuel Azaña, the left republican leader, to form the new government from members of his own party alone. One of the first things the government did was to grant an amnesty to those who had been imprisoned following the Asturian uprising of 1934. Among them was Prieto. 'This Basque demagogue, and very clever politician, with the fat face and portly figure,' McCabe wrote, 'might pass easily for a Carmelite. And, perhaps, fiery Socialist though he be, he may have had the makings of one. He would certainly have made an excellent preacher.'[49] Despite McCabe's assessment of him as a demagogue, it was Prieto, among the socialists, who tried in vain to keep the new republican government from slipping into the hands of the revolutionaries, while his colleague Largo Caballero postured.

McCabe noted an interesting contrast between Spanish and Irish politics. Both were Catholic countries but with very different conceptions of a republic:

The Conservatives laugh at the notion that it would be possible to have 'a Republic with Bishops and all', which is the Republic that most Liberals want. With a little degree of tolerance, I believe that this would be possible. But it is difficult for the Monarchists to abandon their loyalty because they say that the Monarchy is 'consubstantial' – a theological word – with Spain and its history. Then, too, it's difficult for Bishops to be quite at home in a Republic. The two Monarchies, spiritual and temporal, are much better partners, and live more happily together. I cannot imagine any Spanish Bishop voting for a Spanish Republic, even though, in theory, the Church is indifferent to political systems. In practice, it's very difficult to maintain the theory of two complete societies, each with supreme power, living alongside but apart, and governing the same subjects. It's almost like having two souls in the same body. In the case of a Southern, passionate people like the Spaniards, the body politic seems to be possessed by several demons, all struggling for power.[50]

On St Patrick's Day, the college held its annual banquet, which was attended by the bishop of Salamanca, Enrique Plá y Deniel. A native of Barcelona, he was to play an important political role in Salamanca and wider Spain during the civil war. According to McCabe, Plá y Deniel was,

> a dry little Catalan and not as expansive as his predecessor, who was a native of Murcia. We had Padre Celso and Don Francisco for lunch. Don César was not invited. I have broken with him, on account of his wife, who recommended us a housekeeper, and felt that in exchange for this favour, she had a right to run the kitchen.[51]

The months following the election saw Azaña's republican government trying to restore some of the reforms of the *primer bienio* in a febrile political climate. Socialists and anarchists were burning down churches and convents. At the same time, right-wing thugs were committing acts of violence as a means of destabilising the republic. In order to fortify the regime against a possible coup, civil governors were replaced, officers deemed loyal to the republic were appointed to important positions in the security forces and hostile generals were shunted off to remote outposts. Franco, the chief of the general staff since May 1935, was appointed military commander in the distant Canary Islands to prevent him from causing trouble. Various parties, including the bishop of Zamora, wrote to McCabe asking him to sell them sterling. 'This is another case of people trying to transfer their money out of Spain, or open accounts abroad. It would seem that people are afraid of a landslide. Before the fall of the Monarchy, people began to transfer funds abroad in the same way.'[52] The political centre in Spain was collapsing, as the gunmen – blue-shirted Falangists on one side, overalled anarchist and socialist militias on the other – waited for their opportunity to take over the country. In these circumstances, elements within the Spanish army began to plot. These disaffected officers, following in the tradition of the nineteenth-century *pronunciamiento*, believed that it was their job to rescue Spain from disaster. On this occasion, however, they would face resolute armed resistance, leading to civil war.

The military uprising, led by General Emilio Mola, took place on 17 July 1936. Mola was based in Pamplona, made famous by Hemingway and the running of the bulls during the festival of San Fermín. Pamplona was the capital of Navarre, home to the fanatically Catholic Carlists, who had fought on behalf of their pretender to the Spanish throne in two dynastic wars in the nineteenth century. But what was really at the heart of Carlism was a theocratic anti-liberalism. With their soldier-priests at the forefront and their flag, a jagged red saltire on a white background, fluttering in the breeze, the Carlists, wearing their traditional red *boina*, or beret, marched into battle crying '*¡Viva Cristo Rey!*'* Though Mola was the mastermind of the plot, General Sanjurjo, who had launched an abortive coup against the Republic in 1932, was to be the political figurehead.

In the early summer of 1936, Franco, who was languishing in exile in the Canaries, was playing a waiting game. At the age of forty-three, he had rapidly risen through the ranks. A co-founder of the Spanish foreign legion, he was an *africanista*, who had distinguished himself on the battlefields of Morocco. Though often the butt of fellow officers' jokes – he stood at just 5' 4" tall and had a squeaky, high-pitched voice – he was a capable soldier, with a good understanding of strategy and a ruthless streak. His violent repression of the uprising in Asturias in 1934 – including the use of torture and summary executions – had shocked

---

* 'Long Live Christ the King!'

some of his fellow generals, but made him a hero to many on the right. He was politically shrewd and was soon to outmanoeuvre his rivals on the nationalist side.

The plotters' main problem was that the bulk of the professional army was in Morocco. Once he saw that the coup had a chance of success and had joined Mola and the other conspirators, Franco, whose headquarters were in Santa Cruz de Tenerife, was the obvious man to lead the rebellion in North Africa. On the evening of 17 July, the Spanish army garrisons in Morocco rose against the republican government in Madrid. The rebels had been forced to show their hand a day earlier than planned because the government had learned of the plot. The following day, Franco arrived in Morocco from the Canaries and began planning the transport of the battle-hardened Army of Africa – composed of the elite Spanish foreign legion and the *regulares*, the locally recruited Moroccan infantry and cavalry units – onto the Spanish mainland.

On 18 July, the revolt spread throughout mainland Spain. It was successful in a large swathe of conservative, rural Spain, including Galicia, León, Old Castile and Aragón. But in the industrial heartlands, where armed workers were determined to prevent the military coup, the plotters failed to take power. Madrid, Catalonia, Valencia, Asturias, the Basque country and most of Andalusia stayed loyal to the republic, plunging Spain into civil war.

The failure of the coup in large parts of mainland Spain meant that the transportation of the Army of Africa across the Mediterranean was crucial for the chances of the rebels. Franco immediately made contact with German and Italian officials in Spanish Morocco requesting material aid. His success in persuading Hitler and Mussolini to provide planes, fuel and ammunition was to prove crucial to the nationalist war effort and to his own political career. Between 19 July and 5 August 1,500 troops were brought across the straits of Gibraltar by German Junkers Ju-52 bombers in the first major airlift in history. From then on, 500 men were brought across daily. Mussolini also delivered two squadrons of Savoia-Marchetti SM.81 bombers and Fiat CR.32 fighters. Franco himself arrived in Seville on 6 August to take charge of the war effort in the south of Spain.

The nationalist strategy was to launch a two-pronged attack on Madrid. Franco's Army of Africa would sweep towards the capital from the south, while General Mola's forces would drive from the north. Throughout August and September, the legionaries and Moroccan mercenaries of the Army of Africa, under Colonel Juan Yagüe, pushed north through the poor villages of Extremadura in south-west Spain, leaving terror in their wake. The resistance, the little there was of it, was made up of poorly trained militias, who retreated when faced with the nationalist columns, leaving the terrified civilian population defenceless. Working-class men were murdered and women raped. In contrast to Franco's professional, battle-hardened army, Mola's forces were made up of a mixture of inexperienced Carlist militias, Falangists and volunteers, and republican militias soon held them up in the Guadarrama mountains north of Madrid.

By the end of September, the Army of Africa under Yagüe had reached a crossroads, both strategically and metaphorically. At Maqueda, the road led north to Madrid or east to Toledo, where a group of rebels under Colonel Moscardó had taken refuge in the fortified *alcázar** and were being besieged by the republicans in control of the town. On 21 September, the nationalist generals met at an airfield outside Salamanca to name a commander-in-chief. Sanjurjo, who had been the original choice, had died in an air crash in the first days of the war. Now, with a quick victory over the government uncertain, it was important to appoint a new leader. After some hesitation and under pressure from the foreign legion, the generals chose Franco to lead them to victory. The new *generalísimo* decided to divert the Army of Africa towards Toledo to relieve Moscardó, thus enabling the republicans to shore up the defence of Madrid.

Franco now had to select the location for his general headquarters. He chose Salamanca, and over the coming months, the quiet university town in sleepy Castile was to become the centre of the nationalist war machine.

---

* A Moorish palace or fortress.

# Chapter 6
# ESCAPE AND RETURN

During May and June 1936, threats and rumours of a workers' or military revolt percolated throughout Spain, but McCabe decided to go to Pendueles with the students as usual. After spending a few weeks in Asturias, McCabe departed for Ireland in the middle of July, leaving O'Hara in charge. On 19 July, two days after the military rose in Morocco and after McCabe had left for Ireland, the civil guards left their barracks in Pendueles for Oviedo to join the coup. The military commander in Oviedo, Colonel Aranda, had taken over the city by duping the workers into thinking that he was loyal to the republic. The workers had marched out of the city to join battle only to discover that they had been tricked. But the territory around the city was still under the workers' control.

At the start of the war, the rebels had control of most of north-western Spain, as well as the south-western corner of Andalusia. The republican government, thanks to the efforts of the workers, had retained control of the strip of land along the northern coast, encompassing Asturias – aside from Oviedo – Cantabria and part of the Basque country. Pendueles was therefore in the hands of the workers' militias, or the 'rojos', or 'reds', as the rebels described anyone who opposed their revolt.

On 20 July, the last train left Pendueles for Llanes, the closest town. That same day, two of the Irish College students, who were out for a walk, were stopped and searched outside the village by militias. But the first few days after the military rising were still relatively calm. There were no food shortages, except for fruit and a scarcity of butter and sugar, the bread delivery still arrived from Llanes every day, and fish came from Santander. The Irish students were left to themselves and the local people continued to go to mass and work in the fields.

McCabe was sightseeing in Lisieux, which he had first visited in 1926 as a curate, when he learnt that the Spanish military had risen in Morocco against the republican government. It was the first time he had been out of Spain since the middle of 1934 and probably the most restful few days he had enjoyed in more than two years. In France, he felt that he was 'back again in civilised Europe' where 'they don't burn churches and there is less fanaticism in defending them, which gives the churches a better chance to escape'.[1] McCabe immediately left Lisieux for Le Havre after hearing the news. While he was waiting to catch the boat for Southampton, he chatted with the proprietor of his hotel:

> He is very pessimistic about the situation in France. There is no political leadership and French politics are essentially and shamelessly corrupt. He believes that Socialism is the only solution. Europe seems to be as mad as a March hare at present. In Spain, one heard constantly about the danger of Socialism and Communism. Here is a hotel owner who believes that Socialism is the only system that can save France.[2]

In Dublin, McCabe called on the secretary of the department of external affairs, Joe Walshe, and explained his concerns about the plight of the vice-rector and students in Asturias. The Irish government contacted the British Admiralty and the destroyer *Veteran* put in at Llanes, where the captain came ashore and spoke to O'Hara by telephone. O'Hara told the captain of the destroyer that there was no immediate danger and that he did not deem it necessary to evacuate the students. However, McCabe was beset by worry about what was happening in Spain during his first fortnight back home in Cavan:

> I had left it so recently, and saw the whole war so vividly that I could scarcely imagine that any building or any life had escaped. Though Salamanca was on the National or Patriot side, the papers reported that the Cathedral there had been burned. For the moment, I had visions of the College on fire, and of the whole town going up in flames.[3]

In fact, Salamanca had fallen to the nationalists with little bloodshed, though there was to be plenty in the repression that followed.

The parents of the students still in Asturias wrote to McCabe in Cavan anxiously enquiring about their children, and reporters got in contact looking for his views on events in Spain. His instinctive distrust of journalists meant they went away with little in their notebooks. 'It was a curious sensation, too, to walk around and see the external world so tranquil, green hills, quiet trees, cattle grazing, and to have the brain within full up of Spanish fires, Spanish blood and Spanish corpses.'[4] McCabe recalled that the stationmaster in Asturias had said to him, '*No pasará nada*', or 'Nothing will happen', as he was leaving for Ireland that summer. That same man was to be shot by the nationalists for his republican sympathies.

On 28 July, McCabe received a telegram from Joe Walshe informing him that the students in Pendueles were safe and did not wish to leave, information that had come from the commander of the *Veteran* and was incorrect. According to one of the students, a relative of McCabe's, who called on him after returning to Ireland, more than half the students had wished to leave at the first opportunity. At the beginning of August, O'Hara was advised to raise the Union Jack, which had to be made by the servants, on the balcony of the villa, since this was 'the only flag that the combatants on either side would recognise or respect'.[5] Most of the militiamen along the coast of Asturias, the seamen, dockers and fishermen, belonged to the anarchist CNT union. At first, they left the students alone, but the situation steadily grew more tense. A local bridge was mined and military cars were the only ones allowed along the main road. The palace of the Countess of Cortina in Pendueles was turned into a hospital. On 2 August, militiamen travelling in a lorry fired some shots into the air in the direction of O'Hara at the gate of the summer villa because he did not return their 'closed fist' salute. The stationmaster's son and Alejandro Barballa, a friend of the college, came to apologise and said that they had rung up Llanes to have the militiamen arrested. The former later escaped with his sister to France by boat when the nationalists moved into Asturias. Despite being from a monarchist family, Barballa also opposed the nationalists and was executed.

The militias now challenged the students to give the anarchist salute and made 'unquestionably menacing' gestures when they refused to do so.[6] On 3 August, following the advice of the British consul in Santander, O'Hara decided to send the students home. The following day, he and the students travelled by coach to the nearby village of Unquera. Four militiamen preceded them in a car and five accompanied them in the coach as an escort. From Unquera, they took the train to Santander. The militiamen gave them a cordial goodbye and expressed the hope that they would soon return. Militiamen stood guard on the platform at each station as the frightened Irish students passed through on the way to Santander. From there, they were evacuated on board the British destroyer *Valorous* to the French border town of Saint-Jean-de-Luz. On 7 August, much to his relief, McCabe received a telegram from Walshe informing him that the students had arrived in Paris. Already McCabe felt that he was in some way missing out by not being in Spain and guilty that the vice-rector, O'Hara, who had been left in charge for the first time, was the one shouldering all the responsibility. McCabe felt that 'it was a bit shabby to be here safe in Ireland and I should have preferred to be caught in the trouble, and have the responsibility and risk of it – not to mention the experience.'[7]

O'Hara returned to Pendueles to see if he could get the college servants out of Asturias. By now there were no trains, and all the churches in the district had been closed. He told McCabe that he would try to get to Salamanca to check on the college.[8] In a letter written in the middle of August, O'Hara wrote to McCabe: 'There is a battle raging near Oviedo, and it is reported that rebel forces are advancing on Santander. Ávila has been bombed. I am afraid the next important strong-hold to be attacked will be Salamanca.'[9] Conditions were deteriorating in Asturias. Food was scarce and there was no money in the banks. O'Hara was in Llanes to settle bills with the college's suppliers when bombs starting dropping, creating widespread panic. Nationalist airplanes were attacking the airfield at San Roque. 'I took refuge in a house, but I saw very interesting things from a window,' O'Hara wrote on 26 August, 'and I never heard the protection of the angels and saints and patrons, and, indeed, of the whole celestial Hierarchy invoked so fervently.'[10] O'Hara was evacuated from Bilbao at the end of August and taken to France aboard the British destroyer *Comet*.

O'Hara kept McCabe informed of the situation in Pendueles until he left Spain. It was more difficult to get news from Salamanca about the college. Aside from reading the reports in the newspapers, McCabe's other source of news was listening to Madrid radio on a set belonging to the curate in Crosserlough, one of only three in the area. It was a strange sensation to be in the heart of the tranquil Irish countryside listening to urgent appeals to the workers to help prepare the Spanish capital's defences or to the civilian population to donate blood. 'One night in Cavan Town, I heard the Socialist lady deputy, Margarita Necker, make a very bitter appeal to the peasants and workers of Badajoz, her constituency,' wrote McCabe. 'Afterwards, she spoke in French. She had a smooth, caressing, venomous style, like a serpent'.[11]

Towards the end of September, McCabe received news from Francisco Ramos, the college administrator in Salamanca, who described what had happened in the city during the first days of the military uprising:

> On 19 July, the Army came out onto the streets, declaring a state of war. In the *plaza mayor*, a few '*vivas*' were shouted and shots were fired in protest. The Army then opened fire, killing five or six people. Since then, the city has been totally at peace. The majority of the people are on the side of the Army, who are in control of the whole province [author's translation].[12]

Ramos wrote that the authorities were thinking of turning the Irish College into a '*hospital de sangre*' or 'blood hospital'. McCabe had already heard this term while listening to news from Madrid on the radio in the curate's house in Crosserlough. The militias defending the Spanish capital would read out the names of the *madrileños* who had donated blood as they prepared for the nationalist onslaught on the city. 'It made one's imagination drip with blood,' he wrote.[13]

The Irish public's attitude to events in Spain was initially confused because of the different names used to describe each side. Depending on who was doing the labelling, members of the anti-government side were variously called 'nationalists', 'insurgents', 'patriots' and 'rebels'; the government troops and the workers' militias were 'republicans', 'loyalists', 'reds' or 'communists'. McCabe overheard an example of this confusion

between two fellow diners as he ate breakfast in Dublin's Royal Hibernian
Hotel:

> One of them was reading the paper, and the conversation was
> something like this. 'Any news on the paper this morning?' the other
> asked as he got rid of the ham and eggs. 'Not much. The Spanish
> war, of course.' 'How is it going?' asked the other between mouthfuls.
> 'Well, you know, Franco seems to be winning.' 'Ha, ha, who's he? I
> can never tell which is which,' said the other. 'Who are the Loyalists?'
> 'Oh, they're the Nationalists you know,' the reader said, with a slight
> Professorial tone. 'And the Patriots?' queried the eater. 'Are they the
> Government?' 'That's right,' said the other, leaving the paper aside and
> tackling what was on the plate.[14]

Soon, though, due principally to the stance of the Irish Catholic
hierarchy, public opinion became overwhelmingly pro-Franco. Most of
the Irish press portrayed the war as a Catholic crusade against atheistic
communism, and atrocities committed in Spain by anti-clerical mobs
were described in the most lurid terms. However, McCabe noted that
staunch Catholic working men were often admiring of the fight being put
up by the militias:

> On the eve of the Consecration of Mullingar Cathedral, I went into
> a barber's shop. As we waited for our turn, one young man, who was
> looking over a paper, said to another, 'The Spanish workers are putting
> up a great fight.' I heard a man repairing the road make a similar
> remark. But the workmen in Mullingar were all staunch Catholics.
> They were talking about 'the big day tomorrow' (the Consecration),
> and would be shocked to see nuns and priests slaughtered, of course.[15]

For McCabe, this showed a 'spirit of compromise between religious and
political views', which was sorely lacking in Spain. He found depressing
the Spanish Church's alienation from the working class: 'In Spain, there
is too much identification between religion and one system of politics,
on the one hand, and between irreligion and a distinct political creed or
opinion on the other.'[16] McCabe wrote of one Spanish aristocrat he knew

who believed that most Irish priests were 'reds' because they were pro-
Sinn Féin:

> If some of the people on Franco's side read the modern history of
> Ireland since the days of O'Connell, Davis and Davitt, they would
> regard us as very 'Red'. And if some of the Irish people read the
> history of Spain for the past century, they might suffer some mental
> confusion over the present situation. What a wonderful thing it is to
> be ignorant, and yet, to see clearly.[17]

With no quick conclusion to the war in sight, and thus no possibility
of the Irish College reopening for the new academic year, McCabe sought
alternative arrangements for the students. They were initially taken in
by St Patrick's College, Maynooth. Some were then sent to their own
diocesan colleges. On 12 October, McCabe briefed the Irish hierarchy's
standing committee in Maynooth. He was interested to meet these lions
of the Irish Church and remained in Maynooth for the bishops' general
meeting the following day. It was the first time that McCabe had visited
Maynooth and he imagined the contrast with Spain as he wandered
around the recreation grounds:

> I caught a glimpse of a Professor going down to the offices or stables
> in the rere. He was wearing a tall hat, and leggings and carried a riding
> crop, and was going out for a ride in the old-world Victorian style.
> One stared at this peaceful Victorian atmosphere, and it was difficult
> to believe. The life of the people in Ireland is like that of a bird amongst
> the reeds in one of the large Midland lakes. If this were Spain, half the
> Bishops, probably, would be murdered on the way home.[18]

That evening, McCabe and O'Hara, who had arrived back from Spain
at the end of August, were guests at supper in the dining hall where the
bishops and college professors were assembled, 'the cream of the brains of
Ireland'. McCabe described the occasion in his diary:

> At the end, one of the young Bishops at our end of the table handed
> around cigarettes, and Bishops cracked jokes amongst themselves,

or with their old companions, the Professors, like young curates, who were in College together, and who hadn't met for two or three years. If they had a little of this delightful, exhilarating spirit of comradeship in Spain, they wouldn't be murdering, or perhaps, be getting murdered.[19]

By the middle of October, with the weather in Ireland turning wet and cold, McCabe was itching to get back to Spain to see the war, 'risk or no risk,' with his own eyes. 'Between a slow damp death in Ireland, and a quick bloody death in Spain, I'd choose the latter.'[20] McCabe wrote to Cardinal MacRory offering any service he might need in Spain before he departed. MacRory asked McCabe if he could correspond with the Spanish primate, the archbishop of Toledo, Cardinal Isidro Gomá y Tomás, in order to transfer the proceeds from a national church gate collection held to raise money for the aid of Spanish Catholics. 'In case you start soon, perhaps, you may be able, at least by letter, to get in touch with the Cardinal,' wrote MacRory, 'and ask him how he would wish the money forwarded. Also, whether he would wish me to order any dressing, or medical instruments, so that they might be available as soon as possible.'[21]

In Dublin, McCabe called on Joe Walshe at the department of external affairs. Walshe told him that Paddy Belton, a TD and former Blueshirt, was travelling to Spain on the same ship as McCabe, via the English port of Tilbury and Lisbon. Belton was a wealthy businessman and leader of the Irish Christian Front (ICF). The ICF was a pro-Franco, anti-Communist, lay Catholic organisation, which had been founded in Dublin's Mansion House at the end of August. Its manifesto sought 'the success of the Patriot arms in Spain, not that we are the least concerned with the temporal issues at stake there, but that we want the advance guard of the anti-God forces stopped in Spain and thereby reaching our shores.'[22] The ICF claimed to be non-political; its opponents, of which there were many, not least the Fianna Fáil government, saw things otherwise. McCabe had heard neither of Belton, nor of the ICF, when Walshe first mentioned his name. Walshe decided to ring the ICF secretary, since he believed Belton, who had never been in Spain, would be anxious to travel with a fellow Irishman familiar with the country. Though he could not

hear what was being said on the other end of the line, McCabe was left
with the impression that Belton had no wish to meet him in Dublin or
in Spain. He noted that Walshe looked puzzled after putting down the
phone, 'but he also smiled, as if he knew Belton, and what he was up
to.'[23] Afterwards, Walshe invited McCabe and Leopold Kerney, the Irish
minister in Madrid, to lunch at his home. Kerney had been in Galicia
during the military uprising but had managed to return home overland.
'His trip got some publicity in the Dublin papers, and I heard an important
Civil Servant say that this publicity was in very bad taste, diplomatically.
Mr Kerney is a nice, simple, shrewd, middle-sized man, but not in the
least of the "show-off" type.'[24]

At the same time as McCabe was making his final preparations to
return to Salamanca, plans were underway to send an Irish unit to fight
in Spain. Count Ramírez de Arellano, a Carlist aristocrat, had written
to Cardinal MacRory, proposing the creation of an Irish unit that might
fight on the side of the nationalists and asking for suggestions as to who
might lead such a unit. The Irish Church was naturally sympathetic to
the nationalists, given its fierce anti-communism and the anti-clerical
atrocities that had been taking place under the republic. MacRory had
suggested Eoin O'Duffy, the former IRA chief of staff, garda commissioner
and Blueshirt leader. McCabe had first heard of O'Duffy, who came
from County Monaghan, close to his home place, in 1916: '[O'Duffy]
had thrown in his lot with the Irish Volunteers, and was admired as a
promising young man.'[25]

McCabe had not known much about the ICF or the Irish Brigade
up to this point, but was sceptical about what either could achieve in
Spain. Though he had met neither Belton nor O'Duffy, McCabe thought
both had an overly romantic idea of conditions in the country. Based on
his experience of the students in Salamanca, he believed that the Irish
seldom grew accustomed to the people, food, climate or landscape in
Spain. 'From the speeches, I got the impression that Mr Belton was one
of the modern Irish saints, a man like Matt Talbot, who was prepared to
die for the sacred Spanish cause, and who would be probably canonised
later with Matt Talbot,' he commented in his diary.[26] Later on, having met
and studied Belton, O'Duffy and their followers, he developed a yet more
cynical attitude.

McCabe was careful not to express any of his views on the war in Spain in public. He was afraid that comments attributed to him might appear in the press and that it ill-behoved the college rector to take a political stance. His natural inclination was, of course, conservative and pro-nationalist – not that openly proclaiming anything else was possible in Salamanca during the civil war. But he did have a more nuanced view than many of the blowhards in Irish ecclesiastical and political circles.

With a sense of adventure, McCabe set out for Spain in the first week of November 1936, catching the night boat from Dublin's North Wall: 'As it pulled off and we moved down the river, I had a last look at the dim spires and chimney stacks of Dublin. I couldn't tell what I might be walking into, or if I'd ever come back.'[27] In Liverpool, having met one of his sisters, he took the train to London, the 'huge and solid' city where he had worked in his twenties and which he found to be 'so full of civilized life' compared to the anarchic country towards which he was travelling. He wrote that it was 'difficult to imagine these English railway porters running about, yelling, waving, burning and shooting as the workmen do in Spain'.[28]

Visiting the shipping office in London, McCabe discovered that his cabin had previously been reserved for Belton but that the politician had sent a telegram to cancel: 'There's some hocus-pocus in all this, and I feel, somehow, that Belton does not want to travel out with me. And I'm perfectly delighted.' McCabe's ship, the *Highland Patriot*, left Tilbury on 7 November bound for Lisbon. As it reached the mouth of the Thames estuary, McCabe tried to make out Our Lady of Lourdes in Leigh-on-Sea through the sea mist and reflected upon his time there as curate:

In 1928, when I used to have my morning stroll along the Marine Parade, and watch the ships go down, I couldn't have suspected that in 1936 I'd be going down the river, on my way back to Salamanca as Rector of the College. At the time, the idea – going back to live in Salamanca – would have made me laugh until my sides burst. Now this is Land's End, and if the 'Reds' get me, as people threaten, this ship back to Spain is going to be 'Journey's End', without a joke. However, life is always worth the danger, and perhaps Death is too.[29]

McCabe was sharing a cabin with a young Spaniard from a well-off family in the town of Talavera de la Reina whose parents had been trapped in Madrid. The first night, as the ship pulled into Calais, the news came through that the republican government had abandoned the capital for Valencia. It looked as if the war was coming to an end. Four days later, during a storm in the Bay of Biscay when the 'deck stood up at an angle of 30°', the *Highland Patriot* docked in Lisbon. The city was full of Spanish refugees, mostly from Málaga. A woman and her children who had fled the city were in McCabe's hotel:

> The lady sat there at meals, scarcely eating, and heedless of the little children climbing up her knee. She kept staring into space, like one stunned or in a trance. All of this is very sad and affects me deeply. When I was at home, I saw one newsreel of the Spanish War, and, at the end, I had to walk out.[30]

McCabe sought permission from the nationalist embassy in Portugal to enter Spain. He also unsuccessfully tried to secure an interview with Gil-Robles. The CEDA leader had been sidelined since Franco had assumed military and political control of the nationalist zone. Not only was Franco the *generalísimo*, or commander-in-chief, he had also manoeuvred himself into being declared head-of-state at the beginning of October when the nationalists had realised they would have to create some sort of political structure while the war was continuing. Franco had moved to wipe out all political opposition to his new role. Gil-Robles, who had willingly volunteered to work for the nationalists' interests in Lisbon at the start of the war, raising money, buying arms and helping with the propaganda effort abroad, found that he was no longer welcome in nationalist Spain. In the new martial climate, the fact that he had been a gradualist and participated in the democratic politics of the despised Second Republic was held against him. McCabe also visited the Irish Dominicans, who ministered near the city docks at the chapel of Corpo Santo. One of the priests expressed his amazement that McCabe had decided to return to Salamanca.[31]

McCabe arrived in Spain by train on 13 November; he was the only passenger to cross the frontier. A few young men wearing the blue uniform of the Falange and the red and yellow monarchist flag, which had replaced the flag of the republic, were the only evidence of the war. However, there were plenty of soldiers and civil guards on the train to Salamanca. Some of them were on their way to the front at Eibar in the Basque country. McCabe got talking to a civil guard who was attached to a Falangist unit. He had been stationed in Barcelona when the uprising had begun but had managed to escape to France using a fake passport and by passing himself off as a cattle dealer. He had then returned to the nationalist zone and reported for duty.[32]

McCabe had been looking forward to the excitement of a war zone and was, at first, disappointed by the normality of life. The train's carriages were full of women coming back from shopping in a distant town with their baskets, parcels and hens. 'In Ireland, one read the papers, and had a daily vision of all Spain in flame and of blood flowing in torrents down the mountain sides and across the plains.'[33] Many of the women and children were wearing religious medals, and the railway porters wore pieces of yellow cloth embroidered with a silver cross 'to indicate that they have been militarised. This gives them the status and obedience of the soldier, and if they neglect their obligations or create trouble, they are tried for rebellion and treason, and judged according to the Military Code.'[34]

The train stopped at Fuente de San Esteban, which McCabe had visited with the Marqués de Canillejas in 1930. Militias had executed the young noble – who had taken part in the *Sanjurjada*, the revolt against the republic in 1932 – in Oviedo in September. His body had been discovered in the chimney stack of an old factory and was only identified later by a ring he had been wearing. At Fuente, a railway porter asked McCabe for a religious medal. The Irish priest wondered whether this was genuine piety or pretence. Nationalist propaganda was constructing the narrative of a Catholic crusade against atheistic Bolshevism and many Catholics were simply happy to practise their faith, but there were also those who were keen to erase their previous enthusiasm for the republic by showing their adherence to the cause with showy displays of religious devotion. Back on the train, McCabe watched the sun setting from the carriage window:

> As it dies out, the familiar landscape recovers its solidity and stability. How heedless and indifferent landscape is to the tragedies of History. Here we are in Tejares again, making a great noise on the high iron bridge. From the carriage window, I can see the silhouette of Salamanca standing up dimly against the black rain-soaked clouds. There isn't any strange gap in the familiar sky-line, and all the towers and domes still crown the town, and give it the same old air of majesty and serenity.[35]

Stepping down from the train at Salamanca station, McCabe was delighted to see his old friends and colleagues, including Francisco Ramos, the college administrator, and Pedro Salcedo, the vicar-general. At the college, the porter, a former civil guard, took the rector's luggage. 'Though he is usually stiff as a telegraph pole, he almost wrung my arm off. If this man had a revolver and plenty of rounds of ammunition, he'd kill a good many "Reds" before they'd step over his corpse and break in.'[36] The porter had once hesitated before letting in the archbishop of Dublin, a trustee of the college. Once he had admitted the Irish prelate, he had told him that under no circumstances could he make an exception for him to view the upstairs galleries. ·

A set of keys left on his writing table and a thin film of dust on the mantelpiece were enough to reassure McCabe that nothing had been touched in his room. When in Ireland, he had feared that all his books and the valuable college archives had been burnt and scattered. Seeing the college exactly as he had left it was a source of relief and joy. Looking over the patio, he thought: 'It is as peaceful and beautiful as ever. Overhead the stars are twinkling in a clear, cold, deep-blue November sky. It is difficult to believe, in a peaceful atmosphere like this, that tonight, Franco's troops are pounding Madrid with artillery, and that the city is in danger of being destroyed.'[37] Because there were no servants in the college, Ramos offered to put up McCabe for the night. Over supper – while the sound of Unión Radio from Madrid came from the house next door, detailing the atrocities of the nationalist troops – the Spanish priest described Salamanca's fall to the rebels.

# Chapter 7

# THE TWO CITIES

The rising in Salamanca was relatively bloodless. Before dawn on 19 July, machine-guns were set up in all the main squares of the city. Then, at 11am, a company of mounted soldiers entered the *plaza mayor* and their captain read out a statement declaring martial law. There were some defiant shouts from the crowd and the soldiers opened fire, killing four men and a teenage girl. The military took over the town hall, the civil governor's offices, the post office, the telephone exchange and the railway station. They then began removing the socialist town councils throughout the surrounding province. What resistance there was came from the workers in Salamanca, organised by Casto Prieto Carrasco, the republican mayor, and José Andrés y Manso, a socialist member of the Cortes. The military commander in Salamanca, General Manuel García Álvarez, had assured them that he was loyal to the republic but had ordered his forces to join the coup when he had heard that the nearby city of Valladolid was in the hands of the nationalists. A general strike lasted a few days and there was periodic sniping against the military in the working-class areas of Pizarrales and Tejares but any resistance soon disappeared. Carrasco and Manso were arrested and a new mayor and civil governor were installed. Reprisals against the enemies of the new regime began immediately.

McCabe returned from Ireland to a city in tumult. Franco's decision to set up his headquarters in the city had seen to that. His choice of Salamanca was based as much on the proximity of the Portuguese border, convenient should the war go awry, as on proximity to the front. But there was also something symbolic in the nationalists basing themselves in this ornate city in the heartland of rural Castile. Its shimmering, sun-lit towers, grand aristocratic palaces and mighty cathedrals with their soaring spires represented the triumphant glory of imperial Spain, a Catholic, feudal world far removed from the bourgeois liberalism of Madrid or the obnoxious industrialism of Catalonia.

Soldiers and militiamen thronged the streets of the city: blue-shirted Falangists (the Falange, which, from a membership of 75,000 before the war, was numbering close to a million by the end of 1936, also had its headquarters in the city); the *requetés*, the ultra-Catholic Carlist militia from Navarre ('athletic, hard, and a bit dour'),[1] who wore red berets to distinguish themselves and were led into battle by their priests; the members of the Spanish foreign legion, in their green uniforms, who had become battle-hardened while fighting colonial wars in Spain's dwindling possessions in North Africa; the small CEDA militia; and, of course, the *regulares*, the Moroccan or 'Moorish' mercenaries, in their turbans and burnouses, who had earned a fearsome reputation among the enemy. McCabe thought that all this variety in dress suggested a lack of uniformity and unification: 'One has the impression that all the old anarchical divisions of Spain are still too manifest, even though they all call themselves "Nationalists". One wonders why Franco doesn't insist on a military uniform for everybody.'[2]

In September 1936, the bishop of Salamanca, Enrique Plá y Deniel, issued his famous 'Two Cities' pastoral letter in which he compared St Augustine's two cities to the two sides in the civil war: the nationalist cause was divinely approved; the republican government had constructed a city without God and was now being punished. Plá y Deniel further demonstrated his support for Franco by vacating and putting at his disposal the episcopal palace. In the early part of the war, Franco ate, slept and received visitors on the first floor of the building. He worked with his staff on the second floor. There was a permanent guard both inside and outside the palace. 'Each sentry wears a steel helmet, a belt with leather cartridge pouches round his waist, and holds a rifle with fixed bayonet "ground" in front of him. The white gloves on the common soldier look so elegant, and the cold steel of the bayonet looks so murderous, that it is a curious combination.'[3] The nationalist diplomatic service was also based in the palace.

Across a small square was the Gothic cathedral, which housed an air raid shelter in the basement and a siren in the bell tower. Facing the northern side of the cathedral was the Colegio de Anaya, the home of the nationalist press and propaganda department. This was headed by the grotesque figure of José Millán Astray, the fanatical founder and former commander of the Spanish foreign legion, who had lost an arm and an eye in action. McCabe described him as 'crazy and impossible' and 'made of old Spanish steel'.[4] Millán Astray was close to Franco, the *generalísimo* had been Millán Astray's deputy in the legion and they had fought side by side against the Rif tribesmen in the mountains of north Morocco. Millán Astray, who revelled in the nickname '*el glorioso mutilado*',* had inculcated the legion with a poisonous necrophilia: the legionaries were known as '*los novios de muerte*'† and their rallying cry was '*¡Viva la muerte!*'‡

As well as the Spanish military and militias, German and Italian soldiers, diplomats and advisers had arrived in Salamanca. Franco's contacts with Hitler and Mussolini, as well as the fact that he had the bulk of the professional army under his command, gave him a position of strength among the contending generals. At night, McCabe could hear munition trains filled with German shells rolling past his window on their way from Lisbon to the front. He could tell that the nationalists were planning a big offensive when the traffic was unusually high.

Food was plentiful in Salamanca that November, but there was a shortage of manufactured goods. Most of Spain's industry and manufacturing was in the republican zone and the population of Salamanca had shot up since the beginning of the war. There was also a shortage of servants. 'As a last resort, I have this old one in from Calle Espejo, and though she has the sour face of one that has been poisoning people all her life, she's not a bad cook,' McCabe wrote. 'At least, I was able to have supper, and felt no pains afterwards.'[5]

Having spent his first night in the house of the college administrator, McCabe returned to the college on the second night he was back in Salamanca, even though he had no fire or central heating.

> To-night, about 11.30pm, I went into the store-room at the back, where there is no electric light, and went groping for sheets in the

---

* 'The glorious cripple.'
† 'The bridegrooms of death.'
‡ 'Long live death!'

old Spanish chest. I haven't been in here since the night the Rector died. Without students the College is very empty and lonely at this hour. I made my bed, and crept in shivering. It's like camping out in the middle of the night.[6]

The following morning McCabe visited the hospice, which was in the charge of the Vincentian sisters, to say mass. The reverend mother described the actions of the military during the rising, which had resulted in the death of a teenage girl, among others, as a '*bendito tiro*' or 'blessed shot'. Afterwards, he visited the bishop of Salamanca, Plá y Deniel, to see how he might get in touch with Cardinal Gomá y Tomás, the archbishop of Toledo and Spanish Primate, to discuss arrangements for the handing over of the collection gathered by the Irish hierarchy. The bishop suggested he talk to the head of the nationalist diplomatic service, José Antonio Sangróniz.

McCabe had lunch in the Gran Hotel, sitting opposite a middle-aged Spanish officer. 'He had a fine, well-chiselled face, a high complexion, slightly bronzed, and bald temples. He is a fine sturdy type, but he has a very large, unathletic stomach.' The two men discussed Franco's attack on Madrid. The officer believed that Franco wished to save the city, so the entry had to be slow.

> I suggested that Franco has only 20,000 men, which is not sufficient for the assault. In 1935, the Socialists staged a big concentration in Madrid, in which 100,000 took part. If these men are willing to fight, the taking of Madrid won't be an easy affair. 'Numbers do not count,' the officer says. 'Morale is the thing and the Army morale is superior.'[7]

Salamanca's social life revolved around the Gran Hotel, or the 'Gran', as it was informally known. Built between 1928 and 1930, it was the best hotel in the city. Spanish officers, German and Italian diplomats, British spies and American journalists ate, drank and slept there, all looking to pick up tasty bits of gossip. McCabe dined there regularly, hearing the swirl of rumour and opinions about the war. 'The Hotel lounge is full and there are Fascist salutes everywhere,' McCabe wrote after one visit. 'Women sit around knitting for the soldiers. It reminds me of the song "Sister Suzy's sewing socks [*sic*] for soldiers," of Great War days. I met José Juan García [a university professor]. Under his overcoat, he was wearing a Phalange [*sic*] uniform, with black belt and all.[8] All sorts of characters turned up at the 'Gran'. One evening, McCabe met Reg 'Crash' Kavanagh, an Irish stuntman who was flying planes for the nationalists. His companion was a Scottish fascist who wore a dagger in his belt.

The wounded who arrived back in Salamanca from the front were a reminder of the slaughter that was taking place, yet McCabe sensed an indifference to the bloodshed. 'The first impression is that the Spaniards, themselves, are taking it gaily, and with a certain degree of levity.'[9] But many families were suffering intensely, from grief or uncertainty as to the whereabouts of loved ones who were either fighting at the front or trapped in the enemy zone. 'People, for instance, that went to Madrid for a few days' vacation or on business, were caught in the Revolution, and have not been heard of since. In our street, there are two children who came from Madrid to Salamanca for a holiday. They are completely ignorant about their parents and don't know whether they are dead or alive.'[10]

The bloodshed was not confined to the front. A brutal repression was taking place in the nationalist zone. The regime was determined to crush all resistance by executing anyone whose political sympathies were in doubt. Militias terrorised the countryside around Salamanca, rounding up republicans and leftists. The Falange were at the forefront of this murderous campaign. In what were known as *sacas*, or removals, men were dragged out of prison and taken out to the countryside where they were shot and buried in shallow graves. Many were tortured first. The former republican mayor, Carrasco, and socialist deputy, Manso, who had been arrested in the days following the military uprising, were among the most prominent victims of these *sacas*. They were taken out of the provincial prison in Salamanca on 29 July by the Falangist Francisco Bravo and driven up the road towards Valladolid. Their bodies were found in a ditch at a place called La Orbada.

McCabe estimated that 1,300 individuals had been executed in Salamanca by the middle of November. He wrote:

The Phalangists [*sic*] on this side seem to have behaved like the 'Reds' on the other. They shot people by lorryfuls. They used to go to a

village, for instance, drag out their victim, make him dig his own
grave, and then shoot him. Or they put the dead man on the middle
of the road, got into the lorry, and ran over the corpse to iron it out
properly.[11]

Disgusted by the barbarism of the Falange and the endless summary
executions taking place, he added dryly:

> At school, some boys used to play Blind Man's Buff. They robbed a
> bird's nest, put the eggs in the middle of the road, got a stick, closed
> their eyes, and went along beating the road with the stick, until they
> had made 'humpty dumpty' of the eggs. This Phalangist [sic] game
> of making mashed meat of their victims must have been far more
> exciting.[12]

There was a 'complete indifference' to these murders, according to
McCabe, and the perpetrators justified them by pointing to rumours,
spread for propaganda purposes, that Franco had anticipated a 'Red'
revolution. One rumour had it that a list had been found in Salamanca of
those who were to be assassinated once the 'rojos' took power.[13]

The rector of the University of Salamanca, Unamuno, who had
initially supported the military coup, was shocked by the savagery. On
12 October, an infamous incident took place in the university's *aula
maxima*. The occasion was a ceremony to mark the *Día de la Raza* [Day
of the Race], which celebrated the anniversary of Columbus's discovery
of the Americas. Bishop Plá y Deniel, Millán Astray, Unamuno and
Franco's wife, Carmen, were among the luminaries in attendance. After
a fiery speech by one of the university professors attacking Basque and
Catalan nationalism as a cancer, someone in the hall shouted '*¡Viva
la muerte!*', to which Millán Astray, who had arrived accompanied by
an escort of armed legionaries, responded with the nationalist slogan,
'*¡España!: ¡Una!, ¡Grande!, ¡Libre!*'* According to Hugh Thomas,
Unamuno responded:

---

* This was the Francoist motto. It roughly translates as 'Spain!: United! Great! Free!'

General Millán Astray is a cripple. Let it be said without any slighting undertone. He is a war invalid. So was Cervantes. Unfortunately there are all too many cripples in Spain just now. And soon there will be even more of them, if God does not come to our aid. It pains me to think that General Millán Astray should dictate the pattern of mass psychology. A cripple who lacks the spiritual greatness of a Cervantes is wont to seek ominous relief in causing mutilation around him.

In an apoplectic outburst, Millán Astray shouted out, '*¡Mueran los intelectuales!*'* before Unamuno continued:

This is the temple of the intellect. And I am its high priest. It is you who profane its sacred precincts. You will win, because you have more than enough brute force. But you will not convince. For to convince, you need to persuade. And in order to persuade you would need what you lack: reason and right in the struggle. I consider it futile to exhort you to think of Spain. I have done.[14]

Unamuno had to be escorted from the hall on Carmen Franco's arm amid violent rebukes and was shunned in Salamanca for the remaining few weeks of his life. In early December, he wrote to a friend: 'It is a stupid regime of terror. Here people are shot without trial and without any justification whatsoever. Some because it is said that they are Freemasons, and I have no idea what that means any more than do the animals who cite it as a reason to kill.'[15] Unamuno was sitting with a friend in his study on 31 December 1936 when he had a sudden fatal heart attack. He took to his grave his regret at having initially supported the nationalist coup.

There were not enough rooms in Salamanca to accommodate the influx of soldiers, aviators, journalists, politicians and adventurers from Spain and abroad. Most of the large private houses, including the sixteenth-century Palacio de Monterrey, which belonged to the Duke of Alba, were requisitioned for the use of military officers and officials. Callers looking for a bed often woke McCabe in the middle of night.

---

* 'Death to the intellectuals!'

One such was the Irish journalist Francis McCullagh, who arrived at the Irish College in November 1936. He had not been able to get a room in the Gran Hotel and had entertained hopes of being able to stay at the college. From Omagh in County Tyrone, McCullagh was an adventurer who had travelled the globe. He had reported on the Russo-Japanese War in 1904–5, the Portuguese Revolution of 1910 and the Russian Revolution in 1917. In 1918, he had worked as a British propaganda officer in Siberia during the Russian Civil War. His experiences in Russia had left him strongly anti-communist.[16] After meeting him for the first time in the Gran Hotel, McCabe described him as 'a small thin figure' with 'a wizened face', 'long wrinkles down his cheek' and 'weak eyes behind steel-rimmed glasses'. 'He wears no overcoat,' he noted, 'and he looks cold and hungry. From time to time, he gives himself a jerk and a shake, to get rid of the cold.'[17] These were gymnastic exercises McCullagh had learnt in the army.

In the summer of 1936, McCullagh had written an open letter to the President of the Executive Council, Éamon de Valera, which appeared in the *Irish Independent*, appealing to the Irish government to recognise Franco. He mentioned in the letter that he was surprised that no one had stayed behind in the Irish College in Salamanca when the war broke out, if only to put up a Spanish flag.

McCullagh wrote a book about his experiences during the civil war, *In Franco's Spain*, in which he criticised the behaviour of the rector and vice-rector and compared their absence from Salamanca at the start of the war unfavourably with that of their fellows in the English and Scots colleges in Valladolid. This was most unfair given the fact that McCabe was returning to Ireland and O'Hara was trapped in Asturias when the uprising occurred, and both had made every effort to return quickly. McCullagh noted that it was 'startling' that the Irish College was empty in November 1936 given that the military and militias had taken over all the other public buildings in Salamanca. McCabe was incensed at the insinuation of cowardice, and McCullagh apologised when he heard McCabe's explanation. McCabe believed McCullagh to be a fine journalist but was convinced he was working for British intelligence.

After meeting the rector, McCullagh's impressions of McCabe were more positive:

Surprisingly young for his position, he had an old head on his young shoulders, was a shrewd business man, knew Spanish, was precise, practical, not at all imaginative or sentimental. Englishmen sometimes think the good qualities which they associate with Ulster are only to found in the Ulster Presbyterian, but they are also to be found in the Ulster Catholic.[18]

The authorities had called on more than one occasion with a view to taking the college over as a jail or a hospital, and McCabe was determined to deter visitors in order to prevent it from being requisitioned. That McCabe would not grant him a room had irked McCullagh, but McCabe believed that the military authorities would see no reason not to requisition the college if there were already visitors staying there. The Count de San Esteban de Cañongo, a nationalist diplomat, had also asked for a room, but changed his mind once he visited the college and found it too cold for his liking. McCullagh suspected that McCabe had deliberately made the college as inhospitable as possible. 'And, with dogged, Ultonian obstincy he has stuck to his guns. Efforts were made to plant a colony of German aviators on him, but he refused to receive them on the ground that he was, after all, a British subject,' McCullagh wrote. 'A suggestion was made that the college would make a good hostel for the correspondents, but Father McCabe turned it down.'[19]

On the night of 15 November, just as McCabe was getting ready to turn in, Paddy Belton arrived at the college with his interpreter and secretary, a former private in the Irish Guards (the British infantry regiment) by the name of John Michael Coyne. Because the battle for Madrid was raging and Salamanca was full of military personnel, the Irishmen had been unable to find a bed. McCabe located one for Coyne at the house of Francisco Ramos and was returning with Belton to the college along a dark street by the back of the episcopal palace when they were challenged by a Moroccan soldier with a rifle and fixed bayonet who stepped out from a doorway. McCabe shouted out '¡Viva España!' and the guard let them pass.[20]

Belton had left Liverpool in a small ketch the same day that McCabe had departed from Tilbury. The vessel had almost sunk in the Bay of Biscay because of the same gales that had impeded McCabe's journey.

The authorities in Lisbon had welcomed Belton, who was the deputy lord mayor of Dublin, with a public reception. According to McCabe, Belton had rushed out during the ceremony to make arrangements for his journey to Salamanca. 'At the Spanish Junta, he demanded a free car straight-away to take him there,' wrote McCabe. 'He told them that he was taking out a gift of £32,000 from Ireland to Spain, and that if he didn't have a car on the spot, he'd go back to Ireland immediately, taking the £32,000 with him.'[21]

The Irish hierarchy had raised this sum at the end of October in its national church-gate collection for the relief of the Spanish Church. It was meant to go towards the reconstruction of churches destroyed during the war. Belton had instead proposed to Cardinal MacRory that the monies be given to the ICF to enable them to buy medical supplies for the nationalist armies. MacRory was uneasy about the plan, given the antipathy in certain quarters in Ireland towards the ICF. He had asked McCabe to get in touch with Cardinal Gomá in order that the Spanish primate could decide how best to dispose of the funds. Belton, however, was not to be put off so easily. He had instructed the Spanish agent of the ICF, a Chilean-born Irishwoman named Aileen O'Brien, to persuade Gomá to hand over the money to the ICF. O'Brien, who spoke fluent Spanish and French, was the Irish representative of the International Pro Deo Society, a shadowy Christian, anti-communist organisation based in Geneva. At the beginning of November, Gomá had agreed to the proposal and had written to Franco and the archbishop of Dublin to inform them of the new arrangements. The purpose of Belton's trip to Spain was therefore to take control of the monies raised by the Irish hierarchy.[22]

McCabe had a poor impression of Belton. 'It takes all sorts of people to make a world, and it takes all sorts of greedy sharks and cold fish to make an Irish Christian Front,' McCabe observed. 'Belton is a boor of the first order. There is still a certain amount of hugger mugger in his intentions and movements. … He keeps looking at me, in a heavy-headed, bovine way, and we both seem to be playing a game of hide-and-seek with each other.'[23]

Belton had plenty of excitement on his first full day in Salamanca. 'I heard the drone of planes and, looking up, saw three overhead,' McCabe wrote. 'They were flying very high, in close horizontal formation, with their wing tips almost grazing one another, it seemed to us. They looked like birds, flashing their stiff wings in the sunlight.' McCabe was able to make out red markings on the wings of one of the planes and concluded that it was an air raid. 'Immediately, the syrens [*sic*] began to sound, and in a minute the Patio and the whole town was filled with noise and banging. Here and there, at intervals, there was the dull sound of an explosion where a bomb had fallen. The whole gallery was vibrating.'[24]

McCabe and Belton were standing on the upper gallery watching the planes when Coyne came rushing in. He had been returning from nationalist headquarters in a car when the air raid had begun. The driver had stopped in the middle of the street and refused to take him any further. The air raid lasted only a few minutes. 'At the end, we counted seventeen planes high up in the sky, towards the south. They were probably nationalist chaser-planes, and they were floating in loose formation. Against the sky, they seemed to be only tiny balls of white fluff.'[25] During future air raids, McCabe would run around the college opening the windows to prevent them from being smashed by the blast. 'Without shelter, an air raid is a weird – and terrifying – experience,' he wrote later. 'Death seems to brush past one's face (like a large, ugly Bat). One can almost feel its wings, and there's a nervous amazement at being still alive and unscathed.'[26]

Having survived their first air raid, McCabe and Belton had lunch at the 'Gran'.* General Gonzalo Queipo de Llano was dining with fellow officers at an adjoining table and McCabe introduced himself and Belton. Queipo was a mythical figure in Spain. His success in taking control of Seville had been crucial to the nationalists in the early days of the war; he claimed to have done so with just fifteen soldiers. Queipo ruled Andalusia as his own fiefdom for the duration of the war. He had little regard for Franco, regularly disparaging him behind his back.† Queipo's nightly harangues on Radio Sevilla were legendary and included crude sexual descriptions of what his troops would do to the womenfolk of the enemy. Many fellow generals viewed Queipo with distaste because of his avowed republican leanings before the war and suspected freemasonry; he

---

* The popular abbreviation in Salamanca for the Gran Hotel.
† Queipo's nickname for Franco was 'Paquito', which roughly translates as 'little Frankie'.

had been involved in at least two attempted coups against the monarchy before the establishment of the Second Republic in 1931. Queipo, wrote McCabe, 'is not an imaginative Southerner but a Castilian. From his [radio] talks, one might imagine him to have a middle-sized, fat figure, with a round waggish face, and twinkling eyes. He is quite different, with a tall dignified figure, a rather long, serious, somewhat sad face, and though he is all alert, his talk and manner are rather heavy.'[27] McCabe believed that Queipo could pass as a bishop if dressed in episcopal robes. The two Irishmen also met Millán Astray, the grotesque co-founder of the Spanish foreign legion, who made a joke in English about being a little 'astray'.[28]

That evening, Belton and McCabe met José Sangroñiz, the head of the nationalist diplomatic service, who promised to give them a car so that they could visit Cardinal Gomá in Pamplona. They returned to the 'Gran' for supper with McCullagh and Percival Phillips of the *Daily Telegraph*. The latter was an American-born war correspondent whose extraordinary career had seen him cover the Spanish-American War of 1898 and the Great War with the British army on the Western front. He had also reported on the 1916 Rising in Ireland. Phillips, along with most of the foreign correspondents, was disgusted at his treatment by the nationalist press and propaganda service in Salamanca. In the early days of the war, correspondents had been allowed to come and go as they pleased in the nationalist zone, but the authorities had clamped down when reports began filtering out about the atrocities being committed by Yagüe's forces. It was now almost impossible to get accurate information from the front.

The following morning, McCabe and Belton met Sangroñiz, Canon Despujol, Cardinal Gomá's secretary, and a number of Sangroñiz's subordinates, in the Palacio de Monterrey. McCabe was sitting in a waiting room before the meeting when Aileen O'Brien, the ICF's agent in Spain, came in. Belton had instructed O'Brien to soften up the Spanish so that the ICF could use the money from the national collection as Belton saw fit. 'Though she's a clever linguist, and a clever "piece", she looks ordinary enough,' wrote McCabe. 'She has a pale watery face, as if she were anemic or consumptive. We were both on our guard, and didn't talk very freely or comfortably.'[29] O'Brien was well placed with the authorities in Salamanca

– it was rumoured she was having an affair with Sangroñiz, and that a plane had been put at her disposal. The meeting between Belton and the Spaniards was awkward. 'They all gathered around Belton as if he were a big bull that they were trying to shove a step forward,' McCabe wrote.

> It's difficult to know what he wants, what he wants to do, or have done. Sangroñiz asked two or three times, 'Now is Mr. Belton satisfied?' Belton, who doesn't speak Spanish or French, or even English on these occasions, just glares at them under his eyebrows, as if deliberating, like a bull in the ring, which of them he will charge first.[30]

Belton wanted the funds to be diverted to the ICF, ostensibly to purchase medical supplies for the nationalist armies in Spain, though the army would have preferred direct control of the money. McCabe was frustrated at the lack of progress and irritated that he had been put into the position of mediator without being informed of the full facts by Cardinal MacRory, and suggested that both sides draw up a list of points for discussion.

While all this haggling was going on, the nationalists were preparing for what they believed would be their final assault on Madrid. On 6 November 1936, the Condor Legion, comprising about fifty Luftwaffe bombers and fighters, began leaving Germany for Spain. Throughout the early weeks of November, Madrid was subjected to heavy bombing. Only the poorly armed, ill-trained workers' militias stood in Franco's way and there was a jubilant atmosphere in Salamanca since it was believed he would take Madrid within days. The shops were advertising the sale of firecrackers to celebrate the expected victory and special regulations were being put in place to deal with correspondence once the capital was taken. The authorities advised that special broadcasts would be made from Madrid radio to inform people across Spain of their relatives' fate and a commission had been set up to send a telegram to Franco congratulating him on his victory. Those who did not share in the jubilation kept quiet.

On 18 November, McCabe, Belton, Coyne and McCullagh toured the Madrid front in an official car from GHQ in Salamanca, a small sign of appreciation for the efforts they had made towards the nationalist cause. The authorities had not issued a *salvoconducto* [pass of safe conduct] to McCullagh, but his countrymen had issued their own invitation.

McCullagh jumped at the chance since few foreign correspondents in the nationalist zone were allowed so close to the front. Outside Ávila, several cars flew by on their way to Salamanca. Their chauffeur told the Irishmen that it was Franco returning from a visit to the front line.

The four Irishmen stopped for lunch at the Hotel Inglés opposite the cathedral in Ávila. After they had sat down, a large group of German airmen filed into the dining room with a flurry of Nazi salutes. They had spent the morning bombing Madrid. After lunch, instead of taking the main road to Madrid, the driver drove the Irish party towards Navalcarnero, to the south-east of the capital, across a bare, barren landscape. McCabe and the others passed through villages containing ruined houses, a damaged church, broken-down cars and lorries and a burnt-out chassis:

> The villages seem to be deserted except for old men, women and children. Groups of old women sit on chairs in the shelter of the wall, taking the sun, in the old peaceful, peacetime way. At a cross-roads near San Martín, we were challenged by a sentry. He was an ordinary villager or farmer, about 35 years old, dressed in his everyday corduroy. He had nothing to indicate that he was a soldier on guard except the rifle on his back, which he swung round and 'ground' between his toes as we approached.[31]

The driver lost his way in the dark in the Sierra de Guadarrama. Belton was sitting silently in the back of the car, as McCullagh started telling stories of 'Reds' who had been cut off from their units and were wandering around the mountains living like bandits. McCabe asked his companions if they had a revolver. Despite their difficult situation, the Irishmen agreed to carry on towards Madrid.

They passed through more villages, which had once been held by the republicans, where huge crosses were painted in white on the black doors of the houses. This was to signify that the families within were now on the side of the nationalists. In some of the villages, nationalist soldiers stood on guard. Many of the houses were smashed to pieces by shells or had bullet holes in the walls. After climbing and descending for almost half-an-hour around hairpin bends, they came to a fork in the road where another sentry was standing guard. He told them that it was fifty kilometres to

Madrid. In his memoir of the war, McCullagh recalls McCabe showing an impressive resourcefulness. Fearing they were losing light and that they might not have enough petrol to get them home, the Irishmen debated what to do next. The driver was very nervous but McCabe urged him to press on. Ahead, they could see about twenty planes, 'black and sinister', flying into the 'gorgeous flaming sky', off to bomb Madrid with their last load of the day.[32] In Navalcarnero, about thirty kilometres from Madrid, they saw more evidence of the fighting. After filling up at a petrol pump, they set off for the last stage towards the capital. Dusk had set in but McCabe was excited at the prospect of seeing the fighting:

> It is difficult to believe our good luck. In half-an-hour, we shall see the city, which tonight is the centre of burning interest for the whole world. ... It is quite dark, and we meet several pairs of headlights that go flashing past on our left. It seems to be the normal traffic that one meets on the outskirts of any normal European capital. We might be coming back from Bray into Dublin.[33]

As they raced towards the Casa del Campo, the large park and former royal hunting estate in the west of Madrid where the Army of Africa was trying to force its way into the city, they were stopped three or four times by sentries but allowed to proceed, owing to the *salvoconducto* they had been given by GHQ. Military cars and lorries passed them on the road. Finally, McCabe saw the horrors of the war for himself:

> This was our first view of Madrid, and Madrid was on fire. Shells and bombs were doing their work. Tonight or tomorrow night, all Madrid will be a blazing furnace. Its palaces, museums, famous picture gallery, mansions, flats, warehouses, little shops, churches and convents – all will be burnt out and disappear. The end of the siege and of all this madness will be the end of Madrid itself. It was a bit blood-curdling but fascinating to watch that red glow in the sky, and these huge volumes of billowing smoke.[34]

McCabe was mistaken: Madrid was not yet to fall to the nationalists. The International Brigades were being slaughtered in the Casa de Campo but were preventing the *regulares* from punching their way through to the city. In the working-class suburb of Carabanchel in the south-west of the city, where the nationalists' General Varela had launched a diversionary attack, the militiamen and women, many of whom had never picked up a gun before, fought heroically to hold off the *regulares*.

The Irishmen's car was moving along slowly, allowing them to study the inferno that was the Spanish capital, when a sentry came running up to them and told them to turn off the headlights. McCabe wrote:

'The Reds are down there,' the sentry said excitedly, pointing to the road ahead. We all kept cool, got out of the car, and stood on the middle of the road. There was a moon coming up, and the crisp frost air was very cool and stimulating. Behind us, we could hear the faint rumble of the cannon that had passed us by, but there was a deep moonlight silence all around. Suddenly, on our left, the silence was broken by the sharp 'rap' and 'spit' of machine-gun fire. This was followed by the deep boom of a big gun.[35]

There were two sentries standing beside them. The Irishmen took shelter in the abandoned ruin of a two-storey house. They clambered over the debris and climbed up a marble staircase. It must have been an odd sensation, standing in the remains of someone's home watching the flames through a hole in the wall – which had once been a window – and listening to the machine-gun fire and the heavy boom of the cannons. McCabe was struck by the silence that followed each burst of gunfire.

From their viewing point they could see a single light in the Telefonica tower on the Gran Vía in Madrid. The scene fascinated McCabe, but the two soldiers, who had followed the Irishmen into the ruin, were anxious for them to be gone. The Irishmen left the house, deeply impressed by what they had seen. The driver started to pull away without the lights on, so as not to attract fire from the republican forces camped nearby, when he hit a barricade:

There was such a bang that it might have been a shell, or a collision with a tank. We got out to inspect the damage, but the car was all right. As we moved away slowly, we turned around to have a last look at Madrid. What seemed to be a blazing rocket was shooting in a curve of flame across the sky.[36]

Their adventure not yet over, they became lost again on the way home. In Navalcarnero, a sentry told them to be careful to take the right road or they would pass into the republican zone. The advice threw the driver, so at 8pm, and not being able to find the right road, they decided to turn around and head back to Navalcarnero. The town had been badly damaged in the fighting, the church was a pile of rubble and there were ruined houses all around. Navalcarnero was now a military camp and there were soldiers everywhere, sitting beside fires in the middle of the street. The commanding officer in the town told them that the road to Salamanca was quite safe and ordered a subordinate to point it out on the map to the driver. But the driver refused to take the risk of returning that evening. Instead, an officer escorted them to Talavera de la Reina, the site of Wellington's victory against the French during the Peninsular Wars, about sixty kilometres away. McCabe rode in the officer's car while the others followed behind.

Finding accommodation in Talavera was a problem. So, with a letter of introduction from the commanding officer in Navalcarnero in hand, the Irishmen visited the military commander of the town, who ordered an attendant to find them lodgings. After hours of tramping the streets, they found a family who would take them in. The next morning they visited Toledo, passing the 'twisted and charred' remains of cars, lorries, aeroplanes and tanks on the road and women and children who would stop to give them the fascist salute. The area that they were passing through had seen savage violence, as the Army of Africa had fought its way up from the south of Spain towards Toledo and Madrid. The world's attention had focused on Toledo in the early months of the war when republican forces bombarded the *alcázar*, the fortress where about a thousand nationalist army officers, civil guards and Falangists and eight hundred civilians had retreated after the failure of the rising in the town. Bombs and shells rained down on the fortress for seventy days until Franco diverted his forces to relieve the city, delaying his attack on Madrid and allowing Toledo's defenders to organise themselves. A month and a half after the end of the siege, the *alcázar* was a tourist attraction and visitors had to pay an admission fee just to visit the ruins. McCabe and his compatriots clambered over the debris, led by their guide, a corporal who had been in the *alcázar* during the siege.

Back in Salamanca, Belton and McCabe prepared to meet Franco in the episcopal palace. Belton composed his address to the general in McCabe's room in the Irish College. On entering the palace, the Irishmen walked up the stairs past the Moroccan guard through a waiting room and anteroom. Franco received them in the throne room of the palace. 'He's small and friendly,' wrote McCabe of the *generalísimo*, 'but serious and dignified. He has large intelligent eyes, but he hasn't the face, jutting jaw-bone, or sledge-hammer style of Mussolini.'[37] Wearing the ceremonial robes of the deputy lord mayor of Dublin for the occasion, Belton began to read his short speech, which McCabe had to translate at first sight. Franco replied, mentioning the friendly relations that had always existed between Spain and Ireland and pointing out that he, being from Galicia and a Celt, felt all the more sympathy and gratitude for what Ireland had done. 'On the way out, General Franco accompanied us down the long room, almost to the door, and there waited until we bowed ourselves out.'[38] As they were leaving, they met Juan de la Cierva, who had played a key role in organising the plane from London that had taken Franco from the Canaries to North Africa. He was an enthusiastic supporter of O'Duffy's Irish Brigade. A fortnight later he was killed in an air accident at Croydon Airport.

The next day, Belton, Coyne and McCabe set out for Pamplona to meet Cardinal Gomá. The cardinal received them in the convent where he was staying. Belton had drawn up a declaration at the meeting with Sangroñiz and Canon Despujol that he wished Gomá to sign. McCabe believed that he wanted to use it as propaganda for the ICF. 'I gave the Cardinal a respectful hint to be careful, and when he read the Spanish translation, he frowned and said that he couldn't sign this.' Instead, Belton left with a short statement of thanks for the money received. Despujol read it out to a typist. 'We were amazed to learn that the lady, in becoming lay dress, was a nun who had escaped from the "Red" zone. This impressed Mr Belton very much.'[39] The following month, the money was deposited in an account in Ireland under Belton's name. It was reported that the money had been used by the ICF to buy bandages for the nationalist army.

The Irish hierarchy was not pleased that its own collection had ended up in the hands of Belton and the ICF. Neither were the many Catholics who had subscribed to the collection in good faith but were hostile to Belton. In February 1937, Belton responded to the criticism in a letter to Cardinal MacRory: 'I presume that these [questions] will be made by the people so saturated with petty party policies that they resented the inauguration of the ICF and who remain passive in the face of Jewish immigration and the export of food to the Reds in Spain.'[40] At the end of the civil war, Belton was anxious that his own contribution and that of the Irish Christian Front be recognised, and wrote to McCabe to see if he could help organise some honour for himself from the new regime: 'Some of those who helped me to send out the supplies would be very anxious for some honary [sic] token of appreciation of their services to the cause of Nationalist Spain in the darkest hours of its fortunes.'[41]

Having secured control of the church-gate collection, Belton prepared to return to Ireland. McCabe travelled with him and Coyne as far as Hendaye, just over the French border, where he was surprised to see anti-Franco posters everywhere. (It was in Hendaye that Franco met Hitler in October 1940 to discuss the possibility of Spain joining the Axis.) In November 1936, McCabe felt a great sense of tranquillity and was sorry to have to return across the border:

> There is an extraordinary difference between the two countries. It is due, perhaps, to the fact that France's political institutions and traditions date from the French Revolution. They are modern, therefore, and are accepted by all Frenchmen. Spain rejects modern institutions, and has been in a constant state of Civil War since the French Revolution, which tried to impose Modern History on Spain, but half Spain would not have it.[42]

Throughout the winter of 1936, Franco continued to strengthen his position within the nationalist high command. Those close to Franco developed a cult of personality around him to cement his position as the movement's civil and military head. This interweaving of the religious and political in Spain and the attempt to establish 'State Worship' appalled McCabe. One article about Franco, in particular, which described the general as full of grace, infuriated McCabe, who regarded it as 'awful, pious, blasphemous Latin "tosh"'.[43] In December, it was announced that nationalist communiqués would appear in the same position as the leading article in the newspapers. Before the news on nationalist radio, the foreign legion's anthem was played. After the news, either the Carlist or Falangist anthem was played.

The head of the nationalist propaganda machine, Millán Astray, was a familiar sight around Salamanca and not hard to spot, given that he had only one eye and one arm. The general ate lunch in the dining room of the 'Gran' every day. McCabe, who described him as a 'well-known Public Madman', was sometimes present to witness his antics.[44] On one occasion, Millán Astray kept his fellow diners in the Gran Hotel standing with arms outstretched in the fascist salute while he sang the anthems of the Falange, the Spanish foreign legion and the Carlists, the Horst Wessel song, the Italian fascist anthem and the German, Italian and Portuguese national anthems. Millán Astray had been to the fore in popularising Franco in the nationalist ranks, and as a reward had been allowed to set up his own radio station in Salamanca. His broadcasts were extraordinary, rivalling those of Queipo de Llano's in Andalusia.

McCabe spotted General Antonio Aranda in the dining room of the 'Gran' on another occasion. Aranda had been military governor of Oviedo during the uprising and had tricked the workers into leaving the city, telling them that he was loyal to the republic. At the beginning of 1937, Oviedo was surrounded by hostile territory, and it was Aranda who was responsible for its defence. This was 'a task that demands military courage, and administrative genius', McCabe wrote.[45] Aranda was later given a field command in the campaign to take Asturias for the nationalists but fell out of favour with Franco after the war, because the *generalísimo* suspected he was plotting a restoration of the monarchy. Aranda was sitting alone in the 'Gran', dressed in a plain uniform, 'without ribbons or medals' and attracted little attention from his fellow diners. 'He has a round fat figure, stout swarthy face, and looks rather surly, "bull-dog" and brutal.'[46]

The nationalists were purging civil society and removing from their posts those whom they deemed ideologically suspicious. Teachers were fired and university professors were deprived of their chairs because of their political sympathies. At the end of November 1936, it was announced that three university professors in Salamanca had been removed from their positions, including the deceased Casto Prieto Carrasco. 'As the last was executed, and is in another world, they will probably have to notify him,' McCabe remarked.[47]

In order to raise money for the war effort, the authorities imposed fines on those they suspected of having sympathised with the republic. The newspapers published lists of these fines, from five hundred pesetas for spreading alarmist news or making a remark against the nationalist movement to 10,000 pesetas for a breach of public order. The college's house doctor was fined 100,000 pesetas, over £2,000, for having subscribed to the Russian Red Cross. McCabe was disgusted at this form of extortion: 'This is a "Crusade", of course, but a good many things going on here remind me of a Chicago "racket" or "frame-up".'[48] McCabe regarded the Falange as the worst for this kind of behaviour and was dismayed when he was forced that winter to provide accommodation in the Irish College for a group of Falangists working in the nationalist press office.

A fear of espionage was rife in Salamanca. There were rumours that chauffeurs were delivering messages to the enemy. The secret police were also investigating whether chauffeurs, who were all suspected of 'Red' sympathies, were deliberately positioning their cars near important buildings as a signal to enemy aircraft during air raids. Many of the rumours were fantastical but they created a sense of panic in the nationalist zone, which was, of course, the intention. McCabe got caught up in the madness:

[the enemy spies] have a well-organised system of espionage, and they seem to be able to broadcast directly from Salamanca to the Red Zone. They have also the most ingenious ways of communicating, especially by code. Recently, a Nationalist pilot, secretly a 'Red', got up in his plane and flew over to the other side. His sweetheart was a Red spy, kept in touch with him, and sent important messages out through Portugal. One of them was a telegram to say, 'no cloth in town to-day'. This meant that there were no Nationalist planes in the neighbouring aerodromes, and that it would easy and safe for Red planes to come over and bomb the town. The lady was caught, and is being detained, 'until she sings' ... Then she will be 'bumped off'.[49]

The Irish College was not above suspicion. Secret policemen investigating espionage questioned McCabe on a couple of occasions. Not long after McCabe's trip with Belton, McCullagh and Coyne to the outskirts of Madrid, a policeman arrived at the college to inquire how McCullagh, who had not been given permission by GHQ, had managed to visit the front with them. The journalist was then staying at a *pensión* in Salamanca. On the day he returned from the front, he had boasted of his adventures. Unfortunately for him, some civil guards were staying in the same *pensión* and had reported him. After McCullagh had gone to bed that night, a detective arrived to interview him. According to McCullagh, his landlady drove away the detective 'with a humorous violence that would have done credit to a grand old Galway fish-wife, who had "just a drap," but not a "drap" too much or too little'.[50] The detective was not put off for long, though, and returned to the *pensión* the next day, accompanied by a Falangist and another man in civilian dress. At first, McCullagh did not believe that he was a policeman. 'Then it became evident to me that the man was simply the low-class, badly-paid type of detective whom one used to meet with in Lisbon, Venezuela, and Constantinople.'[51] McCullagh also faced an interrogation at GHQ about his visit to the front, and wrote a note to McCabe asking him 'to look him up' in case anything should happen. 'He was afraid of being bumped off as a Red spy,' wrote McCabe.[52] The college housekeeper's brother was another who fell foul of the secret police after making a remark in a café to the effect that the nationalists would not succeed in taking Madrid. A plainclothes detective heard him and the authorities locked him up.

Despite all the intrigue that went with living in a city at war, McCabe was depressed at the end of the year. He ate Christmas dinner alone in the Gran Hotel, describing it as the loneliest day of his life. It was not just McCabe who was glum. Early hopes of a quick resolution to the war had faded throughout Salamanca and the local population was resigned to a protracted conflict.

# Chapter 8

# THE IRISH BRIGADE

At the beginning of August 1936, a few weeks after the military uprising in Spain, and as stories about the slaughter of priests and nuns filled the pages of the Irish newspapers, Count Ramírez de Arellano, the Carlist who had contacted Cardinal MacRory about sending an Irish unit to Spain, wrote to Eoin O'Duffy asking him to lead a group of Irishmen into battle on the side of the nationalist armies. 'What a glorious example Ireland could give the whole of Christendom,' wrote the Navarrese noble.[1] A few weeks later, O'Duffy began appealing for volunteers in the press.

O'Duffy viewed the Spanish enterprise as an opportunity to enhance his prestige after the personal disappointments of recent years. He had enjoyed a stellar early career, having successfully led the Monaghan Brigade of the IRA during the war of independence before succeeding Richard Mulcahy as chief-of-staff. He had supported the Treaty and successfully prosecuted the campaign against the anti-Treatyites in Munster during the Irish Civil War. In 1922, he had become commissioner of the Garda Síochána. His abilities as an organiser and administrator had served him well in that capacity for the ten years that Cumann na nGaedheal were in government. However, when it had looked as if his sworn enemies in Fianna Fáil were about to win office in the early 1930s, O'Duffy had been unable to set aside civil war enmities and had contemplated a *coup d'état* rather than allow the government hand over power. When Éamon de Valera won the election in 1932, O'Duffy's days were numbered. In February 1933, de Valera argued that O'Duffy would be unable to set aside his political prejudices and dismissed him as garda commissioner. O'Duffy refused to accept another role of equivalent responsibility in the public service. Yet within the space of five months of his public humiliation at the hands of de Valera, O'Duffy was the leader of a mass movement in direct confrontation with the government.

The National Guard – or Blueshirts as they became known because of the colour of their uniforms – evolved out of the Army Comrades Association. This latter body had been set up to look after the interests of ex-National Army members, but it soon became a political movement whose declared aim was to defend the country from left-wing and republican elements. The Blueshirts acted as bodyguards to Cumann na nGaedheal speakers at public meetings around the country and were frequently involved in violent clashes with the IRA. The National Guard adopted the accoutrements of European fascism, such as the shirted uniform and Roman salute, as well as much of its ideology. It was fiercely anti-communist and declared itself committed to the corporate and vocational ideas then in vogue. Right-wing Catholicism and opposition to Irish republicanism shaped the Blueshirts' ideology more than the fascism of Hitler or Mussolini. Yet O'Duffy undoubtedly saw himself cast from the same mould as the German and Italian fascist leaders. So much so that in August 1933 he planned a parade through Dublin, in imitation of Mussolini's famed March on Rome. In response, the Irish government banned the parade and declared the National Guard an illegal organisation.

In September 1933, O'Duffy became the leader of the newly formed Fine Gael. The party was the result of a merger between Cumann na nGaedheal, the National Centre Party and the Young Ireland Association (the renamed National Guard). But just a year later, following disagreements with his colleagues, O'Duffy resigned. Many of the members of Cumann na nGaedheal had become uneasy with O'Duffy's histrionics and autocratic style and yearned for a more stable form of politics. He was now free to pursue his own vision, which came to expression in the National Corporate Party, but O'Duffy was never the same political force. It was his desire to regain his relevance in Irish politics that led O'Duffy to Spain.[2]

Public opinion in Ireland was supportive of the Spanish nationalists. The Spanish Civil War was viewed in narrow terms as a battle between traditional, Christian Spain and anti-Christian Bolshevism. The Catholic Church, most of the Catholic press, including the *Irish Independent*, and the Fine Gael-led Opposition were cheerleaders for Franco. Fine Gael used the war to its own political advantage, attacking the Fianna Fáil government for failing to recognise Franco's regime.

In this encouraging climate, O'Duffy's call for volunteers to fight in Spain was well received. Former Blueshirts, ex-British Army and Irish Army officers, bored young men and old-fashioned adventurers rallied to the cause. Many had been followers of O'Duffy during the heady days of the early 1930s, when the Blueshirts were at their strongest, but former members of the anti-Treaty IRA and Fianna Fáil, motivated by their wish to defend Holy Mother Church or with a thirst for adventure, also answered the call. The strongest response was from Munster, especially Tipperary and Cork, the Blueshirt heartland. Monaghan was also well represented, a reflection of O'Duffy's personal popularity in his home county. Such was the initial enthusiasm that O'Duffy believed that he would be leading a small army to Spain.

While there was considerable enthusiasm for the Irish Brigade at home, Franco was less certain about the merits of the project, mostly out of fear for its impact on diplomatic relations with the United Kingdom. Nevertheless, the Spanish high command admitted the Irish volunteers into the Spanish foreign legion and allowed them form their own battalions, or *banderas*. It was deemed an unusual honour to serve in the elite foreign legion and the pay and conditions were significantly better than in the regular army. Each *bandera* was to have its own Irish officers, doctors, chaplains and cooks.

Efforts to transport the Irishmen to Spain were hampered by the Irish government's policy of non-intervention. Despite pressure from Fine Gael, de Valera had refused to recognise Franco and Ireland had committed itself to the Non-Intervention Agreement, which had been proposed by the British and French governments on 25 August 1936 as a means of preventing a proxy war between the Fascist powers on one side and the Soviets on the other. It soon became clear that the non-intervention policy was a failure, as Hitler and Mussolini poured troops, planes and weapons into Spain, despite signing up to the agreement.

An effort to transport the first batch of volunteers from Passage East in County Waterford in October 1936 was stymied by Franco himself, who was anxious to avoid provoking the British. Instead, small groups of volunteers left Ireland and travelled via Liverpool and Lisbon. On

13 December, the largest group of volunteers left Galway aboard the SS *Urundi*, a German-registered cargo vessel, which landed at El Ferrol, Franco's home town in the north-eastern region of Galicia. From El Ferrol, they travelled by train to Cáceres, the capital of the arid region of Extremadura in the south-west of the country, which was to be the Irish Brigade's base. The brigade stopped in Salamanca, where the bishop and the town's municipal authorities welcomed them. Those Irishmen who had taken the pledge were given a dispensation to partake of the local wine. It was the first time many of them had tasted wine and some returned to the train somewhat the worse for wear. Finally, the men reached Cáceres and began their training.

There were about 730 men in the Irish Brigade, well short of the thousands initially envisioned but enough to comprise one *bandera*. They were led by twenty-five Irish officers and twenty-six Spanish liaison officers. Most of the latter were Spanish aristocrats, some of Irish ancestry, who attached themselves to the brigade as a mark of respect and because of their fluent English. After the brigade had returned to Ireland, McCabe wrote that it was 'too top-heavy, perhaps. It was a bit ridiculous to have over fifty officers, between Irish and Spanish, for seven hundred men.'[3] The brigade was divided into four companies, three of infantry and one machine-gun company, as well as a heavy trench-mortar section and a light artillery section. There were also three doctors, two qualified Red Cross nurses, a chaplain and a pipers' band consisting of fourteen men. The brigade was attached to the foreign legion but was commanded by an Irish major, Paddy Dalton.[4]

'The Spanish authorities had the erroneous impression that Ireland would send out a "crack" regiment, veterans, perhaps, of the Great War, and up to the standard of any Continental Army,' McCabe remarked. 'The Spaniards, thought, too, that all the officers would have been trained in a military academy, such as they themselves have in Toledo, Segovia or Ávila.' In fact, many of the men had no military training and little experience, 'except what some of them got in cross-road ambushes in Ireland, during the Black-and-Tan struggle'.[5]

In December 1936, Fr Joseph Mulrean, an Irish-born priest based in Spain, was appointed chaplain to the brigade. Believing that about two thousand Irish soldiers would be based in Cáceres – in fact less than half that number made it to Spain – Mulrean invited McCabe to help with a general confession and communion.[6] Mulrean flew to Salamanca on 4 January 1937 to escort McCabe to Cáceres.

From County Westmeath, Mulrean had come to Spain as a young man after becoming interested in the Order of Saint Jerome and had studied at the Hieronymite monastery of Santa Maria del Parral in Segovia. When the republican government had ordered the monastery closed in the early 1930s, Mulrean had been taken in at the Conciliar Seminary of Madrid. He had been ordained a diocesan priest in Gibraltar in 1932 and had offered his services to O'Duffy when the Irish Brigade was formed. He was a big man – McCabe estimated he weighed sixteen stone – in his thirties, and McCabe's first impressions of Mulrean were mixed. 'Fr. Mulrean is a fine fat, cheery priest, but as I discovered later, he might have been reared in one of these houses with the squinting windows,'* wrote McCabe.[7]

Mulrean had booked a return air ticket to Cáceres, and the two priests visited the nationalist air department – the signs over the doors and in the corridors were in German – to see if they could get a seat for him. They were successful, but the next day McCabe had to give up his seat on the plane to a German colonel. So they asked GHQ for a car to take them to Cáceres instead. While they were waiting for their car, Sangróniz asked McCabe to deliver a few letters that had arrived for Aileen O'Brien, who had been dismissed from the ICF the previous month and had now attached herself to the Irish Brigade:

> Fr Mulrean has an enormous curiosity that makes him itch and scratch himself. In my room, before we left, he asked me to show him the letters. He scrutinised the postmarks, frowned, turned the letters over, looked at the seal lovingly, and I was afraid that he was going to say, 'Let's open this one, and see who is writing to this little witch.'[8]

Mulrean had a 'very filthy opinion' of O'Brien, according to McCabe, and he found her 'nasty and nauseating'.[9]

---

* An allusion to Brinsley MacNamara's 1918 novel *The Valley of the Squinting Windows*.

Mulrean was not the only one hostile to O'Brien. The Irish hierarchy had been displeased that O'Brien had been representing the interests of Irish Catholicism in Spain through her role in the ICF and, according to McCabe, the Spanish officers cracked obscene jokes about her and regarded O'Brien as a 'loose lady with a very high price'.[10] McCabe had thought about giving the letters to Mulrean to deliver but soon changed his mind and handed them over himself when he arrived in Cáceres. McCabe soon came to regard Mulrean as a snoop, a zealot and a gossip, and believed that his loose tongue made the men afraid to confess to him.

Although McCabe was supposed to stay at the Hotel Álvarez in Cáceres, at the last minute Colonel Yagüe, the commander of the Spanish foreign legion, took his room. The colonel was standing outside the hotel when they arrived. 'Yagüe, who is about fifty, has a remarkable head of fine-white hair. Two Aides stood respectfully behind him, carrying sub-machine guns. They say that Yagüe is a stickler for discipline, and that he loves all the military pomp that corresponds to his rank.'[11]

McCabe met O'Duffy in Cáceres, and his initial impressions were positive: 'He has the simple, friendly, hospitable way of all Irishmen with one another, and, especially, of Irish lay folk with their priests. It's so different from Spain, where so many people would like to see all the "Curas" strung up.'[12] O'Duffy spent the meeting criticising the nationalists' mistakes, including their failure to capture Madrid, but McCabe was too tired to take much interest. Despite his exhaustion, McCabe did not sleep well. The house he was staying in was cold and another visitor passed through his room in the middle of the night on his way to his billet. To make matters worse, Mulrean had asked him to preach to the men at a mass the next day and he was mulling over what he would say.

McCabe got his first look at the Irish Brigade in their new home the next morning:

Going down the hill towards the Church, I heard the sound of military music, and when I got to the bottom of the steep street, and in to the little Square in front of the church here, marching and swinging down the street, led by their own Irish officers, come the men of the latest Irish Brigade on the Continent.[13]

The men, dressed in the green uniforms of the Spanish foreign legion, were on their way to Sunday mass. The authorities had reserved the church of San Domingo in the centre of Cáceres for the exclusive use of the Irish Brigade. McCabe was nervous, he had not preached to a public congregation in five years. Mulrean wanted McCabe to exhort the men to 'take the pledge' and abstain from alcohol. He told McCabe that he was worried 'over the drink problem' and that the Irishmen had 'grown too fond of "vino"'.[14] McCabe thought a rousing, upbeat homily was more appropriate for men risking their lives at the front but, in the sacristy, he became uncertain. Mulrean's entreaties had left him with a divided mind, 'which is fatal on entering a pulpit'. Nevertheless, he managed to get through the mass, writing later that, 'to see all these men staring up at one is always a great inspiration. It must be a wonderful, exhilarating experience, to conduct an orchestra, lead a cavalry charge, or to address thousands of people, and hear their cheering.'[15]

After mass, McCabe met some of the Irish officers, including Lieutenant Tom Hyde – who was later killed in a skirmish near the Madrid front – at breakfast at the Café Viena, which had become their informal club. His impression was positive, describing them as a 'friendly crowd' who were 'manly, cheery, refined' and 'good companions'. He contrasted the atmosphere at the Café Viena, 'Irish and jolly', with the 'strained air' of the Hotel Álvarez, where the staff officers were lodging.[16] Afterwards, McCabe watched in the main square as the Irish troops marched past the military governor, Colonel Luis Martín-Pinillos. 'The men looked a bit baggy in their new Legion uniforms, and very stiff and green giving the salute and they seemed to be too tense to be smart-looking and perfectly drilled. However, they looked athletic, clean and muscular and seemed to be a crowd that will give a tough account of themselves.'[17] However, McCabe soon sensed an air of discord. At the Hotel Álvarez, he ate with Mulrean and a Spanish air force captain. The dining room was full of German and Italian officers. 'Some of the Germans with their serious hard-boiled faces, and their sharp military clicks, look the real thing and mean business.'[18]

Mulrean had chosen a table at the head of the room in order 'to keep his eye on people'. Among those he wished to spy on were Captain Thomas Gunning of the Irish Brigade and his wife, Kathleen, who had recently

arrived in Cáceres from Ireland. They were dining in the opposite corner
of the room. Gunning had studied for the priesthood in the United States
and Germany before giving up his vocation to become a journalist. He
was a former editor of the *Standard*, the Catholic newspaper in Dublin,
and was one of the few Irish members of the Irish Brigade who could
speak Spanish and was effectively O'Duffy's right-hand man. McCabe
thought him 'very clever' and 'the brains of the Brigade'. Mulrean and
Gunning disliked each other intensely.[19] Gunning believed Mulrean was
an 'old biddy', while Mulrean disapproved of the presence in Cáceres of
Kathleen Gunning.

On Mulrean's insistence, the two priests ignored the Gunnings in
Cáceres. McCabe thought Mulrean's behaviour odd and believed that
the chaplain's strange attitude was perhaps because Gunning was an ex-
ecclesiastical student. It was likely partly attributable to the chaplain's deep
misogyny, since Mulrean showed similar objections to Aileen O'Brien,
who was also in Cáceres. The chaplain had 'ascetic views about the
relations between a man and his legitimate wife', according to McCabe.[20]
However, McCabe accepted Mulrean's wishes to keep their distance
because he regarded himself as the chaplain's guest in Cáceres.

The military governor arranged for McCabe to visit the Franciscan
monastery at Guadalupe while he was staying in Cáceres. The party that
set out on the day trip included two Spanish Franciscan priests and two
members of the Irish Brigade, including Major Paddy Dalton, O'Duffy's
second-in-command, who had been a member of the IRA, and Captain
Thomas Smyth, a Belfast Protestant who had fought with the British army
in the First World War. McCabe noted that, 'though they were comrades-
in-arms, Dalton referred to Smyth as "that old Protestant".'[21]

As they passed through the Extremaduran countryside, one of the
Franciscans pointed out what little remained of a village that had resisted
the Army of Africa as it steamrolled its way north towards Madrid. At a
blockhouse defended by a group of men with rifles in the middle of the
empty hilly countryside, McCabe was able to look across the front line
towards a village in republican-held territory:

One has the impression of standing on the border of Europe and
looking across into Russia. The land between us and the village is

enveloped in the twilight, and also, in mystery. It seems to be remote in Space and Time, and to be a whole Continent or a whole Century away. It's amazing how War and conflicting Ideologies can separate and isolate two neighbouring villages that are within sight of each other. This, then, is the Front, dividing Spain, and World sympathy into two parts.[22]

McCabe found it exhilarating to be so close to the republican zone, and pondered what life was like on the other side of the front line and whether they had established a new system of government, such as a soviet. Farther along, they passed more evidence of the recent fighting:

> On the twisting road that leads to the Monastery, one of the Franciscan Fathers pointed out a patch of fresh earth, where Reds and Moors have been buried. There is another patch of burnt ground, and a couple of charred rags lying around. The Franciscan, who has a hard, shrewd face, both ascetic and practical, chuckles. A few corpses, or a few bonfires for burning them, do not grate on his finer feelings.[23]

The same Franciscan pointed around at the hills and explained that the 'Moors' and legionaries of Yagüe's columns had appeared just in time to save the monastery, which had been besieged by the republicans. About 5,000 people had taken refuge behind its thick walls. Arriving just as it was getting dark, McCabe and his companions had time for only a quick tour of the monastery.

On the way back to Cáceres that night, the driver told McCabe, Dalton and Smyth – the Franciscans had stayed on in Guadalupe – that occasionally the 'Reds' would cross the front line into the nationalist zone to raid cattle. Two days before, they had come up to the road and attacked a mail-car. Dalton readied his revolver but there was no trouble except a puncture. Once it was repaired, they carried on to Cáceres, singing Irish songs. Smyth sang some of 'the old trench ditties' he had learned in Flanders in the Great War. 'They bought a touch of France and Flanders into this dark, lonely landscape in Extramadura [sic],' McCabe noted.[24]

The religiosity of the Irish Brigade impressed the citizenry of Cáceres. The Irish soldiers attended mass, sang hymns, visited the blessed sacrament, recited the rosary and went to confession and holy communion. While Franco was happy to cloak the nationalist war effort as a Christian crusade against communism and to receive the enthusiastic backing of the Spanish Church, most of the Spanish officers had little or no time for religion – the fiercely Catholic Carlist militias from Navarre being an exception. So when the Spanish officers saw the Irish soldiers performing their religious duties punctiliously, they were amazed. The Irish were conversely disappointed by the religious apathy of their Spanish comrades, given that defending the Church was the brigade's prime motivation. A few of the officers and men, Catholic and Protestant, had, either from purely political motives or a spirit of adventure, come to Spain without any thought of the religious dimension, but most were committed Catholics who had joined up to save the Spanish Church. Yet in Spain, especially in the south, the workers regarded the Church as a reactionary institution that propped up their oppressors, the landlords. Unlike Ireland, where all classes practised Catholicism in public displays of piety, by the mid-1930s the Spanish working class and a large part of the middle class had drifted away from the Church or were vehemently anti-clerical. Most of the workers were on the side of the republican government.

If the Irish in Cáceres might have supposed that they would see more religious feeling among the conservative officer class, they were to be disappointed. In the south of Spain, it was mainly women who practised their religion and, perhaps owing to the vicissitudes of war, with much devotion. McCabe wrote that he had 'never seen anywhere, even in paintings, such a rapt, mystical fervour as on the faces of women receiving Holy Communion. They seem to have a direct emotional contact with the Divinity, as when Our Lady received the Holy Ghost.' McCabe believed that this sacramental communion with God was 'absolutely essential and imperative' and was a strong and visible proof of the need for religion and the satisfaction it could give its adherents.[25]

It took a few days in Cáceres for McCabe to learn that not all was well in the Irish Brigade. Most of the Irish officers and men had come to resent the chaplain's admonishments about their moral failings. McCabe was astonished that Mulrean made each man accept a slip of paper to prove that he had gone to confession. It was an offence to his moderate sensibility. 'Zeal (even when honest) can be dangerous and repulsive,' he wrote, 'when it eats (not the zealot, but) people up.' Mulrean's patronising behaviour especially affronted the officers. 'As Fr. Mulrean talks too much, and is too anxious and unscrupulous about personal, intimate and even feminine affairs, the Irish officers do not want to go to confession to him.'[26] Given that Mulrean was blatantly indiscreet, it was unsurprising that the officers felt uneasy about confessing their sins to him. McCabe attributed part of the problem to Mulrean having been educated in a Spanish seminary, though Mulrean's obsession with sexual morality suggests more a failing of the Irish than the Spanish Church: 'They feel that he sits down in the Box and begins to listen eagerly, just to satisfy his morbid curiosity. They see that he is constantly doing this outside the Box, and it's very hard to trust a Confessor, who is, at the same time an inveterate and unscrupulous gossip and slobberer.'[27]

Mulrean had insisted on being accorded the rank of captain, according to McCabe, which also caused difficulties with his fellow officers, who did not believe he deserved it. 'In the pulpit, he doesn't preach,' McCabe wrote. 'He growls at them, worries them in canine fashion, and is always denouncing them. He does this when the Spanish officers are present in the Church, and it humiliates the Irish officers.'[28] McCabe believed, on the other hand, that the Spanish clergy used the confessional to advise people on how to vote and the people went to confession for advice about their domestic affairs.

Mulrean was on better terms with the Spanish officers: 'whereas he amuses them, while they are winking at one another behind his back.'[29] The aristocratic Spanish officers, steeped in a macho culture from an early age, were contemptuous of the Irish officers because they let themselves be bullied and lectured to by a priest. They most likely regarded the religiosity of some of the Irish as effeminate behaviour. McCabe noted that the Spanish did not have the same respect for priests as the Irish. 'The Spaniards are inclined to regard their own Chaplain as a "*cura*", and though they respect him, it's not the full respect that one man has for another.'[30] While the word *cura* had not the same derogatory connotations that it did in the republican zone, it still carried little weight among the nationalists. It must have caused some confusion to the pious Irishmen who had come to Spain to protect priests and nuns to learn that the bulk of the Spanish officer class had a tenuous respect for the clergy and little time for religious devotion.

The Irish soldiers spent their days in Cáceres drilling, going on long route marches and practising with their Mauser rifles on a range outside the town. The drilling proved particularly problematic, because, instead of forming and marching in fours, as they were used to, the Spanish army marched in threes. One day, the Irish Brigade's commanding officer, Dalton, injured himself on the range while firing at a hand grenade. The officers and men were frequently bored and found it hard to acclimatise to the Spanish food and customs. Because they had been accorded the honour of joining the foreign legion, they were among the best paid in the nationalist forces and enjoyed some of the best food, 'but the Irishmen were squeamish, and could not get used to it. There was grumbling, too, against the Irish Quarter Master about supplies, and about the bad cooking.'[31]

McCabe believed that many of the men were already anxious to get home, even though they had yet to see any fighting. His opinion of the Irish soldiers had changed considerably since his first glimpse of them passing through Salamanca. He found that many were homesick and wished to return home. 'One or two of the men have a crazy look, and a few of them look limp, disillusioned. The Irishmen, compared with the Spaniards, look soft, and they haven't the hard, tough grain of the Spanish climate or the Spanish character.'[32]

Once a week the men held a concert. At one of these, McCabe sang 'Clare's Dragoons' to a packed audience. But drinking was the Irish Brigade's main form of entertainment. The locals admired the Irishmen for their idealism and bravery but it was not long before they began to take a dim view of their excesses. The ordinary Spaniard was astonished at the drunken behaviour of these supposedly devout men. Spaniards, especially those in the south of Spain, simply could not understand drunkenness. 'It's a very serious misdemeanour and loss of dignity, and they never make jokes about it,' McCabe noted.

When, therefore, they see these idealists, and fervent church-goers, drinking and 'having one too many', they are profoundly shocked. In Ireland, people take a lenient view of drunkenness, and a rigid view about sexual excesses. On the whole, the reverse is exactly true in Spain. Here, drunkenness is regarded as unnatural and defamatory, whereas having two or three illegitimate children isn't quite correct, but it doesn't offend against the original Commandment 'to increase and multiply'.[33]

The aristocratic Spanish officers 'could not understand why the Irish officers and men were chumming together one day, and fighting their rows the next'.[34]

The brigade had their own pavilion in the army barracks. The wards were 'neat and clean' with each man's kit, including a gas mask, at the end of his bed. When McCabe visited the barracks with Mulrean, the men were sitting around on the beds cleaning their weapons. There were offices in the pavilion for the use of the officers. In one of them, they met the senior NCO, Staff Sergeant-Major Michael Weymes from Mullingar. Weymes stayed on after the Irish Brigade returned to Ireland and joined another *bandera*. He was killed leading his men at the Battle of Brunete in July 1937. There were three doctors attached to the Irish Brigade. On the day of McCabe's visit, one of them was in bed, 'having a rest from alcohol'. 'Another is a mystic,' wrote McCabe. Though this doctor was cultured and refined, and an excellent teacher, he was 'a bit crazy', 'probably a drug addict' and believed that O'Duffy had tricked him into coming to Spain.[35]

Outside in the barrack square, McCabe watched the Irish Brigade's machine-gun company being drilled by Seán Cunningham, a captain from Belfast and a former member of the British army. A Dublin sergeant was drilling another section, while a third was practising a bayonet charge. Passing one of the other pavilions, McCabe noticed a Moroccan prisoner looking out through the bars of his cell. He had killed a prostitute in a local brothel. McCabe and Mulrean stopped to talk to him and he described to them in detail how he had killed the woman. A young socialist who had been captured on the Madrid front was in the cell with him but refused to be drawn into conversation. On a second visit to the cell block, McCabe came across a couple of young men from Liverpool who had joined the nationalists 'to fight against Bolshevism' and then deserted. The cell beside that contained two Irishmen, one of whom, according to McCabe, was 'completely mad'.[36]

On another occasion, McCabe met two badly bruised members of the Irish Brigade. They explained that they had been in bed when three Irish officers had rushed in, 'swearing and cursing' and threatening to murder them, before giving them a beating.[37] McCabe was unsure what had led to the incident but suspected the officers may have been drunk and that the row was political. McCabe heard one man say that when he got to the front, he was going to shoot one of the officers. Personal and political rivalries were exacerbated by drink and the close proximity in which the men lived. More than once they smashed up the local café where they spent most of their time drinking. Though not an admirer of Mulrean, McCabe conceded that he had a tough job as chaplain.

McCabe thought that many of those who had joined the Irish Brigade were idealists, fighting for Spain and their religion, but that others were adventurers, 'who, in the old days, would take the English "bob", and join the British Army to see the world. It was a change from standing at the corner and staring at the pump.'[38] Indeed, some of those officers and men who had served in the British army during the First World War complained about the lack of organisation in the brigade.

While the men made the best they could of the barracks, O'Duffy stayed at the Hotel Álvarez when he was in Cáceres. He spent much of his time in Salamanca or in Ireland drumming up support for the brigade. Dalton was staying in an old mansion, 'one of the best private houses in town', owned by the Duke of Algeciras. The duke was a producer and exporter of sherry and one evening he invited some of the Irish officers to a tasting. McCabe attended with Mulrean and described the atmosphere as 'strained' owing to the presence of the chaplain. 'Finally, Mulrean and I left, and I expect that the party felt more at home when we had gone.'[39]

While McCabe and Mulrean were visiting some of the Irishmen who had already ended up in the military hospital in Cáceres, they looked into a large ward full of wounded Spanish soldiers. It left McCabe feeling depressed and ill:

Most of the men have bullets or shrapnel in some part of the body. Here, in another bed, is a man with a bullet in his brain who is raving all the time. ... Some are recovering, some don't know if they will even recover and some are dying. Nearly all of them feel dreary and depressed. It can't be very cheery to be wounded, and to look around at all the other wounded, and to see them dying, too, and their corpses being carried off ...[40]

The Moroccan wounded were housed in a separate hospital.

One evening, in Mulrean's room, the two priests tuned in to Madrid radio. It was something of a risk because listening to an enemy station was forbidden:

The speeches were fierce, with a real revolutionary ring in them and a high pitch of bitter defiance. They have no speakers like that on this side – so hot and passionate in appeal and invective. But after half-an-hour of it, I had a genuine pain in my head. The wireless, which is so modern, has become just another instrument of barbarous, medieval torture.[41]

They turned off the radio when the family with whom Mulrean was staying became understandably nervous.

While in Cáceres, McCabe took a trip to Mérida to visit the Roman ruins. The town had been the scene of fighting in the early stages of the war and many of the houses had been destroyed. On the Roman bridge, a young Spanish boy described the nationalist assault on the town in detail, pointing out the positions of the *regulares* and their artillery emplacements. The boy had hidden in the cellar of his house with the family during the bombardment. Down by an ancient well in the town, some families, 'looking hungry and panic-stricken', had made their home. The frequent air raids terrified the residents, as the republican air force pounded the town, an important crossroads in south-west Spain, hoping to hit the bridge.

McCabe had a lucky escape before he returned to Salamanca. He had been scheduled to travel on the regular air service between Seville and Salamanca. Twice he had visited the aerodrome in Cáceres but the plane had failed to show up. Eventually, bored of waiting, he decided to return to Salamanca by train on 13 January 1937. The plane in which he was supposed to travel crash-landed in the Sierra de Gredos outside

Salamanca and all the passengers, German officers, were found days later, frozen to death.

Back in Salamanca, McCabe applied himself to the task of preventing the Irish College from being commandeered by the authorities. At the beginning of February, an official from the town hall and Salamanca's police chief had arrived to inspect the building, while Falangist officials were frequent visitors over the following months.

Though life continued as normal for those in the favour of the authorities, it was not so for the families of republican prisoners. One day, McCabe saw a group of old women carrying mattresses down a hill towards one of the jails for their sons. The brother of McCabe's housekeeper was one of them. McCabe suspected that she was pilfering supplies from the college kitchen to give to him in jail.

On 2 February, Mulrean wrote to McCabe telling him that he expected the Irish Brigade to be sent to the front the following week. The orders had been delayed, according to Mulrean, because the Spanish military authorities were unwilling to 'take the responsibility of sending so many men with officers unfit to lead them'. Discipline among the men was poor, he added:

> The attendance at the Kips [brothels] has increased, to my knowledge, from 5 the 1st fortnight to over 40 a week now. Several cafés were broken this week, the proprietor of one injured, a Spanish major ditto. Our name is now below 0. My work gets more difficult every day. Drunkenness is a curse. I told them they were trying to make a national virtue of it, and the language vile.

Mulrean also accused Gunning of stealing one of his letters. 'I laid a trap for him and two days afterwards he fell into it. I have several witnesses including a Spanish officer or two. Such is the life of the Irish Brigade.'[42]

On 6 February, returning to Salamanca from Seville where he had been supervising preparations for the assault on Málaga, Franco stopped off in Cáceres and inspected the Irish Brigade. The *generalísimo* was satisfied with what he saw and issued instructions for the brigade to form part of the offensive across the Jarama valley south of Madrid. Two days later, the nationalist Army of the South under Queipo de Llano, aided by 90,000 Italian troops equipped with light tanks and armoured cars, captured Málaga. Salamanca celebrated the victory the following day. The square between the episcopal palace and the cathedral was thronged with people shouting Franco's name. McCabe witnessed the scene:

> Over the heads of the crowd, dozens of National, Falange and Requeté flags floated and flapped in the wind. It was a gay inspiring scene, and though this little square was too small for the occasion, the two Cathedrals and the old University gave character and tone, and a note of tradition to the scene. It called up the past, and one thought of the 16th Century, and of the Spanish 'Tercios' that fought in Italy, Flanders or the New World. The old Spanish troops must have entered many a Continental town with flags flying gaily like this. There is one thing that Spaniards can do. They can give a bright colour, or a tragic intensity, to their daily lives and their history.[43]

The crowd let out a roar when Franco appeared, but McCabe was unimpressed by his speech. 'He has a cold, buttoned-up style, and cannot let himself go. Besides, when he speaks, he seems to have a slight catch in his nose and he looks small and stodgy for a Dictator and a Generalísimo.'[44]

McCabe had the opportunity to appraise members of the *generalísimo*'s family when Franco's sister, Pilar, his niece and his daughter, Carmencita, visited the Irish College, accompanied by two private detectives. 'The two small cousins ran and romped about in the Aula Maxima, and we commented on how happy and carefree they were in the midst of all this tragedy, and of all the worry that the Franco family has had.'[45]

The Irish Brigade left Cáceres for the front by train on 17 February. Nationalist forces under General Orgaz were trying to sweep north-east to capture the Madrid–Valencia road, thus cutting off the capital from the sea. After several delays, the brigade arrived at the village of Torrejón la Calzada, on the outskirts of Madrid, from where they marched twelve kilometres to the village of Valdemoro.

On the morning of 19 February, the brigade set off for the front at Ciempozuelos. They were walking through a narrow valley when the leading company spotted a group of troops some 600 yards in the distance. The company commander, Captain Diarmuid O'Sullivan, went forward with his Spanish liaison officer, Lieutenant Pedro Bove, a Spanish interpreter, Captain Calvo, and two other Irishmen. A party of men also detached themselves from the opposing line. The party from the Irish Brigade established that the opposing troops were nationalist (a Falangist battalion drawn from the Canary Islands) but the opposing commander mistook the Irish Brigade for republicans and opened fire. The two Spaniards were killed instantly. The Irish soldiers managed to escape back to their lines and an engagement lasting about an hour took place, during which two Irishmen, Lieutenant Tom Hyde from Midleton and Private Dan Chute from Tralee, were killed. A third Irishman, Corporal John Hoey from Dublin, was seriously injured.[46]

It was an inauspicious introduction to the front for the officers and men of the Irish Brigade. But despite the fatalities, the men were in good spirits when they arrived in Ciempozuelos, believing that they had got the better of the enemy in their first engagement: the Canary Islanders had withdrawn. Yet the true savagery of the war was soon brought home to those who were under any illusions about what they had got themselves into. O'Duffy's account of the Irish Brigade, *Crusade in Spain*, is full of flowery, self-serving prose, but his description of the horrors the Irishmen witnessed in Ciempozuelos required no embellishments:

> Ciempozuelos was a town of the dead when we arrived. Apart from Moorish troops, who left next day, and half a dozen Civil Guards, there was not a living person to be seen in streets or houses. Only a few days before our occupation the town had been taken by Franco's troops in one of the bloodiest battles of the war. When the Reds were driven out they left over a thousand dead, many still unburied or only half-buried with a few inches of clay. One of our first duties was to dispose as best we could of the decomposing bodies which were to be seen everywhere; in the gardens and yards, in the river which runs through the town, and in the olive grove through which our main line of trenches ran.[47]

Particularly horrific was the fact that one of the biggest institutions for the mentally disabled in Spain was in Ciempozuelos. With the fighting taking place all around them, the nuns in charge continued to look after the patients. The Irish soldiers could hear their screams when the shells rained down on the village. Mulrean described the Irish Brigade's situation in a letter to McCabe written a week after they had arrived:

> Last Sunday night we were fairly well bombed. On Wednesday evening several shells burst on our first line trenches. Our men had miraculous escapes. While going up the first line trenches on Tuesday morning on a very bare spot, the shells began. I was 22 minutes on my stomach and 56 shells flew over our heads, 3 of them burst as near as 10 yards away.[48]

While the officers and men on the front got used to the discomforts of life in the trenches, the brigade's staff officers enjoyed a more comfortable existence behind the lines. O'Duffy, Gunning, O'Duffy's interpreter Lieutenant Walter Meade, and Captain Camino, the chief Spanish liaison officer, were frequent visitors to the Irish College. Camino was a devout Catholic who wore the Carlist cross. They would have parties in McCabe's room where the conversation flowed, thanks, in part, to liberal amounts of Irish whiskey.

McCabe got to know the foreign correspondents who were flocking to Salamanca to cover the war.[49] He was not impressed by many of them. 'It's amazing to see the crowd of queer birds that are coming out to Nationalist Spain to do propaganda for Franco. They know nothing about Spanish History, or about the political events of the past few years, and, generally, they don't know Spanish.'[50]

The foreign correspondents hung around the nationalist press office in the Palacio de Anaya at all hours but found it difficult to get reliable news from the front. Among them was the Irish journalist Gertrude Gaffney, who covered the progress of the Irish Brigade for the *Irish Independent*, visiting the front at Madrid, Talavera and Oviedo and being ambushed by the republicans. The American journalist Reynolds Packard of the American United Press (UP) news agency was another acquaintance. In January 1937, Luis Bolín, the former London correspondent of the monarchist *A.B.C.* newspaper who had been instrumental in leasing the Dragon Rapide that had flown Franco from the Canary Islands to

North Africa, summoned Packard to Salamanca. Bolín worked for Millán Astray's press and propaganda department and was responsible for dealing with the journalists flooding into Salamanca. He was angry with Packard over an article that had appeared in the Paris edition of the *New York Herald Tribune* under the American journalist's name about the massacre of innocent civilians in Badajoz by Yagüe's African troops in August 1936. Packard denied having written the story and was sufficiently intimidated to cable the European bureau chief of UP to get him to convince Bolín of the fact.[51] McCabe thought that Packard was 'a nice, breezy chap, all alive, and typically American' but that he did not understand the religious significance of the war because he was not a Catholic.[52] McCabe believed that Packard had retracted the story about the Badajoz massacre under pressure from Bolín.

Arnold Lunn* was another visitor to the Irish College. McCabe had met Lunn, an English Catholic convert and apologist, whose mother was a Protestant from Midleton, County Cork, while touring Greece and Turkey. 'He is very humble, and simple, and though a bit crotchety, not hard to please. He carries his luggage in a ruck-sack, and his whole outfit suggests that he regards his Spanish trip as a sort of Alpine expedition.'[53] McCabe and Lunn had lunch with Pembroke Stephens, the *Daily Telegraph* correspondent. Stephens was to die in Shanghai in November 1937 while reporting on the Japanese invasion of China. The right-wing Catholic Francis Noone, an associate of Aileen O'Brien, and ostensibly reporting for the *Catholic Times*, was another acquaintance.

On 10 March, Leopold Kerney, the Irish minister to Spain, arrived at the Irish College. The Duchess of Tetuán, Blanca O'Donnell, who had succeeded to the title upon the death of her brother and who was taking a particular interest in the fortunes of the Irish Brigade, accompanied him. Kerney had fallen ill in May 1936 and returned home from Madrid to Ireland. In February 1937 he had reopened the Irish legation to Spain in temporary accommodation in Saint-Jean-de-Luz, across the border in France, where many of the diplomatic missions accredited to the

---

* Lunn was lame, having injured himself skiing. He was later knighted for services to skiing and was instrumental in popularising downhill and slalom skiing. He had just returned from Canada where he had been training the British skiing team and was in Spain to write a book about the war.

republican government had moved at the outbreak of the war. He had been sent to Salamanca to 'secure material for a full report to enable the [Irish] government to come to a decision about the recognition of the authorities there' and repatriate minors who had joined the Irish Brigade.[54] But he was also charged with keeping an eye on O'Duffy for the Irish government. In a letter dated 6 March sent to Joe Walshe in the department of external affairs, he wrote that Franco's agent in Biarritz, the Visconde de Mamblas, was worried that O'Duffy's hostility to de Valera 'might have an adverse effect on the decisions of the Irish Government' in relation to recognition.[55]

McCabe was hosting two officers from the Irish Brigade, Gunning and Camino, when Kerney showed up with the Duchess of Tetuán. McCabe feared an awkward situation, given the Irish government's antipathy to the brigade and O'Duffy's dislike of Kerney, but the Irish minister, unsurprisingly, given his mission in Salamanca, said he had no difficulty meeting Gunning and Camino. The conversation drifted onto the Irish Brigade and Camino took out a letter he had received from General Aranda. The postscript to the letter had asked '¿Y esos irlandeses?'* Kerney was 'clever and shrewd', according to McCabe, though he looked 'rather stockish and plain', and did not miss the contemptuous tone of the question, which suggested that the nationalist high command was dismissive of the brigade.[56]

The following morning, McCabe accompanied Kerney and the duchess to nationalist GHQ. Kerney was trying to secure an interview with Franco, and was driving his own car with diplomatic plates and an Irish tricolour flying from the bonnet. A detective took down the details of Kerney's passport and, ten minutes later, Sangroñiz, the head of the nationalist diplomatic service, sent for him. McCabe waited in the lobby, which reminded him of a barracks guardroom. Moroccan troops in turbans and cloaks stood silently on guard beside stacks of rifles leaning against the walls. Streams of people filed into the building where they made inquiries of a couple of civil guards, while officers saluted superiors and clicked their heels. Three notices hung on the glass doors. One warned the local population to beware of spies; another advised giving all

---

* 'And those Irishmen?'

information to superiors, and no one else; and a third requested visitors not to ask for favours. After a long wait, Kerney left with his companions, without having seen Franco.

At lunch in the 'Gran' later that day, McCabe, Kerney and the duchess met Fr Charles O'Daly from Enniskillen, who had been appointed auxiliary chaplain to the Irish Brigade. Afterwards, they bumped into the pro-Franco *New York Times* correspondent William Carney and the Marqués de Hoyos, a descendant of the O'Neills, who had been minister of the interior at the fall of the monarchy, and who corresponded regularly with McCabe. He and his nephew, the Duke of Almodóvar, were owners of a sherry and brandy firm in Jerez.[57] The Irish party was also introduced to the Conde de Rodezno, the leader of the Carlists, and Victor de la Serna, the editor of the right-wing *Informaciones* newspaper.

That evening, Kerney and McCabe had an interview with Manuel Hedilla, the Falange leader. 'We went through a couple of offices, past hieratic figures stretching out a rigid arm in a tremendous Fascist salute. The Spaniard is so restless and indisciplined that all these automatic Jack-in-the-box movements must be very uncomfortable. The old-fashioned Spanish bow, though less assertive and aggressive, was a much more civilized form of salute.'[58] Hedilla received them in a small, plainly furnished room. A tall, heavily built man, the Falange leader was a former machinist from Cantabria who had joined the party in 1934. 'He might be a coal-heaver, disguised in a blue Falange uniform.'[59]

Hedilla had become the *de facto* leader of the Falange upon the imprisonment of José Antonio Primo de Rivera, the son of the former dictator. The republican authorities had arrested Primo de Rivera on 14 March 1936 and he was executed in Alicante in November of that year. In the nationalist zone, however, no one was sure about his fate, despite reports of his death in the international press. This power vacuum suited Franco's manipulation of the Falange, and he encouraged the cult of the absent leader, or '*el ausente*,'* as Primo was known. Hedilla was therefore in the awkward situation of being second-in-command to a dead man.

'He looks plain,' wrote McCabe, 'but he is intelligent, very clear, and talks directly, to the point without mincing words, or indulging in polite

---

* 'The absent one.'

evasive formulas.' Hedilla told his interlocutors that the Falange was going to solve the land problem. '"And the aristocracy?" I asked. "We'll solve that, and the church problem, too," he added with a smile.'[60] Hedilla and the atmosphere in the Falange headquarters left a favourable impression on McCabe. He thought the officials working there looked 'slicker, more energetic and more efficient' than those in the GHQ. 'There's an air of silent reverence, too, and they have caught the Fascist trick of a gradual hierarchical ascent leading up to the Chief in his lonely room.'[61] It soon became clear that Franco was not going to see Kerney and the Irish minister left for Paris with the duchess a couple of days later.

At the front, the Irish Brigade was preparing for its first major offensive after several weeks of inactivity in Ciempozuelos. On 12 March, the Irishmen were ordered to take the village of Titulcia on the other side of the Jarama valley. According to historian Robert Stradling,

> even by the high standards of the Tercio [the foreign legion] – the capture of Titulcia would have been an amazing achievement. Apart from its physical location on the crest of a cliff which towered 150 feet above the river bank, the place had been heavily fortified, was bristling with machine-guns … and garrisoned by elements of the elite communist 11th Division.[62]

O'Duffy, who was a rare visitor to the front, was in Cáceres when he received word that the brigade was to launch an attack at dawn the next day. He immediately set out for Ciempozuelos, arriving about midnight.

The assault on Titulcia required an advance across the open flood plain of the River Jarama. A cavalry squadron led the advance and was cut down by enemy machine-gun fire. O'Duffy watched the slow progress of the Irishmen as the republican artillery launched salvo after salvo. 'The shells fell four at a time, and the smoke of one set had not subsided when the whistle of the next was heard,' he wrote in *Crusade in Spain*. 'Now, a soldier moved to take cover [behind] a clump of hay, then, the hay was enveloped in smoke. About midday, when the troops had advanced about three miles from the town, no fewer than four hundred shells had been estimated to have fallen.'[63] In the afternoon, the republicans brought an armoured train from behind Titulcia. A party of Spanish engineering officers had prepared for this by mining the railway track, but the mine failed to detonate. A second attempt resulted in damage to the track but failed to destroy the train. By nightfall, the brigade had reached the Jarama but Major Diarmuid O'Sullivan (who had replaced the ill Patrick Dalton as commanding officer) ordered them to retreat. Despite the heavy shelling, the brigade had suffered relatively light casualties: one man, John McSweeney of Tralee, had been killed in action; nine had been injured, three of whom, Sergeant Major Gabriel Lee of Dublin and Privates Bernard Horan and Tom Foley, from Tralee, were to die of their injuries.[64]

'The operation was disappointing to the Irish *bandera*,' O'Duffy wrote. 'They had anticipated getting into close contact with the enemy, and instead had been obliged to endure eleven hours' continuous shelling from enemy batteries miles away.'[65] As the brigade regrouped, orders came through to resume the attack at dawn the following day. O'Duffy disobeyed the order, citing a lack of tank or air cover. 'I had a consultation with the Spanish staff of the sector, the artillery officers, and the Irish officers,' he wrote. 'All were of the opinion that there was no chance whatever of the success of the operation, and that in the attempt to carry it out there would be a huge loss of life.'[66] O'Duffy was adamant that he was opposed to a renewed attack from the outset. However, Stradling cites testimony from an Irish sergeant that it was only after objections from his officers that O'Duffy decided to refuse the order.[67]

The refusal to advance on Titulcia probably spelt the end for the Irish Brigade, whether O'Duffy's mind was changed for him or not. It seems odd that the brigade suffered no sanctions for refusing direct orders but perhaps, as Stradling suggests, the Spanish generals 'merely accepted that, in the circumstances, which its leader had (both consciously and inadvertently) brought to their attention, any further action by the XV *bandera* was likely to be counter-productive'.[68] Nevertheless, the sector's commander, General Saliquet, and Franco must have been singularly unimpressed by the behaviour of O'Duffy and the Irish Brigade, especially because there had been such a slight casualty list relative to losses in other sectors.

On St Patrick's Day, Franco inspected the brigade once again during a tour of the entire front. Less than a week later, the Irish Brigade was pulled out of Ciempozuelos to the tiny village of La Marañosa, within sight of Madrid. Here, the Irishmen occupied the trenches alongside the *requetés*, the fiercely Catholic militia from Navarre. The climate in La Marañosa was warmer and drier but it was difficult to get water. Many of the men were sick and, after the events of 13–14 March, morale was low and there was endemic infighting. Some of the Irish soldiers ended up in hospital in Salamanca, where McCabe visited them. The head of the foreign legion, the uncompromising Yagüe, paid a visit to the brigade shortly after their arrival at La Marañosa. In a report to Franco, he proposed dissolving the Irish *bandera* and redistributing the men to other legion battalions. He cited as his reasons indiscipline, exacerbated by drunkenness, disobedience among the men and a lack of military efficiency.[69]

In Salamanca, the threat of air raids meant the cancellation of the traditional Holy Week processions, but public piety was not affected despite the now familiar daily wail of the air raid siren and the frequent appearance of republican aeroplanes in the sky. On Holy Thursday, McCabe was walking through the centre of the city when he came across Franco on his way to church with his wife and daughter. 'People clapped and cheered as the Franco family went past,' McCabe wrote. 'Franco looked well, and walked with a smart, light youthful step, and a little smile on his face. He wore a Legion cap, and his hair is turning grey around the temples. He does not look very worried or very dictatorial to-day.' McCabe continued: 'The Señora looks very shy and retiring, and little Carmencita looks more grave than when she was in the College a few weeks ago.'[70]

Another public ceremonial event took place at the beginning of April when the Italian ambassador presented his credentials at the town hall in Salamanca's *plaza mayor*. Spectators poured into the square, which was decorated with the Italian, German, Portuguese, monarchist, Carlist and Falange flags. A film camera operator and photographers captured the proceedings from a platform while various militia bands played martial music. Moroccan cavalrymen escorted Franco from the episcopal palace to the town hall. Generals Mola, Queipo de Llano and Kindelán, Admiral Cervera, and Nicolás Franco, the *generalísimo*'s elder brother and chief political adviser during the early part of the war, were present. After the speeches, an infantry regiment marched past and a squadron of aeroplanes performed stunts over the *plaza mayor*. 'One of them was amazing,' wrote McCabe. 'The pilot flew low over the roofs of the houses, until he arrived at the centre of the Square, and then he shot up, with roaring engines, in a vertical line, for a couple of thousand feet.'[71]

The following day the German ambassador presented his credentials. That evening, Carlists marked the occasion by hosting a concert, to which McCabe was invited. The theatre was decorated with swastikas, Italian flags and the Spanish monarchist flag. According to the *Adelanto* newspaper, as quoted by McCabe in his diary, these were 'flags and friendly ensigns that we carry in our hearts … because these two nations have known how to appreciate our aspirations for civilization and the grandeur of the *patria*'. The florid prose continued:

> The place was completely filled with hundreds of red caps [Carlists], and here and there, the uniforms of the glorious Spanish Army, the blue shirts of the Spanish Falange, the green caps of Spanish Renovation [the Alphonsine monarchists], the red crosses of Popular Action, and the white Moorish turbans, giving a marvellous spectacle of the unity of the New Spain.[72]

Of course, the nationalists were far from unified, something McCabe noted while reading the newspaper: 'If this is unconscious, it's delicious, but then, the "Adelanto" was always Republican, and so it may be an ironic "dig".'[73] The programme for the evening's entertainment included Beethoven, Wagner and Verdi, in honour of Salamanca's distinguished German and Italian guests.

Meanwhile, nationalist propaganda continued to promote a cult of personality around the image of Franco. In Salamanca, posters began appearing on walls ascribing great virtues to the general. They had slogans such as '*un caudillo, un patriota, un estadista – Franco*'\*; '*honor, heroismo, fé, autoridad, justicia, eficicacia, inteligencia, voluntad, austeridad – Franco*';† or

---

\* 'A chief, a patriot, a statesman – Franco'.
† 'Honour, heroism, faith, authority, justice, efficiency, intelligence, will, austerity – Franco'.

*'Franco, caudillo de Dios y de la Patría. El primer vencedor en el mundo del bolchevismo en los campos de batalla.'\**

The nascent nationalist state emphasised public acts of religious piety. Though Franco himself was not particularly devout, he made sure to be seen attending mass, and decrees recognised the place of the Roman Catholic religion at the heart of the regime. In April, a decree ruled that a statue of the Virgin Mary, preferably that of the Immaculate Conception, had to be hung in a place of honour in every school; the devotion known as the month of Mary had to be practised in schools; on entering the classroom every morning, children had to call out, 'Ave María Purisima', and the teacher had to reply, *'sin pecado concebida'* (conceived without sin); and the teacher had to lead the children in reciting a prayer for the victory of the nationalist forces in the war. These measures were instigated in a vindictive spirit to test the loyalty of mostly republican schoolteachers.

On 9 April, O'Duffy wrote to Franco indicating that he wished to bring the Irish Brigade home and requesting transportation to do so. He blamed the 'official attachés' to the brigade for causing discontent and undermining the loyalty of the Irish troops. Four days later, Franco wrote to General Luís Orgaz, who was in charge of the Jarama front, announcing the disbandment of the brigade.

McCabe and the Duchess of Tetuán tried to reconcile the Spanish generals with O'Duffy and the Irish officers. On 21 April the bishop of Gibraltar, Richard Fitzgerald, a former vice-rector of the Irish College, arrived in Salamanca with a native Gibraltarian, Salvador Gómez-Beare. The latter took the 'Beare' part of his surname from his wife, who was descended from Donal Cam O'Sullivan Beare, one of the most famous seventeenth-century Irish exiles to Spain, whose portrait hung for many years in the Irish College in Salamanca.†

Gómez-Beare was an extraordinary character. He had served in the British armed forces during the Great War but resigned his commission in protest at the behaviour of the Black and Tans in Ireland. 'He was in the motor business in Madrid and seems to have been in everything,' wrote

---

\* 'Franco, God and the Fatherland's chief. The world's first victor over Bolshevism on the battlefield'.
† It was later hung in the office of the president of St Patrick's College, Maynooth.

McCabe. 'He is very heavy and swarthy and speaks English with a slight "Gib" or Andalucian accent.' The Duchess of Tetuán was sceptical about all the people Gómez-Beare claimed to know. 'She cannot quite make him out. He talks about "my old friend this", and "my old friend that" at GHQ. The Duchess knows most of them, and most of these "old friends" don't know Gómez-Beare.'[74] McCabe suspected that Gómez-Beare was a spy. The college administrator, Francisco Ramos, and the vicar-general, Pedro Salcedo, were visiting the college one evening and the latter made a remark about the progress of the war. Gómez-Beare took out a pencil and notebook and wrote something down.

> The Vicar looked at him, blushed up to the ears, laughed artificially at something, and remained almost silent for the rest of the visit. Gómez-Beare really gave the impression that he is an agent collecting information but it is really silly to be doing it so obviously. At present there is a spy-fever raging, and Gómez-Beare has already excited a certain amount of suspicion.[75]

McCabe was right; Gómez-Beare *was* a British spy, who was to play a key role in an operation that altered the course of the Second World War.

In early 1943, with the Allies assembling their forces in North Africa in preparation for the invasion of Sicily, British intelligence began working on Operation Mincemeat.[76] This was a plan to dupe the Germans into thinking that the invasion would take place in Greece, not Sicily. The idea was to have a corpse dressed in the uniform of an airman, with fake identification contained within a briefcase chained to his wrist, fall into the hands of the Germans. Also in the briefcase would be fake documents pointing to an invasion of Greece. The elaborate hoax was concocted in a basement room underneath the Admiralty in London. The problem was where to land the corpse. This was where Salvador Gómez-Beare came in.

In 1939, Alan Hillgarth, the naval attaché at the British Embassy in Madrid, appointed Gómez-Beare as his assistant. 'As you will see, my Service record is somewhat varied as during the last War I served in the Army, Royal Air Force and now in the Navy!!' Gómez-Beare wrote to McCabe in January 1940 shortly after the appointment. 'I shall have to do a bit of sailing in the lake in the Retiro!!'[77] In fact, Gómez-Beare was one of Hillgarth's chief spies, and in 1943 was invited to London to help with Operation Mincemeat. It was Gómez-Beare who suggested landing the corpse – that of a Welsh tramp, Glyndwr Michael, who had killed himself in a disused London warehouse by drinking rat poison – near Huelva on the southern Spanish coast, because of its large German community, its pro-German police chief and the existence of a German spy network. The British fear was that somebody would discover that the body was that of a Briton and the documents would be handed over to the authorities in Gibraltar.

The plan worked smoothly at the beginning. A Royal Navy submarine dumped the body into waters close to Huelva where local fishermen retrieved it. However, instead of the local authorities handing over the briefcase to the Germans, they sent it to Madrid, and the Spanish decided to hang on to it. The British, hoping to move things along, sent cables to Spain inquiring after their missing airman and documents in the hope that the Germans would intercept them and be duped into thinking the briefcase was significant. The Germans eventually managed to photograph the contents of the briefcase and, despite some suspicions, notably on the part of Goebbels, Hitler believed that the British were going to attack Greece and proceeded to shift men and materials away from southern France and Sicily, easing the way for the Allied invasion of Sicily.

The bishop of Gibraltar, Richard Fitzgerald, had met O'Duffy in Cáceres and was in Salamanca to persuade Franco to save the Irish Brigade. McCabe was afraid that Fitzgerald, who was still enthusiastic about the brigade and unaware of the Spanish high command's contempt for it, would make a fool of himself in front of Franco. He informed the bishop of the full facts at a meeting in the Irish College attended by McCabe, Fitzgerald, Gómez-Beare, the duchess and the vice-rector.

McCabe explained that the Spanish authorities were dissatisfied with the discipline of the Irishmen and military capabilities of the officers. McCabe was sympathetic to the Spanish point of view, and while on good terms with the Irish officers and friendly with the Irish soldiers who were in hospital in Salamanca, he believed that the Spanish high command was not in a position to tolerate the lax discipline of the Irish Brigade when compared to the standards set elsewhere in the nationalist forces – especially the legion to which the brigade had been accorded the honour of joining. He believed that Franco, Yagüe and Mola could not understand the 'tom-fooling' of the brigade.[78] McCabe's assessment impressed his guests. Although Fitzgerald secured an interview with Franco, the bishop was not able to prevent O'Duffy and the Irish Brigade from returning home.

A few days later, General Kindelán, the head of the nationalist air force, who was also of Irish ancestry, called to the college for another meeting, which was attended by McCabe, Fitzgerald and the duchess, in the Blue Room. 'He is tall, is turning grey, has a flabby sort of face, and a sad expression,' was McCabe's description of Kindelán. 'He looks delicate, without any trace of the iron soldier. He is more cautious, too, and less voluble than the average Spaniard.' Kindelán was courteous in his references to the brigade, according to McCabe, simply saying that some men had 'exceeded the measure'. McCabe thought it funny to hear a Spaniard criticising Irishmen for their excesses but conceded that drunkenness was not acceptable in Spain. 'Then too, the Spaniards have military service, and they find it more easy than the Irish to submit to military discipline,' wrote McCabe, a touch defensively. 'On the other hand, we have more discipline in the family and the school than they have in Spain and the general behaviour of Irishmen is more orderly and peaceful than that of Spaniards.'[79] In an interesting aside, McCabe heard Kindelán remark to the duchess, 'Your father and my father were liberals', noting that men were being shot in the nationalist zone for such statements.[80] McCabe believed the presence of Fitzgerald had prevented Kindelán from being more candid, but still thought that the general had become sick of the Irish Brigade.

McCabe was unsure of O'Duffy's intentions at this stage and still believed that there was a chance he would stay in Spain. It was only later that he discovered that O'Duffy had already made up his mind to go home. An article in the *Irish Independent* announced the brigade's departure for Ireland a few days after the meeting between O'Duffy and Fitzgerald, which meant that the former had already made his decision by the time the bishop was trying his best to intercede on his behalf. McCabe was scornful of O'Duffy and wrote that 'he never intended to die in Spain or for Spain' but was only interested in forming a 'Blueshirt' government in Ireland by armed force, 'if there was no other way'.[81] He believed that the Irish Brigade had been ill-conceived and was little more than a tool for O'Duffy's political ambitions at home.

McCabe's opinion of the Irish soldiers who had come to Spain to fight for the nationalists had changed dramatically in three months, but he reserved most of his criticism for the Irish Brigade's officers. A couple of the Irish soldiers had been confined to hospital shortly after arriving in Spain, which McCabe believed demonstrated a careless recruitment process and 'crude ignorant illusionism about the Spanish climate', and 'Coming out to Spain to fight for an ideal is all right but to send out a hopeless case of TB, who has to go to hospital as soon as he arrives, is a bit ridiculous'.[82]

McCabe showed some of his own prejudices when writing about his compatriots. Four members of the Irish Brigade were in hospital in Salamanca: a man called Brogan from Kildare, Thomas Doyle from Roscrea, Eunan McDermot from Ballyshannon and Gus King from Kenagh in Longford. The Irish soldiers had no change of linen and were wearing filthy shirts. In contrast, the German soldiers had 'splendid uniforms, clean linen, piles of books, and a wireless set'.[83] The Irish had no money and had to cadge cigarettes off the Germans. The comparison is a little unfair, given that the German soldiers were members of a professional army equipped with the latest in military technology and who were afforded luxuries because of their position in the nationalist pecking order, while the Irishmen, rightly or wrongly, had volunteered mostly out of unselfish motives, with next to no logistical or financial support. Nevertheless, McCabe noted that one of the Germans could speak English, another French and that all of them had a 'good smattering' of Spanish. The Germans were all learning Spanish methodically. He contrasted them favourably with the Irish officers, including O'Duffy, who had not bothered to learn a word of Spanish. 'People in Ireland spend too much time talking gossip and drivel, when they should be working or learning something.'[84]

Even though O'Duffy was intent on bringing the Irish Brigade home and Fitzgerald had returned to Gibraltar, McCabe and the Duchess of Tetuán continued to work to reconcile the nationalist military authorities with the Irish Brigade officers. At this stage, the Spanish were determined that the Irish Brigade should have a Spanish commanding officer and more Spanish officers if it was to remain in Spain. On 29 April, Captain Meade, the senior Spanish liaison officer, put forward the Spanish command's position regarding the Irish Brigade. Meade was unimpressed with the behaviour of the Irish officers, not least because he had put his own car at O'Duffy's disposal and it was now a 'wreck'. Meade told McCabe that he believed the Irish officers had spent too much time 'gadding about' and that Gunning was 'too reckless in spending money, and too careless in accounting for it'.[85] The Spanish high command was particularly insistent on replacing Diarmuid O'Sullivan, who had himself replaced the sick Paddy Dalton, with a Spanish major as commanding officer. McCabe suggested a compromise whereby the new commanding officer would be a Spaniard of Irish ancestry; 'there should be some of the old O'Donnells, O'Neills, O'Reillys, O'Dwyers or Sarsfields still left in the Spanish Army'.[86] The two men then decided to ask the Duchess of Tetuán to use her influence with O'Duffy in order to get him to come to stay in the Irish College in the hope of brokering a deal.

The following morning, McCabe sat down with Meade in the college to draw up a list of points to be discussed. The Spanish wished to see all complaints addressed to superior officers; all offences committed against superior officers resulting in strict disciplinary measures; closer contact between O'Duffy and GHQ; and an end to O'Duffy consulting with his company commanders, but instead making his own decisions. McCabe told Meade that the Irish would insist on new clothing; a change of front – the Irish wished to serve with the Carlists, with whom they shared a religious feeling and motivation; a change of liaison officers; that Captain Camino be aide-de-camp to O'Duffy; and that a senior Spanish officer would be aide-de-camp to O'Sullivan.[87]

McCabe and Meade drew up a number of further points upon which they thought it might be possible to have an agreement between O'Duffy and the nationalist military authorities. These were that the brigade should have a Spanish commandant, but one of Irish descent with an Irish name – 'this would reconcile the demands of the Spanish military authorities, and, on the other hand, the demands of Irish sentiment'; that the brigade be allowed to join another *bandera* of the legion; that the Irish soldiers be allowed serve on another front, preferably in the north of Spain; that all the Irish officers would be allowed to retain the same command except for Major O'Sullivan; and that the Spanish liaison officers be changed.[88]

O'Duffy arrived that day accompanied by his private secretary and interpreter, Captain Arthur O'Farrell, a Canadian of Irish descent who had served in the British army before joining the Spanish foreign legion. According to McCabe, O'Farrell was 'slightly below medium height, has a slight limp, carries a cane, looks square and squat, carries his shoulders well back, his chest out, has glassy, fishy eyes, and a bulldog face and expression'. McCabe thought him a 'first-class performer' and a 'bumptious bounder full of himself' and he also suspected him of being a spy.* 'He would seem to be an agent and I am surprised that O'Duffy took him with the Brigade, much less into his confidence.'[89]

By this stage, McCabe was heartily sick of O'Duffy. That evening McCabe, O'Hara, the Duchess of Tetuán and O'Duffy had supper. O'Duffy's unwillingness to adapt himself to the Spanish diet clearly irked McCabe. 'The General has a silly horror of eggs cooked in olive oil. It is little trifles and "fads" like this, to which the Irishmen should be quite accustomed by this time, that are helping to create mountainous troubles in the Brigade.'[90] The next morning, O'Farrell and Meade called into McCabe's room. McCabe was inside chatting to O'Duffy after breakfast. When O'Farrell entered the room, he 'clicked his heels together, saluted and barked out defiantly, "*A sus ordenes, mi General.*"† O'Duffy, standing with his back to the fire, did not know quite what to do, so McCabe pulled a couple of chairs out and bade his guests sit down.[91]

O'Duffy confirmed McCabe in his view that he had no real desire to save the Irish Brigade. He told McCabe that the brigade would do more good if it formed a musical band and went on a propaganda tour of Spain, which would suggest that he was more interested in gaining political capital in Ireland than being of practical use to the nationalist war effort. He defended his officers and men against charges of drunkenness with the limp excuse that they were all respectable individuals, some of whom were national heroes, noting in particular

---

* O'Farrell later claimed to McCabe to be working for the nationalist secret service and to have formerly been employed by British intelligence. 1 September 1937, Diary, *agosto 6*, AMP, Ms 50,555/4/10.
† 'At your orders, General!'

the fact that O'Sullivan had been imprisoned by the British following the Easter Rising. O'Duffy added that most of his officers and men were daily communicants and total abstinence pioneers.[92] In his *Crusade in Spain*, O'Duffy wrote that he was 'proud to say that I did not observe one member of the Brigade under the influence of drink at any time, and I was in close touch with all ranks'.[93] This was in direct conflict with the testimony of the Spanish officers. McCabe was less than impressed with O'Duffy's boast that most of the men in the brigade were daily communicants and pioneers. The latter, he concluded, 'probably are the very heavy drinkers'.[94]

O'Farrell, who stayed behind in Spain after the departure of the Irish Brigade, later regaled McCabe with a telling story about this clash of cultures, which the rector regarded as 'really typical' of both the brigade's good spirit and defects, and which he copied down in his diary:

> One night, the men, who had been out drinking, were getting back to barracks pretty drunk. The group of Irishmen saw an old Spanish priest ahead, and quickened their pace. The priest looked round, and from their appearance, concluded that they were after him, and going to murder him. He, too, quickened his pace and doubled a corner. The Irishmen broke into a staggering sprint, and doubled the corner after him. When he saw them bearing down on him, the priest decided to get his back against a wall, and die a martyr's death. The Irishmen rushed at him, and surrounded him. The priest must have been greatly relieved and positively amazed when the Irish men took off the Legion cap, dropped down on one knee, and said, 'Your blessing, Fadder.' The priest very gladly gave them his blessing, and went off home, pondering, perhaps, over this strange mixture of Irish Faith and Spanish alcohol.[95]

Whatever his sympathy for the Irishmen's weaknesses, McCabe described O'Duffy's remarks about his officers' respectability and military records in fighting against the British as 'rather puerile'.[96]

O'Duffy and McCabe had grown up only twenty-five miles from each other – the former was born in Cargaghdoo in County Monaghan, the latter in Drumkilly in County Cavan – but their political outlooks and temperaments could not have been more different. O'Duffy was the youngest son of a poor farmer. At forty-seven, he was ten years older than McCabe; he was volatile, a man of action and not prone to reflection. The former IRA chief-of-staff was intensely nationalist, anti-British and a devotee of Gaelic culture. On the other hand, McCabe, the eldest son of a national school principal, was cool, measured and analytical. He was Anglophile and interested in classical music, art and architecture. Aristocratic by temperament, McCabe was disdainful of what he saw as the new, narrow-minded Ireland. O'Duffy's bombast led McCabe to make unfavourable comparisons between Spanish and Irish military prowess: 'Perhaps O'Duffy is finding out that Spain has its own ways, which are different from the Irish and that the Spaniards in the War are not old idealists, like Patrick Pearse.'[97]

On a previous occasion, O'Duffy's lack of discretion had caused McCabe acute discomfort. O'Duffy had been working to bring another battalion of Irishmen to Spain, and Fr Charles O'Daly, a curate from Enniskillen, had arrived as a second chaplain. In the event, the battalion never materialised but O'Daly stayed on. As commander of the foreign legion, the brusque Colonel Yagüe had been asked to admit O'Daly as the second chaplain to the Irish Brigade. According to McCabe, Yagüe dismissed the suggestion along the lines of: 'Let the Padre O'Daly, Female Section in Ciempozuelos, go home to Ireland. Let him not have a post in the Legion.' The female section referred to the mental institution in Ciempozuelos, which was divided between men and women, and which was where the chaplains were quartered. O'Duffy had written this reply down on a piece of paper, which he had then shown to McCabe. He asked the rector what he thought of it. McCabe had replied that, as Spaniards were usually very polite, he thought it 'abrupt, gruff and nasty', presuming that he was talking to O'Duffy in confidence. However, O'Duffy repeated McCabe's opinion to the Irish and Spanish officers and the rector's remarks found their way back to Yagüe. According to McCabe, Yagüe, 'a first-class soldier, but a nasty fellow', resented the suggestion that he had meant anything by his remark and summoned Mulrean to find out who McCabe was and what he had meant by his remarks. It was an unpleasant experience for McCabe and summed up O'Duffy's shocking lack of discretion.[98]

O'Duffy and McCabe had very different attitudes to the war in Spain but there was some common ground. Though sympathetic to the nationalist cause, McCabe was critical of the more brutal methods employed by its generals and shared O'Duffy's abhorrence at seeing Spanish officers whipping their own men. Yet McCabe scorned O'Duffy's ignorance – and unwillingness – to learn. 'O'Duffy had a "pet" idea (cherished from Black-and-Tan days, perhaps) that Franco would have won the War long ago, if he had adopted a campaign of ambushes,' he wrote. 'This in a War with fixed lines and Fronts, and in a country with no trees!!'[99] McCabe believed that O'Duffy had no understanding of modern warfare. He also sensed in O'Duffy an unwillingness to risk the lives of his men and a tendency to self-deception. An exchange between Franco and O'Duffy, as recorded by McCabe, sums up the Irish Brigade leader's bumptious self-regard: 'Franco asked O'Duffy if he had any experience of military command. O'Duffy replied that he had commanded a million men on one occasion. Franco asked him when. "At the Eucharistic Congress in Dublin," O'Duffy replied proudly, and innocently, like a child. Franco merely smiled.'[100] O'Duffy's dreams of martial glory were shattered by the brutality of the Spanish war – incomparable to the fighting during Ireland's war of independence and civil war – and the number of Irish fatalities, even if relatively tiny. He was incapable of adapting to Spanish conditions and lacked resolve.

On 2 May, McCabe attended mass in the Irish College's chapel with O'Duffy, the Duchess of Tetuán and O'Farrell. The vice-rector, John O'Hara, was the celebrant. Afterwards, McCabe made another attempt to persuade O'Duffy to concede a Spanish commanding officer in the hope of preventing the break-up of the Irish Brigade. But O'Duffy had already made up his mind that he wanted out of Spain.

> As we walked in the sun in the upper gallery, I came to the point, and asked O'Duffy if he would drop Captain O'Sullivan, and for the sake of the Brigade, have a Spanish Major instead. O'Duffy got quite thick and obstinate, and began to splutter, something about O'Sullivan's merits, and then he shouted out violently, 'No, I'll take the Brigade home. I wouldn't stop here for the Duchess of Tetuán, or all the O'Donnells in Ireland. And we'll close the Irish College,

too.' I was not prepared for this outburst, and I remarked drily, 'We'll see about the College later on.' He almost jumped about in his rage, and he looked a coarse, rough type, that reminded me of a 'pub' on Saturday night.[101]

The next night, McCabe and the duchess again tried to convince O'Duffy to stay in Spain but found him unresponsive. McCabe told him, rather disingenuously, that history would remember him as a 'second Sarsfield' if he stayed, but O'Duffy remained unconvinced. 'A glass of whiskey usually makes an Irishman genial, and responsive, and it helps to warm up his imagination and speech,' McCabe lamented. 'O'Duffy is not like that. He's not open to conviction, reasons or persuasions of any kind and we failed hopelessly to convince him.'[102]

The Irish Brigade had left the front and was temporarily stationed in Talavera. McCabe remained convinced that O'Duffy and the rest of the Irishmen should have gone through with what they had promised back in Ireland. He was dismissive of the fanfare that had launched the brigade as 'a lot of talk, clap-trap, and "codology"' and described the unit as a 'complete "wash-out"'. He was contemptuous of the officers for not spending more time at the front. Still, efforts to save the Irish Brigade continued. On 4 May, the Duchess of Tetuán spoke to the Conde de Mirasol, the secretary of Nicolás Franco, the *caudillo*'s elder brother and political factotum. He told her nothing could be done.[103] 'He was so frigidly polite and obviously sarcastic,' wrote McCabe, 'that the Duchess isn't going to take any further interest in the Brigade. Her romantic interest in Ireland, home of the O'Donnells, has suffered a bad collapse.'[104] Five weeks later, the Irish Brigade was back in Ireland, except for those whose injuries were sufficiently serious to prevent them from travelling and those who had decided to stay on and join other units of the legion.

The Irish Brigade was an ill-conceived adventure and its officers woefully unprepared. Less than a handful of officers had any idea about the historical and political context of the war. Only one or two of them could speak Spanish or made any attempt to learn it. More forgivable, perhaps, was their lack of military preparedness. Arthur O'Farrell, who was on O'Duffy's staff, told McCabe after the brigade had gone home that the Irish officers 'couldn't read a map, know nothing about triangulation or range-finding and some of them couldn't understand how a shell could be fired directly to a target out of sight'.[105] This may have been true but it was not their fault. That lay with O'Duffy, who deceived the nationalist high command about the military training of his officers and men. It is surprising that the nationalist authorities, especially the commander of the legion, the ruthless Yagüe, who were not renowned for their leniency when it came to disciplinary matters, did not take a harsher line towards insubordination among the Irish ranks. This was probably due to diplomatic considerations on Franco's part. In any event, McCabe was happy to see the back of them.

# Chapter 9

# FRANCO TAKES CHARGE

During the spring of 1937, Franco and his brother-in-law Ramón Serrano Suñer, who had supplanted Nicolás Franco as the *caudillo*'s foremost political adviser, and so acquired the nickname *cuñadísimo*,[*] discussed the best way of unifying the competing interests in the nationalist zone into one party under Franco's leadership. Hedilla, the acting Falange leader, was becoming too politically ambitious and was overly radical for Franco's taste. At the same time, the Falange was riven by a power struggle between Hedilla and a more aristocratic clique centred on the immediate family of Primo de Rivera, including Agustín Aznar, head of the Falangist militias, and Sancho Dávila, the party chief in Seville. As Hedilla prepared to face down his opponents in the Falange by travelling to the north of Spain to secure armed support, Franco informed the Carlists that he was establishing a single political party. Hedilla was encouraged to put down Dávila's revolt against his leadership of the Falange and was led to believe that he would be the leader of this new single party. With an extraordinary general meeting of the Falange's national assembly due to take place in Salamanca to elect a permanent leader, truckloads of armed militia started arriving in the city. On 16 April, those opposed to Hedilla entered the party's HQ and informed him that he was to be replaced as acting leader for consenting to the unification decree. Hedilla reported what had happened at Franco's GHQ before planning a fightback. When one of Hedilla's bodyguards attempted to arrest Dávila, he was shot dead. The shooter himself was then killed.[1]

Salamanca was full of rumours in the aftermath of the shooting, one of which was that the whole affair was a 'Red' plot engineered by the moderate

---

[*] *Cuñado* means brother-in-law in Spanish. Translating roughly as 'highest or most important brother-in-law', *cuñadísimo* was a play on Franco's title of *generalísimo*.

socialist leader Indalecio Prieto to shoot Franco and start a revolution in the nationalist rearguard, which would see the Falange throw in their lot with the workers. In fact, Franco had manipulated Hedilla so that he himself could assume control of the Falange. While Hedilla was elected the new leader of the Falange at a hastily rescheduled meeting of the party's national assembly, Franco announced the merger of the Falange and the Carlist party under his authority. McCabe described Franco's announcement of the new party, the *Falange Española Tradicionalista de las Juntas de Ofensiva Nationalista Sindicalista* (FET y de las JONS), in his diary. 'The shooting took place on Saturday night,' he wrote. 'On Sunday night, Franco spoke over the Radio. His first words were an appeal for "unificación" and unity. He asked his collaborators to drown their personal differences, which are being "nourished by the enemy with his habitual perfidy".[2] Hedilla had won the battle for control of the Falange only to be eclipsed by Franco at the last minute. When Hedilla refused to acquiesce to Franco's authority, he was arrested, tried and sent into exile. When Falangists who had been billeted in the Irish College moved out shortly afterwards, McCabe found bullets scattered around the floor of their rooms.[3]

Because Asturias remained in the republican zone, McCabe and O'Hara spent the summer in Salamanca. Every morning they would take a brisk walk along the River Tormes. At the beginning of June, McCabe attended a requiem mass in the church attached to the Dominican monastery of San Esteban in the centre of Salamanca for General Mola, who had died in a plane crash on his way to the front. Mola, who had been buried in Pamplona, had been the last great threat to Franco's position as nationalist leader. A catafalque draped in the monarchist flag with a wreath at each end stood in the transept, surrounded by stacks of rifles, cavalry lances, helmets and brass cornets.

They looked rather out of place at a religious function. And to make it look less Christian, there were two trench mortars and two machine-guns as well. The Bishop sat on the Gospel side, and General Varela [one of the foremost nationalist commanders] had a prie-dieu on the other. He is small and black, and he seemed to be very worried. All the time he kept passing his hand over his forehead, and around his jaw. He seemed to be a bit bored, too, by the long ceremony.[4]

Members of the Irish Brigade receiving communion at La Marañosa, spring 1937. (P13/81, Stradling Collection © Image courtesy of Special Collections and Archives, Glucksman Library. Copyright of the University of Limerick.)

Eoin O'Duffy (centre) with Irish Brigade officers, Cáceres, May 1937. (P13/83, Stradling Collection © Image courtesy of Special Collections and Archives, Glucksman Library. Copyright of the University of Limerick.)

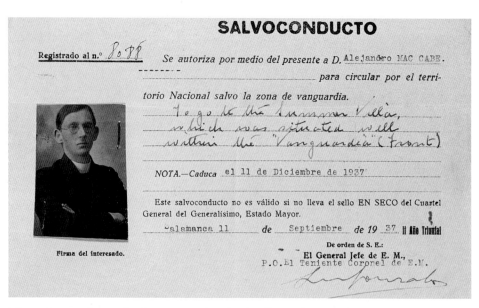

## SALVOCONDUCTO

Registrado al n.° *8088*

Se autoriza por medio del presente a D. Alejandro MAC CABE.

-------- para circular por el territorio Nacional salvo la zona de vanguardia.

*To go to the Summer Villa, which was situated well within the "Vanguardia" (Front)*

NOTA.—Caduca el 11 de Diciembre de 1937.

Este salvoconducto no es válido si no lleva el sello EN SECO del Cuartel General del Generalísimo, Estado Mayor.

Salamanca 11 de Septiembre de 19 37. II Año Triunfal

De orden de S. E.:
**El General Jefe de E. M.,**
P.O.El Teniente Coronel de E.M.

Firma del interesado.

The *salvoconducto* (military pass) which allowed McCabe to visit Pendueles in September 1937 after it had been taken by nationalist forces. McCabe later wrote on the pass: 'To go to the Summer Villa, which was situated well within the "Vanguardia" (Front).' (Courtesy of the National Library of Ireland.)

McCabe (right) with Otto Timm, head of the German press and propaganda department, in the Irish College, summer 1939. (Courtesy of the National Library of Ireland.)

Kathleen and Tommy Gunning in the Irish College patio, c.1937. (Courtesy of the National Library of Ireland.)

McCabe in the Irish College during the German occupation of the building, c.1938. (Courtesy of the National Library of Ireland.)

McCabe (left) and the vice-rector, John O'Hara (right), in the gallery of the Irish College, spring 1942, with an unidentified couple, possibly a naval attaché at the US embassy and his wife. (Courtesy of the National Library of Ireland.)

McCabe standing in one of the air-raid shelters built for the German press and propaganda department underneath the staircases of the Irish College, summer 1939. (Courtesy of the National Library of Ireland.)

Ceremony awarding the 'Y' decoration to members of the Sección Feminina (Female Section) of the Falange, which was held on the patio of the Irish College, 15 October 1941. (Courtesy of the National Library of Ireland.)

Another view of the ceremony awarding the 'Y' decoration to members of the Sección Feminina (Female Section) of the Falange, which was held on the patio of the Irish College, 15 October 1941. (Courtesy of the National Library of Ireland.)

McCabe (back row, third from right) attending a fiesta in Buelna, Asturias, on 2 September 1942, to commemorate the fifth anniversary of the 'liberation' of the village by nationalist forces in 1937. (Courtesy of the National Library of Ireland.)

McCabe (on horseback) in the Picos de Europa, Asturias, in August 1943 with the parish priest of Pembes (centre) and Emiliano Celis. (Courtesy of the National Library of Ireland.)

McCabe standing in front of the Irish College in October 1947. The photograph was taken by the Bishop of Galway, Michael Browne, who was in Salamanca to assess the future of the college. (Courtesy of the National Library of Ireland.)

McCabe (left) off the Asturian coast, 1949. (Courtesy of the National Library of Ireland.)

McCabe (right) with the bishop of Gibraltar, Richard Fitzgerald, in the gallery of the Irish College, 1949. (Courtesy of the National Library of Ireland.)

The *Casona de Verines* in Pendueles was bought by the Irish College in the early 1920s. The Irish clerical students studying in Salamanca holidayed there every summer, sometimes reluctantly, until the outbreak of the civil war in Spain. (Author's photograph.)

On 19 June, Salamanca celebrated the fall of Bilbao to the nationalists. The capture of this major industrial city was a significant victory: the nationalists had hitherto controlled mainly rural, agricultural areas. Groups of soldiers and civilians ran around the *plaza mayor* yelling for joy and there were more speeches from the balcony of the town hall, the scene of celebrations after each nationalist victory. McCabe was sitting in the Café Novelty when he heard the news. 'A gentleman and his wife sat at an adjoining table. They may be Basques. They were both very silent and sad, and the lady's face was almost full of tears.'[5] The Basques were something of an anomaly. Despite being fervent Catholics, they also knew that any chance of hanging on to their traditional liberties and independence would be crushed under the nationalists and so they sided with the republic. The men of the Irish Brigade were sympathetic to the Basques. Upon arriving in Spain, O'Duffy had made it clear that he did not want the Irish Brigade to serve in the Basque country, so as to avoid his men having to fight devout Catholics.[6]

At the end of June, McCabe went to hear the rector of Manila University, Fr Silvestre Sancho, at San Esteban. When Sancho had finished his lecture, General Millán Astray jumped up onto the platform to congratulate him and answer Sancho's charge of frivolity in the rearguard. He started telling Sancho that he could let the world know that Franco was going to win the world and started gesticulating wildly. 'One man beside me put his forefinger on his right temple, and began to screw it around. The gesture was as much as to say, "Cracked, you know."' A detachment of *regulares* were staying in the Dominican convent and, when McCabe was making his way out, he could see them praying towards Mecca.[7]

After the departure of the Irish Brigade from Spain, Tommy Gunning and his wife, Kathleen, came to stay in the Irish College. According to McCabe, he was 'on-the-run' from Cáceres for not paying his bills. Gunning and O'Duffy were no longer on speaking terms and the former had no compunction about giving his uncensored view to McCabe of what had gone on behind the scenes of the Irish Brigade. Gunning's tales of the antics of O'Duffy and the Irish Brigade provided great entertainment, though McCabe thought Gunning 'a bit too bitter and bilious'.[8] Though McCabe enjoyed hearing Gunning's stories, there was a part of him that also felt a deep sadness that the Irishmen who had come to fight for Spain for what he had initially regarded as largely chivalrous and romantic reasons had let down their country. Over whiskey parties in McCabe's room, he tried to pump Gunning for information about O'Duffy's real motives, but, despite the feud between the former comrades, McCabe 'could never get him – drunk or sober – to admit that the whole thing – the Brigade and the Christian Front, was a purely political "racket"'.[9] That was nevertheless the view that McCabe took of both Belton and O'Duffy's involvement with the nationalist cause.

The bulk of the Irish Brigade had returned home by the middle of 1937 but a few had decided to stay in Spain. Some joined other units in the legion, while a couple of former members of the Irish Brigade, Eunan McDermot and Thomas Doyle, remained seriously ill in hospital in Salamanca. Another, Seán Donnelly, was in hospital in Burgos. The remainder had been left behind in Cáceres. McCabe found the visits to the hospital difficult. 'The ward this morning almost gave me nausea. Doyle was expectorating all the time, and there is a heavy atmosphere of medicine and corpse all around. I don't know how the sisters and attendants can get used to it.'[10] In July, McDermot died in the city's Hospital de la Santísima Trinidad. He had been suffering from a high fever, yet the nurses had trouble keeping him in bed; one day he had climbed out to see a bullfight. Doyle died in the same hospital the following month. Both men were buried in the municipal cemetery.

Another casualty was Tommy Gunning. Despite his reservations about Gunning, McCabe found him good company. He and his wife, Kathleen, knocked about Salamanca with some of the other remaining members of the brigade, including Arthur O'Farrell. Reuters subsequently appointed Gunning as its correspondent in Spain, and the Gunnings moved to Burgos. But in the spring of 1938, he was diagnosed with tuberculosis in both lungs. Gunning wrote to McCabe from his sick bed while he tried to build his strength so that he could leave Spain for a sanatorium in Germany or Switzerland: 'I was inclined to blame myself for it, but the specialist said no, and fixed the date of the beginning of the disease, so that I can only add it as one more debt to the list I already owe to O'Duffy.'[11] Despite his infirmity and intimations of mortality, Gunning still had enough strength to harbour some old-fashioned Irish hatred. He wrote to McCabe:

Frank Ryan of An Phoblacht, a great ruffain [*sic*] and murderer of repute was taken it seems in Aragon with the International Brigade gang of cut-throats there. I have got all sorts of appeals to help him out so that he can go home and murder more of my friends. [Leopold] Kearney [*sic*] too has asked [Robert] Hodgson [the British representative to Franco's government] to pull for him. It may not be Christian charity but if I could get my hands on him myself I'd shoot him with pleasure. I don't know what they'll do with him but I hope they won't be too lenient.[12]

Gunning successfully encouraged the nationalist authorities to shoot Ryan.[13] He himself died in Berlin on 11 June 1940 after undergoing treatment in a Black Forest sanatorium.

Andrew O'Toole was another former brigade member who had chosen to remain in Spain, having arrived in November 1936. When the brigade returned home, he volunteered for service in the foreign legion.[14] In July 1937, Leopold Kerney tried to secure his discharge on the grounds that he was a minor. The legion ordered his discharge on 7 July 1938, but O'Toole was not aware of the fact and on 16 July 1938, after receiving a letter from his father telling him his brother had been killed, he got drunk, deserted and was subsequently arrested. It was not until April 1939 that Kerney was officially informed that O'Toole had been arrested. Kerney travelled to Burgos to plead his case personally with General Francisco Gómez-Jordana, who was notionally the head of government in the nationalist zone. Despite the fact that O'Toole had committed the grave offence of desertion, the military authorities informed Kerney that the Irishman would not be shot and he was released on 8 May 1939. The military judges had found him not guilty. McCabe helped O'Toole in Salamanca as he awaited official permission to return home to Ireland.[15]

McCabe also helped a Tipperary man who had remained in Spain after the departure of the Irish Brigade and rejoined the legion. John Madden from Roscrea had intended to join the planned second *bandera* of the Irish Brigade. By the time he arrived in March 1937, however, the Irish Brigade was already breaking up. According to Madden, he became 'very unpopular' with the Irish officers when he tried to persuade the rest of the men to remain, and was slapped in jail for five days for joining the legion without permission. After having to get special permission from the military governor at Cáceres to join up, because he was over age, Madden went on to fight at Brunete and, later, at Fuentes del Ebro.[16] 'I am not much good except to fight because of my lack of Spanish, but my record is clean,' he wrote to McCabe, 'except that twice I was tight, that would not matter only each time I had the bad luck to meet the Commander. I cannot blame myself very much because I meet other Irishmen in Talavera, and naturally for us, we must celebrate, but it is [sic] very serious offence in Spain and in the Legion.'[17]

Many of those who were linked to the brigade remained bitter about their experiences long after the unit had returned to Ireland. Mulrean and Gunning could not stand the sight of each other. O'Duffy, who wrote to McCabe in 1938 inquiring about the remaining brigade soldiers still in Spain, was scathing about Mulrean, whom he said was 'back in Ireland spreading falsehoods about the brigade'. O'Duffy was also dismissive of McCullagh, who had subsequently written his book, *In Franco's Spain*, about his experiences of the war, including his impressions of the Irish Brigade. O'Duffy wrote to McCabe: 'Because of the attack on his fellow countrymen, shown up by Irish reviewers in the papers, [McCullagh's book] had no circulation here in Ireland. I made enquiries from the booksellers and find that it was returned to the publishers – no sale.'[18]

The foreign correspondents, many of whom McCabe met in Salamanca, were increasingly irritated by the attitude of the nationalist press and propaganda department. Priority was given to the Germans and Italians, while the British and Americans were viewed with suspicion at best. The truculent personality of Luis Bolín managed to upset nearly everybody. Another who managed to alienate many foreign correspondents with his ill-considered views was a former cavalry officer and landowner, the Conde de Alba de Yeltes, Gonzalo de Aguilera y Munro. Among the bizarre cast of characters in the nationalist zone – a long list – he was one of the strangest. According to Paul Preston in his book about the repression in Spain, *The Spanish Holocaust*, Aguilera's 'cold and calculated violence reflected the belief, common among the rural upper classes, that the landless labourers were sub-human.'[19] At the outbreak of the war, Aguilera summarily executed six of his workers to set an example. He was a frequent visitor to the Irish College, expounding on all manner of subjects. 'He was a magnificent talker and theorist, and interested in everything,' McCabe wrote. 'He regarded peasants as serfs – "slave stock" – that should be wiped out. He was a poor Churchman, and had no respect for "scallywag Bishops" and "snivelling clerics". His mother was a Scotch Protestant and a great reader, but had no piety.'[20]

Fr Edward J. Ferger, an American correspondent with the *Buffalo Catholic Union and Times*, stayed with McCabe at the Irish College in June 1937. Ferger was uneasy in Salamanca, not least because he could not stand the sight of so many Germans. The American also did not understand certain attitudes common among the nationalists. One woman, whose husband had been executed in Málaga, told Ferger that all the lower classes should be wiped out. Ferger had been prepared to work hard for Franco's cause, but when he realised the level of class hatred among the Spanish aristocracy, and the disdain with which sympathetic correspondents were being treated by the nationalist press and propaganda department, he returned to the United States.

It was not just Ferger who found this class hatred among the aristocratic and landowning classes difficult to swallow. Cecil Geraghty of the *Daily Mail*, an enthusiastic pro-Franco propagandist who wrote *The Road to Madrid* about his experiences in Spain, told McCabe that he could not understand the bloodthirstiness of the nationalist supporters. Geraghty had been in Málaga drinking cocktails with a young woman when she announced that she had to be off because she wished to attend the execution of the man who had killed her father and have her revenge.

While McCabe was not shocked by this woman's hatred for the man who had killed her father – 'it may not be very Christian or womanly, but it is human' – he eventually began to despair of the animalistic desire for revenge in the nationalist zone. He himself attended the trial of an official in Llanes in Asturias in 1937. He wrote of it a few years later: 'I was amazed (later I got used to it) at the vengeful, un-Christian spirit of "pious" aristocratic ladies who were present at the trial. I found the same spirit in Oviedo in 1938. By this time I was less amazed. The spirit of revenge became a physical lust.'[21]

There were those among the Spanish military and aristocracy who wished for a return to an economic system comparable to medieval feudalism. A well-educated army captain told McCabe that he thought Spain would be a happy country when the people were as ignorant as in the days of the fifteenth-century Spanish monarch Isabel the Catholic. McCabe found these attitudes extraordinary. He had a great belief in education, instilled in him by his father, and thought that it was 'not difficult to understand why there are so many untamed savages and assassins about' when 'half the young lads in Spain never went through the discipline of a Primary School'.[22]

One of McCabe's most interesting encounters in Spain occurred in July 1937, when he met the London *Times* correspondent Harold Adrian Russell Philby, known to friends and family as 'Kim'. Philby had first arrived in Spain in February. Returning to London in May 1937, he had managed, with the help of his father, to secure a job with *The Times*, and was back in Spain the following month. When they met on that first occasion, Philby questioned McCabe 'with professional eagerness' about his views on what would happen in Spain after the war,[23] while McCabe later witnessed him having a 'stand-up row' with Captain O'Farrell, formerly of the Irish Brigade.[24] Little did McCabe or the nationalist authorities know that Philby was working for Soviet intelligence. It has been claimed that Philby was sent to the nationalist zone by his Russian controllers to gather information on Franco's personal security, with a view to an assassination attempt. Whether or not Philby was to be involved in the actual execution is unclear.[25] Though most of the British foreign correspondents were regarded with distrust by the nationalist press and propaganda department, Bolín seems to have taken a shine to Philby and regarded him as a gentleman. An incident at the end of the year added to his lustre in the eyes of the nationalists. Dick Sheepshanks of Reuters, Edward J. Neil of the Associated Press, Bradish Johnson of *Newsweek* and Philby were covering the Battle of Teruel on the Aragon front when a shell hit their car. Sheepshanks, Neil and Johnson were killed instantly; Philby escaped with minor injuries. Three months later, in March 1938, Franco personally decorated Philby with the Red Cross of Military Merit in a ceremony in Salamanca. Ironically, given that it had been a Russian shell that had nearly killed him, the medal gave Philby even greater prestige in the nationalist zone and opened a number of doors for him during the rest of the war.

On 6 July 1936, the republicans attempted to relieve pressure on Madrid with an assault on nationalist lines fifteen miles west of the capital. After initial success, the nationalists drove the republican army back, causing them heavy losses. McCabe noticed the increased aerial activity in Salamanca and there were claims that the artillery could be heard in the *plaza mayor*. On 14 July, Franco received the foreign press to tell them that the Battle of Brunete was over. There were correspondents from the United States, Japan, the United Kingdom, Italy, Germany and Poland, as well as a cameraman from Fox Movietone. In fact, the nationalists were still preparing their counterattack to coincide with the anniversary of the rising on 18 July.

In Salamanca, the bloody repression continued. Executions were frequent, one or two a week, according to McCabe. In an entry in his diary for 16 July 1937, McCabe wrote:

Lying awake at dawn, with my windows open, I can hear the sparrows chattering outside in the garden. Then suddenly, I hear the cars whirring in second gear as they climb the hill. When they have come around the Faculty Corner, they change into top, and I can hear them racing past outside the old City walls, which bound the College garden and 'corral'. Then the sound gets lost somewhere on the Cemetery Road. In about ten minutes afterwards, the silence is broken by the sharp crack of the volley, and I know that one or two or three souls, perhaps, have gone somewhere into eternity. The sharp report sounds like little bits of iron, smashing glass to pieces. Then, in about half-a-minute, two or three isolated pistol shots ring out. They are the 'golpe de gracia', a 'coup de grâce' – funny word – fired into the victim's brain to finish him off if he be still alive, and to make sure of his death. On these beautiful mornings, when there is a touch of divinity about the Earth, all these killings in Spain are a diabolical mystery.[26]

McCabe thought the Spaniards were 'absolute' in their 'indifference to the pain and death of others' and that their attitude shocked 'even the Germans'.[27]

Accommodation in Salamanca was still scarce. Diplomats, soldiers, journalists, adventurers and militiamen all had to be housed, and requisitioning of rooms in private houses was common. Throughout the first half of 1937, McCabe had potential house guests looking at the college, including Falangists and members of the Spanish Air Force. At the beginning of June, officials from the German embassy had called on McCabe with a view to installing offices in the college. Wilhelm von Faupel, the German ambassador, inspected the rooms himself. Von Faupel was a retired general and a staunch Nazi.

> He has large ears, a broad, bony chalky face, and sunken features, as if he had an ulcer or cancer somewhere inside. He is plain, but brusque and energetic, and he has hard fanatical eyes. He lacks completely a suave, diplomatic manner, and he might be an old Sergeant instead of a General. The two Secretaries, who accompanied him, pay him extreme deference – rather in head-waiter style – and wait for any suggestion or order, as if he were an oracle.

McCabe was embarrassed about the state of the Irish College – 'too much old junk', 'all the 15V bulbs, and old strings that convey the current, ought to be thrown into the lumber-room' – but the ambassador had put him at ease, telling him the Irish and the Germans would get on well together. Von Faupel had gone into each room to inspect its suitability for the embassy's purposes, prompting McCabe to muse on the differences between the Spanish and the Germans:

> When the Spanish Air Force officers came in to see the rooms, they spent all the time admiring the Patio and talking Art, and they went away without seeing the rooms. The German Ambassador scarcely looked at the Patio, and said nothing about it. He was intent on one thing. He came in to see the rooms, and he saw them.

Von Faupel remarked on the floors and made a joke about the central heating in case the war lasted into the autumn. 'I smiled. He laughed and asked if I thought it would be over before then. I laughed and said that there might be time to try [the central heating] out at least. We all laughed. The Germans don't think that the Spanish War will end in a hurry.'[28]

Throughout June and July Spanish tradesmen prepared the Irish College for the arrival of the German embassy staff. They painted the rooms and doors, wired new electric lights, fitted new locks to the doors, installed new lavatories and laid down a new water main outside in the street. Spanish army engineers built concrete air raid shelters packed full of sandbags for the Germans under the arches of the granite staircases that led up to the gallery. McCabe spent his time rearranging books in the library.

On 19 July, embassy officials started to move into the college. The Nazi press and propaganda department also began operating surreptitiously from some rooms upstairs. 'I never saw harder workers than the Germans, and they were ambitious, enthusiastic, and anxious to learn,' wrote McCabe. 'Even the minor officials wanted to take English lessons. But most of the men had deep hollow voices that seemed to come out of an empty barrel and they used to bellow a lot.'[29]

In August, the career diplomat Eberhard von Stohrer replaced von Faupel. While von Faupel had antagonised Franco with his constant military advice, the rumour around Salamanca was that his anti-clericalism had caused the Spanish to ask him to be replaced.[30] McCabe was friendly with the embassy officials and found himself in the strange position of being invited to diplomatic functions held in the college. In November, an exhibition of German books was organised by the local representatives of the Nazi Party in Spain, as was a ceremony honouring those who had died for the cause of National Socialism. At the end of January 1938, the embassy organised a ceremony and concert in the Irish College to celebrate the fifth anniversary of Hitler's coming to power. The German Embassy moved to San Sebastián in April 1938, but the Nazi press and propaganda department remained installed in the Irish College until shortly after the end of the war in April 1939.

In August 1937, the nationalists controlled most of north-western Spain, except for a strip of territory along the northern coast, comprising the regions of Cantabria and Asturias. Having concentrated on repelling the republican attempt to break through their lines outside Madrid – in the Battle of Brunete – the nationalists renewed their campaign in the north, striking west towards the Cantabrian capital of Santander. At the beginning of September, having taken Santander, the nationalist forces pushed west to Asturias and soon marched into Pendueles. On hearing the news, McCabe went to the nationalists' military headquarters in Salamanca to see about getting a *salvoconducto* in order to check the summer villa.

McCabe travelled to Santander and then caught a ride on a munitions lorry heading for the front. 'The three soldiers in charge, two of them foreign volunteers, had each a rifle within easy reach, and as we rushed along between the mountains and the sea, the beautiful harvest night seemed charged with the atmosphere and dynamism of war and death.'[31] After passing through countless ruined villages, McCabe arrived in Pendueles to discover that the summer villa was still standing but that the village school next door and the church had been set on fire and only the walls remained. Many of those McCabe had known in the village since he had first visited in the early 1920s had been arrested. The mayor, who was also the local butcher and a fervent republican, had been executed.* His wife had been forced to take his corpse home in a sheet and was then ordered to go and work for the civil guards. 'They put her on the job, just to teach her a lesson,' wrote McCabe. 'It seems a bit hard to persecute a widow like this, and she has several young children to support. I can't for the life of me see how this un-Christian spirit is going to help Religion.'[32]

During his stay in Asturias, McCabe met a couple of engineers, who were repairing bridges at a local beach. They told McCabe that 103 civilians had been captured and executed on the beach by republican forces during the retreat from Bilbao and Santander. Their bodies were buried in the sand.

> As we talked the tide was coming in full. We were suddenly amazed, looking at the edge of the water, to see first a head and then a shoulder and the arm of a dead man appear. Finally, the trunk and legs seemed to be wrenched out of the sand by some invisible force, and there the dead body lay, face downwards, tossing on the surface of the water. Two more bodies were thrown up in this gruesome

---

* His last words had been '¡*Viva Azaña!*', the name of the republican president of Spain.

fashion. It impressed all the bystanders to watch the sea, not only returning its dead, but as it seemed, coming right up to the shore and digging them out of the beach.[33]

This grisly description was contained within the pages of McCabe's report to the Irish bishops, which he wrote in the summer of 1938. The image of the bodies being churned up in the sand on that Asturian beach had an undoubted impact on McCabe. His description of the scene is less detached than most of his diary entries.

While he was in Pendueles, McCabe witnessed a dogfight between nationalist and republican fighters. On another occasion, a German artilleryman explained to him the workings of an anti-aircraft gun. He was amazed at the freedom he had to ramble around the front, stumbling upon 'rearguard secrets'. Similarly, in Salamanca, he was able to wander up to a hill in the poor suburb of Pizarrales, the location for an anti-aircraft battery, and chat away to some of the artillerymen.

The nationalist victories in the north of Spain – Gijón fell on 21 October – meant that Franco had access to the coal mines of Asturias and the important ore deposits in the Basque country, as well as the northern ports. Tens of thousands of republican soldiers and militias had been taken out of action. Franco now turned his attention to shoring up his own political control of the nationalist zone. That same month, a proclamation, issued on behalf of the *caudillo* and *jefé nacional*, announced that the only shouts permitted during public manifestations were: *'¡Franco, Franco, Franco!'*; *'¡Arriba España!'*;* *'¡Viva España!'*;[†] and *'¡España, Una, Grande, Libre!'*. Monarchist, Carlist and Falangist slogans were forbidden. This was designed to neutralise threats to Franco from within the nationalist spectrum and promote the cult of the *caudillo*. Propagandists, such as Ernest Giménez Caballero, a visitor to the Irish College, busied themselves creating the Franco legend. Despite the intervention of Germany and Italy on the side of the nationalists, much of the regime's propaganda was xenophobic. In October, the prominent monarchist writer and intellectual José María Pemán, who had been

---

* 'Up Spain!'
† 'Long live Spain!'

named minister of education by the nationalist junta, made a sniping remark about the Irish College in a newspaper article, suggesting that it was not really 'Irish' – in other words, that the building should be returned to the University of Salamanca – much to McCabe's annoyance. It was the beginning of a long campaign by the local authorities to force the Irish hierarchy to hand over ownership of the building.

Much of the nationalist symbolism borrowed heavily from the Nazis and Blackshirts and attempted to establish continuity between Spain's glorious imperial past and her modern-day crusade against 'atheistic' communism. On 29 October, the nationalist army commemorated its dead at an open-air mass in the *plaza mayor*. On the south side of the square, a large black, figureless cross was hung over an altar. On either side there were columns with the legion's slogan, '*presente*', written about them and a smoking urn in a wooden frame. Franco and his fellow nationalists had perhaps learnt something from their attendance at the Nazis' Nuremberg rally that September. Certainly, McCabe did not think it representative of Catholic Spain. 'It looked a bit Protestant, modernistic and Teutonic, and it suggested to me an altar erected to celebrate the German Victory at Tannenberg, or Hindenberg's funeral.'[34] Behind the chief celebrant, armed Falangists stood guard, while the crowd was asked to observe a minute's silence in memory of the founder of the Falange, José Antonio Primo de Rivera, and give the fascist salute. McCabe found this increasingly prevalent mixture of the military and religious bordering on the sacrilegious. The mass was followed that evening by a Nazi-style torchlight procession through the centre of Salamanca.

The Spanish hierarchy played a key role in lending legitimacy to the new regime. The bishop of Salamanca, Enrique Plá y Deniel, was one of the foremost supporters of Franco among the Spanish hierarchy and was awarded for this support by becoming Spanish primate and archbishop of Toledo in 1942. He believed in the interdependence of the civil and religious spheres and described communists and anarchists as 'sons of Cain, fratricides, assassins of those whom they envy and martyr merely for cultivating virtue.'[35] In May 1939, at the end of the war, upon the victory of Franco, he wrote another pastoral entitled 'The Triumph of the City of God and the Resurrection of Spain'. There were dissenters; the bishop of Vitoria, in the Basque country, was a notable exception and was forced into exile, while many Basque Catholic priests were executed for opposing the nationalists.

The Church was to the forefront of the nationalist propaganda effort abroad, and the anti-clerical violence in the republican zone, including the assassination of priests and nuns and damage to church property, was a great boon to their efforts. McCabe corresponded with Fr Teodoro Rodriguez, an Augustinian, who was one of the editors of *De Rebus Hispaniae*, a publication established in 1938 to counter criticism abroad of the nationalist cause. A vehicle of the Centre of International Catholic Information – the driving force behind which was the primate of Spain, Cardinal Gomá – *De Rebus Hispaniae* acted as a kind of news agency disseminating information to Catholic publications across the world.[36] In the United States, after a visit to Spain, during which he had met McCabe, Fr Joseph Wolfe of Philadelphia embarked upon a lecture tour, extolling the virtues of the nationalist 'crusade' to Americans. 'I do not mention the word Jew or the word Mason; but I give to the atheists and the communists all that is coming to them,' he wrote to McCabe of his lectures in February 1939. He told McCabe that his lectures were being well received, though there were some dissenters:

We have the Spanish Communists licked in this country, nevertheless many Americans still think that the wrong side won. Recently, Mrs Roosevelt in her daily newspaper column entitled 'My Day', stated that the Loyalist Government was what we would call in this country, 'a kind of democracy'. She is not thought of well in this country, outside of those women who go in for women's clubs.[37]

The Enniskillen curate Fr Charles O'Daly, one of the Irish Brigade's former chaplains, was also eager to do his bit for the cause. He wrote to McCabe in the middle of 1937 with an unusual petition. 'The request is to approach Generalissimo Franco to have a postcard size photo taken of himself, his daughter Carmencita and his charming wife', wrote O'Daly. The former chaplain's idea was to have the photograph reproduced as a postcard for sale in Ireland, with the proceeds going towards the relief of wounded and hard-up members of the Irish Brigade. O'Daly's instructions about how the photograph would be taken were quite precise:

I should like the Generalissimo taken in uniform with the daughter smiling on his right with his right hand on her right shoulder and Madame Franco on the daughter's right again looking a little towards the Generalissimo. Then I should like a brightness like the dawn for a background behind the Generalissimo's head. I don't expect the Generalissimo would autograph the photo. However, use your judgement.

In the postscript to his letter, O'Daly wrote, 'To describe further what I want, it would be good if Madame Franco stood behind Carmencita looking over her head thus making for the fullest figures in the limited space.'[38] McCabe's exasperation can only be imagined.

In early November, there was what McCabe described as a 'necrological concert' organised by the German embassy in the college's *aula maxima* in memory of the Nazis who had died during the Munich Putsch of 1923.[39] German Embassy officials and Spanish, Italian and Portuguese diplomatic representatives all attended. The college's reception room was decorated with swastikas for the occasion and the chancellor addressed the audience before Otto Timm, the Nazi chief in Salamanca and head of the German press and propaganda department, gave a history of the party. Beethoven's Fifth Symphony was then played.

McCabe declined an invitation to attend. The embassy secretary, Rudolf Bobrick, who lived in one of the student rooms, called to McCabe's room after the concert. McCabe thought him a typical German. 'He is sceptical of everything (he probably thinks that I'm the same), as if he were a disciple of Kant, and he loves to deny what people have said – like Luther.'[40] During their chats, Bobrick would attempt a little proselytising.

He knows that I don't like the Nazis, and he is always trying to do a little propaganda for the Fuehrer-Chancellor, and bring me around. Bobrick never calls him plain Hitler, but gives him his full title and always pronounces it with marked solemnity. I asked him how many Germans have been killed in the Spanish War. He doesn't know, he answered blandly. This isn't a lie, but ordinary 'diplomatic ignorance'.[41]

McCabe gave English lessons to Bobrick, though he suspected he was more interested in picking up news and gossip than learning a language in which he was already fluent. Though they were to spend a lot of time together and became friends, Bobrick often irked McCabe. On one occasion, representing the German embassy at a special mass, Bobrick refused to kneel at the consecration, instead remaining standing with his head bowed. It clearly annoyed McCabe, 'even the Ya-hoos from the German Propaganda Department knelt down'.[42]

Although McCabe was uncomfortable with the German occupation of the college, he considered himself fortunate – given that it was only a matter of time before the building was commandeered – to be living with embassy officials rather than soldiers. He regarded the Germans as hard workers – von Stohrer began work at the crack of dawn in his office in the college library – but thought them 'a bit mad and fanatical' and was unimpressed by the constant shouts of 'Heil Hitler' and the Nazi salutes.[43] The German presence could often prove awkward, such as when the Nazi flag was hung from the front of the college to celebrate the capture of Gijón. On another occasion, a German chaplain tried to hold a Protestant service in the college chapel. It required McCabe's diplomatic efforts to prevent it.

One evening, McCabe hosted Bobrick and two Dominicans, Fr Alberto Colunga y Cueto, Professor of Sacred Scripture, and Fr Sabino Alonso Morán, Professor of Theology. Morán quizzed McCabe over whether or not he was allowing Protestant services to take place. 'I almost laughed outright, and felt inclined to tell him that they are. He says he's sorry that the Germans are here. He has cold, glassy, protuberant eyes, a frosty face and mouth, and an anemic, dehumanised, Inquisitorial expression.'[44] Alonso was of the opinion that McCabe should try to convert Bobrick. The Dominican order had been the driving force behind the Spanish Inquisition at the end of the fifteenth century; McCabe remarked in his diary that some members of that order were in favour of it being re-established.

During this period McCabe gained an insight into the diplomatic tensions that existed between the Spanish high command and their German allies. One evening, McCabe was with Bobrick when the latter received a telephone call from Burgos. It was a message from Franco's office saying that the *caudillo* would see von Stohrer – but not at the hour requested. Throughout the war, Franco was determined to maintain his authority in the face of German might.

Nazi propaganda was disseminated throughout Spain from the Irish College during the war. Wooden cases, weighing about sixteen stone (100kg) each and full of German newspapers, would arrive at the college for distribution to the airmen and technicians of the Condor Legion along the front. The department also produced a journal in Spanish, *Actualidades Semanales de Prensa Alemana (ASPA)*,* which contained articles detailing the *führer* and the Nazi hierarchy's views on various subjects. The last issue's editorial noted that the journal's purpose had been 'to show to the Spanish public the support of the German press for the cause of the true Spain and its glorious Caudillo Franco' and 'demonstrating the common fight of both countries against Bolshevism'.[45] In the same issue, an article was given over to some of the ideas and achievements of National Socialism. A British official from the consulate in Vigo later remarked to McCabe how amused he and his colleagues were to receive Nazi propaganda from the Irish College – the address of the college was written on the first page of each edition. Though enthusiastic, the members of the embassy staff were quite cynical. One of the Spaniards working in the office told McCabe that the nationalists would be ashamed of reading their own propaganda after the war was over, while the head of the press and propaganda department, Timm, told McCabe bluntly that he never read newspapers.[46]

In the anteroom off the college library, the Germans showed McCabe their teletype machine, which had been installed for receiving news and messages from Berlin. They also had a radio receiving set to which they would listen throughout the night, mostly to 'Red' propaganda. With all this modern surveillance technology in the college, McCabe was understandably anxious for his own privacy. 'I sometimes suspected – without reason, I suppose – that they were able to tap the long confidential conversations that Spaniards, Irish, English – and Germans – had in my room, which I maintained as an oasis of absolute confidence and security. A friendly German told me to be careful.' One night, McCabe

---

* Weekly news from the German press.

had visitors in for a few drinks in his room and a challenge was made to give the raised-fist salute. Three or four stood up, one a German, and clenched their fists. 'Everybody was in good humour, and it was only fun, and dare-devilry. But men were shot for less, and with high-class German technology around, one couldn't be too sure'. Another night, a couple of the Spaniards working in the press and propaganda department gave McCabe a guided tour of a room they used on the gallery. It was clean, well furnished and looked nothing like the old room McCabe remembered. There were portraits of Franco and Hitler on the wall. The embassy officials showed McCabe a collection of photographs of undesirables: European politicians and 'agitators'. He was also shown old photographs of Lenin and the Soviet diplomat Maxim Litvinov, from when they were both on the run.[47]

A small circle of officials, soldiers and diplomats attended most of the parties to which McCabe was invited during this period. An event in the town hall to welcome the representatives of the Saxon Youth Movement, a forerunner of the Hitler Youth, was typical. All the guests were later invited to the German ambassador's house for a drinks reception. 'The place was full of Falange and Nazi uniforms, and it was a relief to come away'.[48] This event took place not long before McCabe was invited to attend the function marking the fifth anniversary of Hitler's accession to power in Germany in the *aula maxima* of the Irish College.

At the end of 1937, during one of the worst winters in Spain in living memory, McCabe wrote: 'This has been an exciting year, but every day, I have wished that I were far away from all this Spanish War, because it's simply "horrible, horrible, horrible" – worse than "Hamlet"'.[49] On the Aragon front, the Battle of Teruel had begun. It proved to be one of the bloodiest confrontations of the war and a crucial turning-point. When the battle was over, the republicans had lost tens of thousands of men. Throughout 1938, the nationalists, aided by the German Luftwaffe, moved inexorably, if slowly, towards victory. In April, they reached the eastern coast of Spain, cutting off Catalonia from the rest of the republic. At the beginning of June, McCabe wrote in his annual report to the Irish hierarchy that it was agreed that 'the war has reached a decisive stage' but made no comment on when it would come to a conclusion, only venturing the remark that 'if the war retains its character right to the end, the final resistance will be stubborn and desperate, and will prolong the end of the struggle.'[50]

The German embassy vacated the college in the spring of 1938, moving to San Sebastián. McCabe wrote to the Irish hierarchy that the college had gained by the Germans' presence, primarily because they had renovated much of the building for their own use. Though the embassy officials departed, the Nazi press and propaganda department continued its work from the college, spreading itself into the rest of the building with an increased staff. 'Spain deserves well of Ireland, and as the Nationalists have felt that the English-speaking world, in general, is hostile or indifferent to their cause,' McCabe wrote, 'I have a special obligation to give every facility to the authorities, and to maintain good relations with the avowed friends of Spain.'[51]

In October 1938, McCabe became involved in the case of Domingo Sanmartín Barrera, the son of the caretaker who had looked after the summer villa in Pendueles since the college had bought it in 1920. The nationalists alleged that Domingo had been a member of the local revolutionary committee in Pendueles. These committees had sprung up in towns and villages across Asturias in the aftermath of the military rising. They were made up of members of the UGT and CNT, respectively the socialist and anarchist unions, as well as some communists. Domingo was also accused of having been involved in the murder of a local Falangist, a charge that he strongly denied. Domingo was imprisoned in the Colegio de los Escolapios, the school run by the Piarist Fathers in Bilbao, which had been turned into a jail. He was later transferred to Gijón for trial. His brother, Victoriano, and sister, Margarita, who had worked in the college in Salamanca for many years, wrote to McCabe pleading with him to use his influence to prevent Domingo's execution.[52]

McCabe wrote to the military governor in Oviedo. He explained that he had not been in Asturias when it had been under 'Red' control, and so was unable to give personal testimony about Domingo's behaviour during that period, but he mentioned his good character and the fact that he had played football with the Irish clerical students. McCabe condemned the fact that Domingo had been a member of the village committee but spoke in praise of the Sanmartín family.[53] The following year, McCabe travelled to Burgos to plead Domingo's case, but to no avail. Domingo was executed in 1940. He was only twenty-five.

Domingo's niece, Concepción Sanmartín, believed that her uncle was apolitical and completely innocent. She said that a man from nearby Buelna, who was jealous of Domingo's relationship with a local girl, had denounced him to the nationalist authorities. Many such incidents, involving the local settling of scores, occurred during the Spanish Civil War. The Sanmartín family, like hundreds of thousands of families across Spain, suffered terribly. Concepción Sanmartín's mother and grandfather were also imprisoned during the war for their republican views. Her grandfather died in Cádiz. When her mother was released from jail in the Basque country, she had to present herself at the local *guardia civil* barracks every week.[54]

In January 1939, Barcelona fell to the nationalists. Hundreds of thousands of men, women and children fled to the French border. Two months later, Franco's forces entered Madrid and by the end of March, the whole of Spain was in their hands. In his report to the Irish hierarchy at the beginning of June, McCabe hoped that Irish students would be able to return to Salamanca the following September 'if the situation on the Continent permits'.[55] After three years of warfare, McCabe must have been looking forward to the return to normality and the reopening of the college. The outbreak of the Second World War was to prolong his agonies.

# Chapter 10
# THE FINAL BATTLE

While the end of the war brought some degree of normality to Salamanca – at least for those on the right – the Francoist repression continued and the fear was that Spain would be sucked into the approaching conflict in Europe. At the end of July 1939, the Nazi press and propaganda department moved out of the Irish College. They left behind a typewriter, a desk, a flag and a portrait of Hitler. McCabe immediately advised the eleven students studying in Irish colleges on Salamanca pensions to return to Spain. That same month, Cardinal Gomá asked McCabe to undertake a mission to Australia to collect aid for the ruined Spanish churches.[1] For such an enthusiastic traveller, it must have been a great temptation to see this distant part of the world, but McCabe declined, citing a lack of experience for this type of work. The Spanish hierarchy was forced to abandon the idea at the outbreak of the Second World War.

The looming conflict also affected McCabe and O'Hara's preparations to reopen the Irish College. In Ireland, McCabe met with Cardinal MacRory, who advised postponing the reopening. On 10 September 1939, McCabe cabled O'Hara to tell him that the students would not be returning to Salamanca for the foreseeable future and wrote to the Irish hierarchy informing them of his decision. Aside from the difficulty in getting the students to Spain from Ireland, there was the problem of the college investments, which were tied up in the Philippines. Without a steady income, the college was not in a position to provide free places.

On 21 September, O'Hara in Salamanca wrote to McCabe in Ireland that there was 'was still a feeling here that the war may end soon. Chamberlain's constantly harping on his desire for peace and pacific negotiations seem to give some small ground for optimism, but the entry of the Red Army into Poland has rather shocked people and the Press does not seem to know very well how to regard it.' In his report to the Irish hierarchy in April 1940, McCabe wrote: 'It is tedious to have to wait like this from one war to another, but the Spanish war was a lesson in difficulties, and a good many Continental institutions, similar to our own, have been obliged to close down'.[2]

Throughout the first couple of years of the Second World War, McCabe hoped that conditions in the Mediterranean would permit the return of the students. In April 1941, despite food shortages in Salamanca and rising prices, McCabe again made an effort to reopen the Irish College and wrote to the presidents of the diocesan colleges in Ireland offering free places to willing students. He was anxious to have students in the Irish College again, because he feared that the University of Salamanca was eager to get its hands on the college building. Seven applications from Ireland were received for the academic year of 1941/42 but the war prevented any of the students from travelling. Another blow was the Japanese invasion of the Philippines in December 1941, which threatened the college's substantial investments there. McCabe was not only worried about the effect on college revenue, but he was also fearful for the safety of the archbishop of Manila, Michael O'Doherty. To add to his considerable woes, the college building in Salamanca and the villa in Pendueles had suffered extensive material damage during a storm that swept through Spain at the beginning of 1941, leaving an expensive repair bill.

McCabe's sense of isolation in Salamanca was exacerbated by two family bereavements. In February 1941, McCabe's brother James Charles died. He had been an invalid for most of his life and had suffered from a mental disability. He was the first person to be buried in the new cemetery in Drumkilly, right behind the house where the McCabes had grown up. Five months later, on 21 July, McCabe's father died after an illness. He was buried in the same plot as his son. At the time of his death, James McCabe's children were scattered around Ireland and abroad. Alex was in Salamanca, Patrick was living in New York, while Kathleen and Maura were working for the ministry of labour in England. In Ireland, Michael, Susan, a civil servant with the department of agriculture, and Helena, who worked for the department of finance, lived in Dublin. Another sister, Brigid, or Babs as she was known, was working as a national schoolteacher in Carrick-on-Shannon. James McCabe had died intestate, ironically, given that he had spent his life writing wills for his neighbours. Since the eldest son was a priest, James Charles was deceased and Patrick lived in New York, their mother, Katie, decided that the farm at Corlislea, where the family had moved after James had retired as principal of the school, would go to Philip, the second-youngest boy, who, along with Margaret, still lived there.

The business of looking after the college's financial affairs aside, McCabe was increasingly restless. In the autumn of 1942, he replaced the old monument that marked the college plot in the municipal cemetery with a granite cross and tombstone. He was proud of the new Celtic cross, which introduced 'a little Irish touch'.[3] Interesting visitors, such as the British ambassador, Sir Samuel Hoare, who was playing a crucial role in keeping Spain neutral, helped alleviate the boredom.

In 1942, after the invasion of North Africa and the total occupation of France, Franco ordered a mobilisation of troops. On the morning of 4 December, three Spanish officers arrived to inspect the Irish College with a view to requisitioning it for the army. That afternoon, a group of soldiers arrived and the officer-in-charge gave McCabe a piece of paper from the military governor ordering him to hand over the college for the use of a regiment of engineers. McCabe was told that appealing the decision would be useless and he decided not to protest. The soldiers arrived shortly afterwards. Having managed to prevent the college falling into the hands of the military during the civil war, McCabe now found himself living in a barracks. He made sure that anything breakable was removed.

In the early days of the occupation, there were over 1,000 soldiers living in a building that had previously accommodated a maximum of forty clerical students. By the spring of 1943, about 500 soldiers were in the college; this number slowly dwindled as the threat of invasion receded. The army remained mobilised, however, and the continuation of the war put paid to any chance of the students returning.

In 1944, McCabe started lecturing in English in the University of Salamanca, which must have provided some welcome relief from the Irish College's financial and administrative problems. In the spring of that year, he reported to the Irish bishops that thousands of pounds were required in order to modernise the building. McCabe wished to refurbish the chapel, replacing the plain benches with stalls and the paper prints of the stations of the cross with more expensive ones. He also wished to replace the furnishings in the students' rooms. Again he expressed his desire to the Irish bishops that the college should reopen as soon as possible, but he remained pessimistic about the prospect of students returning that autumn.

In September 1944, the rector of the University of Salamanca, aware that there had been no Irish students in the college since the spring of 1936, told McCabe that he was trying to acquire old buildings in Salamanca that had once belonged to the university and had started to make inquiries about the ownership of the Fonseca building, the home of the Irish College. 'This is part of a general scheme to extend the University and establish a residence for the students,' McCabe wrote in his report to the Irish bishops in May 1945. 'It also responds to a new patriotic and cultural spirit which is anxious to restore what had formerly been neglected, and to recover property that had been lightly abandoned.'[4] The building had historically been a *colegio mayor* (a constituent college) of the university. The Irish College had been in the building since the 1830s but it did not have title.

The University of Salamanca was not the only body with designs on the building. The cathedral authorities in Salamanca also had a claim. Towards the end of the month, the bishop of Salamanca, Francisco Barbado y Viejo – who had replaced Plá y Deniel when the latter had become archbishop of Toledo and Primate of Spain in 1941 – paid a visit and explained to McCabe that he was having difficulty finding a suitable residence for ordained priests taking degrees in the city's Pontifical University. Pope Pius XII had founded the Pontifical University in 1940 to replace the University of Salamanca's faculties of Canon Law and Theology, which had been abolished by liberal governments in the nineteenth century. The bishop, who was also the chancellor of the Pontifical University, asked McCabe for temporary use of the Irish College building, indicating that he would use his influence to have the soldiers moved elsewhere. He reassured McCabe that once students started arriving from Ireland again, he would find alternative accommodation.

McCabe felt it was better to have ecclesiastical students in the building rather than soldiers and preferable to deal with the bishop of Salamanca than the Spanish army. He wished to see the back of the soldiers and welcomed the idea of students living in the Irish College once more. It had been almost a decade since students had strolled across the patio and through the college galleries. If students were not to be accommodated in the building, McCabe believed the army might be in residence for another four or five years.

The bishop said that he wished to see the Irish students return in order to enhance the international prestige of Salamanca as a university city. McCabe took the bishop at his word. He was hopeful that future Irish clerical students of a sufficiently high intellectual calibre who came to Salamanca would study for degrees in the Pontifical University rather than just attend the diocesan seminary. He told the Irish hierarchy that Barbado y Viejo had formerly been bishop of Cáceres during the Irish Brigade's time there and had shown kindness to the Irish soldiers. 'All during our history here we have lived, not so much on our rights, as on Spanish hospitality, and it would be ungracious to grudge a return, when the occasion offers, or difficult circumstances demand it.'[5] The Irish bishops accepted the request provided that a formal legal document was drawn up between McCabe and Barbado y Viejo. The Spanish clerical students moved into the Irish College on 9 October. Four days later, the last of the soldiers left; they had been drafted north to the Pyrenees to guard against a border incursion from France.

The war in Europe came to an end in May 1945. McCabe warned the bishops that it was 'extremely important' that 'normal possession' of the Irish College, meaning the return of the students, take place as soon as possible, in order to ward off the attempts to seize it by various interested bodies in Salamanca.[6]

Difficulties remained, though. In the post-civil war period, the income from the college lands in the province of Salamanca had decreased, while the cost of living had trebled. There were also issues surrounding the title to these lands. Though modern contracts were in place between the college and the tenants, the lands had never been registered. The college held the deeds, but they were often hundreds of years old and indecipherable. With the college vacant and rival educational and ecclesiastical institutions attempting to get their hands on the vacant building, McCabe sought to register the college lands but it was a bureaucratic nightmare.

Furthermore, the college's investments in the Philippines looked precarious and the building in Salamanca was in need of repair. Not only had the wear and tear of the soldiers left their mark on the rooms, requiring extensive repairs, the old structure of the building was crumbling. The news that the archbishop of Manila, Michael O'Doherty, had survived the war safe and well provided welcome relief, though the college's assets in the Far East remained frozen.

After ten long years of holding the fort as rector, McCabe wished to go home. In May 1945, against the objections of friends and colleagues who were anxious to see him stay in Salamanca at a critical juncture, he offered his resignation to the Irish hierarchy:

> During the past troubled decade, in which there have been so many changes, it has been my modest obligation and ambition to save the College property and to see Irish students back again in their old 'Alma Mater'. Including my student days, I have spent twenty-one years in Salamanca, which is a very long time, and the best part of a lifetime. I feel that a change ought to benefit the College, and as I am anxious to return to Ireland, I wish to resign my post as Rector.[7]

In August 1945, the bishop of Gibraltar, Richard Fitzgerald, wrote to McCabe asking him to reconsider. 'May I suggest that the present is not the time to leave the old ship,' he wrote. 'You may plead that you are fed up with so many difficulties and the future is still so obscure. But it seems to be that precisely because of the difficulties of the situation and those that still may come, you ought to remain.'[8]

The Irish College had continued subsidising places for Irish students at seminaries in Ireland since 1936. Fitzgerald believed the money should have been left to accumulate instead and used for refurbishment and modernisation. He was unimpressed during a visit in the summer of 1945. 'I thought a lot of improvements had been effected at the time the German Embassy had been installed there,' he wrote to McCabe. 'Except for the few lamps and the air-raid shelter (?), I could not see them.'[9]

The vice-rector, John O'Hara, was also anxious to go back to Ireland. He returned home to Sligo in August for a holiday and met the bishop of Achonry, Patrick Morrisroe, who told him that it was the 'prevailing view among the Bishops that the present superiors of the College should continue'.[10] Bishop Morrisroe recommended that some form of announcement should be made if the college were to reopen in October and that O'Hara should discuss the matter with one of the four Irish archbishops, the trustees of the college. Three days later, O'Hara met the archbishop of Tuam, Joseph Walsh, and asked his approval to send a cable to McCabe in Salamanca inquiring, on behalf of the hierarchy, if the college would reopen in October. Walsh then recommended that O'Hara report to the archbishops after hearing from McCabe. O'Hara inquired at the Dublin offices of the shipping companies to see if they would be a position to take any of the students to Spain or Portugal. Two of the companies refused, but a third, the Limerick Steamship Company, agreed to take students in groups of two to Portuguese or Spanish ports at the end of September.

In the meantime, a surgeon in Dublin's Mater Hospital had informed O'Hara that he needed an operation for a duodenal ulcer and that there was a danger of serious complications, but that 'with care' he would 'possibly be safe for some little time'.[11] O'Hara still planned on returning to Salamanca so that McCabe could return to Ireland to discuss the college's future with the trustees. The archbishop of Cashel, John Harty, also wrote to O'Hara, expressing his wish that the college reopen, but there was a blow to the chances of this happening when the shipping company in Limerick wrote to say that they would no longer be able to accommodate any passengers on their vessels. In reply to the news, Cardinal MacRory wrote to O'Hara saying that the matter would be discussed at the hierarchy's October meeting. O'Hara informed Bishop Morrisroe that, although he needed an operation, he was returning to Salamanca for a few months to enable McCabe to return to Ireland. He also wrote to the Bishop of Ferns, James Staunton, the secretary to the Irish hierarchy, explaining that he would be able to remain only six more months in Spain before he would have to return for the operation and he asked the bishops to accept his resignation.[12]

O'Hara travelled to London on 3 October to wait for a plane to Lisbon or Madrid. It was while in London that he received a cable telling him that the bishops had accepted his resignation at their meeting in Maynooth. O'Hara cancelled his flight and travelled back to Ireland.[13] He was appointed a curate in Bohola in County Mayo shortly afterwards. While content with his new life performing pastoral work in a rural parish after a tumultuous decade in Spain, in a letter to McCabe that Christmas, O'Hara confessed to missing the weekly visitors, the conferences at the university, the concerts in the *conservatorio* and the '*elegancias*' of Salamanca.[14]

McCabe was now alone in Spain, with no prospect of the college reopening. During a visit to Ireland at Christmas, he pleaded with the bishops at their January meeting to ensure its survival. Yet returning to Salamanca must have been painful. With O'Hara gone, he was now reliant on the company of the Spanish students and old acquaintances.

Among the latter was the Conde de Alba de Yeltes, the landowner Gonzalo de Aguilera, who – supposedly to set an example – had shot six of his workers upon the outbreak of the civil war. He was a well-known eccentric figure around Salamanca and would hold court at the Café Novelty in the *plaza mayor* about his favourite subjects, including politics and science. He was also a regular visitor to the college, keeping McCabe up to date with the local gossip. At the beginning of 1946, Aguilera wrote to McCabe about the three days he had spent with Randolph Churchill, the former prime minister's son, in Madrid. The American news agency UP had invited Randolph Churchill to write a series of articles. Questions had been asked in the House of Commons about the visit, alleging that Churchill's true mission was to blacken the name of the new government in Britain. Churchill was a hard-drinking, bad-tempered man whose political career was as rocky as that of his father, Winston, and grandfather, Randolph. Unlike his illustrious relatives, however, his time as an MP was both brief and inconsequential. Aguilera wrote:

I got an idea that [Churchill] thought things were simpler than they are. He had a kind of secretary-interpreter from the U.P. (american) [*sic*] but not an anglo-saxon type at all, who was ladling out stuff that did not fit at all, made one wonder whether he had been squared to dish out his spiel. This guy had been picked up locally. What with the whiskies, coffies [*sic*] and other hard drinks in Madrid I've come back a wreck with my stomach and am on strenuous diet.[15]

In another letter to McCabe, Aguilera was dismissive of the Paris Peace Conference, which aimed at settling some of the outstanding issues in post-war Europe.

> That Paris conference is a huge farce. What I can't understand is how the Anglo-Yanks are standing the truculence of Moscow & Co. to say nothing of the Stern gang in Palestine. I can imagine my old friends [sic] the colonel Blimps at the Atheneum and similar clubs, if they exist, chewing their Mustaches and saying, not without reason, the country is going to the dogs.[16]

Aguilera developed a persecution complex in later life. His tragic end is related at the end of Paul Preston's history of the repression in Spain, *The Spanish Holocaust*. In 1963, Aguilera's wife, Magdalena, became so afraid of her husband's violent rages that she asked her two sons to come home to the estate at Matilla de los Caños to live with her. His eldest son, Gonzalo, a retired cavalry officer who had been seriously injured during the civil war, was forty-seven. He had settled in Lugo in Galicia where he was married to one of the nurses who had tended to him when he was in the military hospital there. Gonzalo's marriage to someone he believed to be a social inferior had enraged Aguilera. The younger son, Agustín, was thirty-nine, a farmer who lived in Jerez de la Frontera. He too had a difficult relationship with his father. The family eventually conceded that Aguilera would have to be committed, after he was diagnosed as a paranoiac. Yet the process was lengthy and, at the end of August 1964, Aguilera's madness got the better of him when he shot dead his two sons with an old revolver. He spent his last few months in a mental institution in Salamanca, before dying on 15 May 1965.[17]

At the end of 1945, after a decade of war in Spain and Europe, a disillusioned McCabe decided to destroy his diaries covering the years 1938 to 1945, as well as several notebooks, in all about 800,000 words, an invaluable record of life in Spain during and after the civil war.[18] He was an inveterate diarist but then, periodically, would consign dozens of journals and notebooks to the fire, a possible sign of violent mood swings. His isolation in Salamanca and his near constant disappointment at his understandable failure to reopen the college was having a deleterious effect on his health. Events were conspiring against him.

He was not helped by the attitude of the Irish bishops, whose decision-making about the Irish College was based on economic rather than cultural or educational reasoning. The hierarchy regarded the college and its property as a financial asset to be protected. They were not concerned about maintaining a cultural, educational and ecclesiastical link with Spain that was over 350 years old. There was also a sense that there was little point in sending clerical students to be educated in a foreign ethos in Spain when the national seminary at Maynooth was the jewel of the Irish Church. From their point of view, the fact that the Irish College could not prove title to the Fonseca building and that it required substantial investment was a major headache.

McCabe battled on, however, and again raised the question of the future of the college in his annual report of 1946: 'I am anxious to save the College, as other Rectors did in difficult periods, and I feel that I can count on the support of the Irish Bishops. The College may not be absolutely necessary, but with the intensification of international life in Church and State, it can still serve a useful and noble purpose.'[19]

In 1947, he pointed to the historical and religious links between Ireland and Spain:

Every educated Irishman knows that, in the past, Spain sent expeditions to Ireland, and a certain Spanish atmosphere still survives in Kinsale, for example, or Galway. In the same way, every educated Spaniard, whether he be from the extreme North, or the extreme South, associates Salamanca with Irishmen and Ireland. This may be a small item, but it is an important part of our national heritage on the Continent. Beside, it is important to have an Irish centre in modern Spain, which can rightly boast of its traditional title of 'Catholic', and which is the Mother country of twenty-one Spanish-speaking nations in America.[20]

McCabe also put forward the tangible assets of the college, which included the use of a 'magnificent' sixteenth-century building; a 'small, but valuable' library of sixteenth- and seventeenth-century books, and three black-letter incunabula; the college estates; and the summer villa in Asturias. Again, McCabe was keen that the students would study for degrees in the Pontifical University. 'I might add that I, myself, have no Degree, but it would be easy to appoint a Rector that has, and for the necessary time being, I should give him all the assistance possible. My only interest is to see the College survive and thrive under new Superiors, if necessary.'[21]

In October 1947, the bishop of Galway, Michael Browne, travelled to Salamanca on behalf of the hierarchy to assess the situation. He, along with the bishop of Meath, John Kyne, was charged with dealing with the future of the college. In an article written for *The Furrow* in 1971, Browne spelt out the problems from the hierarchy's point of view. The college was in need of 'very extensive repairs and required heating and sanitary facilities of modern standards'. It had accommodation 'for only thirty students, while Maynooth had one hundred rooms vacant and the Irish College in Rome had many externs', while the new Pontifical University in Salamanca wanted only students who would study for academic degrees.[22]

The Pontifical University was making efforts to get its hands on the Fonseca building. An article written by a professor of the Pontifical University, which was published in the Catholic magazine *Ecclesia* in May 1948, made only a fleeting reference to the fact that it was the home of the Irish College, much to McCabe's annoyance. The writer instead praised the bishop of Salamanca and Pope Pius XII for restoring the old *colegios mayors* and giving a home to priests studying for degrees in the Pontifical University.

McCabe remained holed up in the college. The years spent whiling away his time in Salamanca were taking their toll. He had given up walking, one of his great pleasures, and had started to drink heavily. He felt lethargic and unhealthy. The porter would call McCabe in the mornings, telling him what the day was like. If the weather was bad, he would recommend that the rector stay in bed. The mood swings, tendency to melancholia, heavy drinking and the fact that he was spending so much time lying in bed indicate that he may have been suffering from depression.

For the first time in his life, McCabe felt homesick and, ruminating on his childhood and his late father, he felt intimations of his own mortality.

The smell of the charcoal *brasero* in his room, where he would spend hours writing, reminded him of a wake and the burning candles that were laid out around the corpse. At the beginning of 1949, he wrote: 'I allow my mind to brood and brew too much – some men are more feminine and feline than they, themselves, advert to ...'[23] 'As we grow older, we begin to feel more keenly the death of people of our own generation, because we are beginning to feel death in our bones. If it isn't knocking at the door, at least, we can see it approaching in the distance. So our sympathy is largely self-pity'.[24]

McCabe recalled how Salamanca had changed in the three decades since his first visit. New buildings had been erected at the end of the civil war, including the Bank of Spain. McCabe remembered the scenes he had witnessed outside the old hospice, which had now become a seminary:

> There used to be a hole in the wall, with a notice 'Expositos' overhead. I once saw a pair put in a foundling. They had an awful black glass-less hearse to take the paupers to the Cemetery. The road was flinty, and full of 'pot-holes', and they used to drive along, trotting hard, 'rattling his bones over the stones'. Another vanishing feature was the unpainted wooden box, not unlike a coffin, in which soldiers and poor people were conveyed from the Hospital to their last resting place. The 'hurdy-gurdy', too, has gone off the streets, and I shan't forget the dirty blood-stained stretcher from the Hospital, on which they dragged out the old house-keeper. Though she was in a dying condition, they jolted her along as if she were a sack of meal.[25]

While many things had improved in Salamanca, postwar food rationing and electricity and water shortages made daily life uncomfortable.

In April 1949, the Irish hierarchy wrote to the Sacred Congregation of Seminaries in Rome requesting authority 'to dispose of the College, to realise all its assets and to devote them to bursaries for the education of priests'.[26] The Spanish bishops, however, did not believe it was for the Irish bishops to give away. Citing a law of the early nineteenth century that all ecclesiastical property belonged to the Spanish state, the Spanish hierarchy wrote to the papal nuncio in Madrid in 1950 stating that the college and its associated properties did not belong to the Irish hierarchy.

They claimed that the suppression of the college 'would break the glorious tradition linking Spain with Ireland, would diminish the status of the Pontifical University of Salamanca and would injure the international links of Spain with other nations, which the present government was most anxious to maintain'.[27]

The Irish hierarchy disputed this claim to title, saying that they held the college by *donatio* [gift]. They claimed that the king of Spain, Alfonso XIII, had 'recognized their full property rights to the college and that the villa, lands and investments of the college were derived from gifts of Irish ecclesiastics, soldiers and merchants during the previous centuries'.[28] The Irish bishops declared that they were prepared to hand over the college to the bishop of Salamanca in return for a bursary for Irish students in the Pontifical University and again asked the Congregation of Seminaries to obtain the permission of the Holy See for the transfer as soon as possible.

During a visit to Rome, the Irish primate, Cardinal D'Alton, and the bishop of Meath, John Kyne, raised the matter with the prefect of the Congregation of Seminaries and Universities, Cardinal Giuseppe Pizzardo. He told them that the Irish hierarchy's statement had been sent to the nuncio in Madrid, who had proposed the establishment of a committee of two Irish bishops and two Spanish bishops to work out an agreement regarding the future of the College. In January 1951, the bishops of Galway and Meath, Browne and Kyne, were appointed as the hierarchy's representatives. They met their Spanish representatives, the bishop of Salamanca and the archbishop of Valladolid, in the episcopal palace in Salamanca on 9 April 1951. According to Browne, 'a full discussion of over two hours took place but the Spanish bishops adhered rigidly to their contention that we had no right of ownership of the college, or even of the villa and lands which had been acquired at various times, or of the college funds invested in Spain'. He added,

> When we rose to depart I mentioned that we had arranged to pay a courtesy call on General Franco, as we were in Spain on official business. Whereupon the Bishop of Salamanca said: 'Oh, he can settle it.' I asked: 'Settle what?' 'This college business', he replied. We then realized how strong is the position of the State in Spain in regard to ecclesiastical affairs.[29]

Browne and Kyne then travelled to Madrid where they had the Irish Loreto Sisters help them draw up a document in Spanish. On 11 April, they read the document to General Franco at an interview. They made it clear that 'the Irish departure from Salamanca was not due to any lack of confidence in the political situation of Spain – a point that we had encountered in some quarters' and insisted that the change was for 'purely ecclesiastical and academic reasons'. They added that the Irish bishops were 'most anxious' to maintain their links with Spain and that was why they wished to transfer the college to the Spanish government in exchange for two scholarships, lay or clerical, in Spanish universities. They also requested that the historical archives of the college be transferred to Ireland and that the villa, lands and Spanish investments be realised and also transferred to Ireland.

'Although General Franco had no notice that he would be presented with this intricate legal problem,' wrote Browne, 'he made no demur and treated us with the greatest courtesy.' Franco accepted the proposals in principle and he asked Browne and Kyne to meet the Spanish ministers of foreign affairs and of education to work out the details. 'Before we left he gave us an assurance which had a certain piquancy – that if ever Ireland needed help or refuge again, Spain would be there.'[30]

The meetings between Browne and Kyne and the Spanish government ministers were successful, and the Irish hierarchy applied to the Sacred Congregation of Seminaries for formal approval of the transfer to the Spanish government on condition that the money realised from the sale of the villa, lands and investments would be given to the Irish College in Rome – partly in the form of bursaries, to be called Salamanca bursaries, and partly as capital funds of the college.

The decision to close the Irish College was met with disapproval from many quarters, not least in Salamanca, where some suspected the Irish bishops were pulling out of Spain for political reasons, a view they felt had been borne out by the fact that the Irish hierarchy did not explain its decision to close the college publicly. McCabe was undoubtedly disappointed at the decision of the bishops. On 16 November 1949, he handed the keys to his temporary replacement, Fr Francis Stenson, a former Salamanca student, and returned home to Ireland. Fr Joseph Ranson, another former Salamanca student from the diocese of Ferns, soon replaced Stenson, becoming the last official rector of the Irish College. Ranson was a keen historian and spent his time in the college arranging the books and manuscripts in the library for transfer to Ireland. Four years later, the college was officially closed and Ranson returned home, leaving the Irish embassy in Madrid to wrap up its affairs.

The legal and financial wrangling took over a decade and the college was not officially handed over to the Spanish state until 1962, thus ending a link between Ireland and Spain stretching back over 350 years. The sum realised through the sale of the summer villa in Asturias, lands and investments was two million pesetas or £20,000, which went to the Irish College in Rome. Two scholarships were established, one lay and one clerical, and ownership of the college passed to the University of Salamanca. It was subsequently restored and is now a residence for professors and guests of the university.

# Chapter 11

# BACK HOME

McCabe celebrated his fiftieth birthday in Ireland on 12 May 1950. Bar his brief period in Staghall in the late 1920s, he had been away from Ireland since first leaving home as a nineteen-year-old and had spent the last twenty years of his life in Salamanca. He had been an able student, sufficiently well regarded by Denis O'Doherty, his predecessor as rector of the Irish College, that he had been appointed vice-rector at the age of thirty. Five years later, he was rector of one of the Irish Church's most distinguished ecclesiastical institutions. He was a respected figure in Salamanca, a man whom the great and good held in high esteem.

Yet the decade that followed his appointment as rector had been full of disappointments. Year after year, he strove to reopen the college, but his efforts went unrewarded. For all McCabe's yearning to leave Spain, the prospect of returning to Ireland was not one that filled him with pleasure. In 1949, during the Bishop of Galway's visit to Salamanca, he tried to lobby the hierarchy to give him a position in the United States – but without success.

Back in his home diocese, McCabe must have looked at his own future with great anxiety. He was a fiercely intelligent, curious man with many talents, who had been offered a lectureship in the University of Salamanca, yet he had never taken a degree. The fact that the Bishop of Kilmore, Patrick Lyons, had died in April 1949, and his successor had not been named by the time McCabe returned home, added to his uncertainty over his future.

Spending time with his family was some consolation and McCabe's sisters doted on him. Three of them, Maura, Kathleen and Babs, none of whom had married, lived together in Ballinagh, about six miles from Drumkilly, when they retired. Fr Alex was a frequent visitor and everything had to be just right for their brother, the priest. Unfortunately, McCabe's mother, Katie, did not get to enjoy having her eldest son back home in Ireland for very long. She died at the age of seventy-eight on 11 July 1950, eight months after he had returned home. Eight days later, the new bishop was appointed for the diocese. An Armagh man who had previously been the parish priest of St Peter's in Drogheda, Austin Quinn was consecrated on 10 September in Cavan cathedral. On 23 September, the new Bishop of Kilmore appointed McCabe curate to the parish of Lurgan in south County Cavan.

It must have come as a terrible disappointment to McCabe. The world had opened up to him, first as a student in Salamanca, then in London and Leigh-on-Sea, and finally back in Spain and during his many trips through Europe and farther afield. McCabe had spent most of his adult life in the rarefied world of university professors, canons, diplomats and aristocrats. He was interested in art and literature, philosophy and politics. He was an educator who had cruelly been robbed of his life's work by the outbreak of two wars.

McCabe had realised in his twenties that he was not cut out for hearing the confessions of farmers and publican's wives and found it difficult to readapt to Irish rural society. One occasion serves as an example of his inability to accept his new position in life. In rural Ireland at that time it was quite common for farmers to pay their parish dues in produce rather than cash. Once, a farmer, not finding the curate at home, had left a bag of oats on the table for him. When McCabe returned home and saw the oats, he swept them from the table in anger.

McCabe's drinking had become a problem in Salamanca and this was probably one of the factors that influenced the bishop's decision to appoint him to Lurgan: Quinn was not known for showing mercy to priests who transgressed, and ruled his diocese with an iron fist. By sending McCabe to a small rural parish, the bishop exacerbated the problem. With little to engage his intellect, McCabe turned to the bottle. His drinking became heavier and his behaviour spiralled out of control. The bishop's response was to punish McCabe by transferring him to an even poorer, more remote parish. In 1954, Quinn sent him to Corlough, a parish in the wild, hilly north-west part of the county, on the border with Northern Ireland.

McCabe's treatment at the hands of his bishop was not unique. A small number of priests were permanently or temporarily suspended from ministry for alcohol problems. According to the author of the official history of the diocese of Kilmore, Daniel Gallogly, 'the priest's drinking was seen by his superiors as a vice, which he himself was expected to conquer by will-power'. Bishop Quinn was particularly strict on priests with a drink problem. Gallogly writes:

> The unfortunate priest was repeatedly reprimanded, changed from parish to parish in rapid succession, usually to poorer parishes where he would have less money to spend on drink. He was made do retreats to mend his ways, suspended for periods but allowed resume. If all this failed and only as a last resort he was removed permanently.
>
> The Kilmore Clerical Fund which was in operation from 1843 to provide for sick or disabled priests made no provision for the support of priests suspended for alcoholism. In the words of its own charter it catered only for 'priests of good standing' and the alcoholic priest wasn't seen as such. He was turned loose to fend for himself by going abroad or else returning to live at home with his family surviving in penury, bartering the efficacy of his Office and prayers to earn enough money to survive and to feed his addiction.[1]

McCabe's transfer to Corlough was part of this punitive policy. From his lofty perch as rector of the Real Colegio de San Patricio de los Nobles Irelandeses, a man who had witnessed the world pass through Salamanca, he was now an embarrassment to his bishop: a poor curate with a fondness for the drop. It was a desperate humiliation and, of course, served only to intensify his drinking. Fellow priests were shocked at the bishop's treatment of McCabe. One priest who knew McCabe thought that 'a man of his ability and experience' should never have been sent to 'a place like Corlough'.[2]

McCabe spent five years in Corlough. In 1959, after nine years as a curate, he was appointed administrator of the parish of Ballaghameehan in County Leitrim, at the north-east end of the diocese, close to the border with County Fermanagh. The parish church was in Rossinver and the new priest made quite an impact on the parish. Having had little need to drive in Spain, McCabe had never become accustomed to looking after a car. He would drive around the parish in first gear or leave the car in the middle of the road when it broke down, steam rising from the engine. While out walking, he carried a sword stick, with which, out of cussedness, he would stab boxes of biscuits in the local shop.

McCabe drank mostly at home – his favourite tipple was wine – and he would often load up before arriving at the church. Sometimes he would assemble the men waiting outside into formation and drill them up and down, ordering them to give the fascist salute. He could be unreasonable when drunk – once he arrived at the house of a local man and accused him of stealing a bag of turf from the parochial house – but when sober, he was gentlemanly and polite. While many of his parishioners did not approve of his behaviour, others liked him and took a tolerant view of his drinking. In 1961, the bishop removed McCabe from ministry and sent him to Belmont Park.

Belmont Park is on the edge of Waterford city but located in County Kilkenny. The building, formerly the grand home of the Barron family, had been bought by the Brothers of Charity in the late nineteenth century. It opened its doors in 1885 as St Patrick's Hospital for the Insane. In the 1960s, the order was operating a psychiatric hospital at Belmont Park. McCabe was admitted voluntarily to the hospital on 21 October 1961 with a diagnosis of schizophrenia. Patients were initially placed in a ward accommodating about twelve to fourteen beds. Once they were settled and the consultant deemed it safe, they were given their own room. The hospital catered for both clerical and lay patients. Priests were able to say and attend mass in St Patrick's chapel on the campus.

McCabe's consultant psychiatrist was Dr Denis Lane O'Kelly, and his initial treatment included a course of electroconvulsive therapy (ECT). Patients undergoing ECT are given a muscle relaxant and anaesthetic – McCabe was administered with atropine and Sodium Pentothal™ – before seizures are induced through a series of short, sharp electric shocks via electrodes placed on the temples. Lane O'Kelly administered ECT to McCabe six times in November 1961. McCabe was 'very nervous' before undergoing the treatment, according to the Belmont Park records. It is not clear if McCabe underwent further courses of ECT because most of the medical file is missing. Lane O'Kelly may have treated McCabe as a private patient after he was discharged from St Patrick's and held on to the file. Lane O'Kelly died in 2002, two weeks before he was due to stand trial on multiple charges of indecently assaulting female patients in Belmont Park.

McCabe was discharged seven years after entering Belmont Park on 16 July 1968. He was appointed chaplain to St Joseph's Nursing Home in Fort Lurgan in Virginia, County Cavan, where he was also a full-time resident. It was a premature end to a career that had once promised so much. He was to spend the last twenty years of his life in St Joseph's and became increasingly reclusive, though he was invited to give a few classes in religious doctrine at the vocational school in Cavan town in the early 1970s.

A priest who got to know him at that time remembered McCabe as 'a colourful character', a 'great conversationalist' and 'a good man'. This same priest believes the bishop wanted to get him out of the way: 'I would say a man can be forgotten about, out of sight, out of mind. He was a bit of a nuisance.'[3] With nothing to keep him occupied, McCabe retreated into himself. He lived out his days in St Joseph's, the wallpaper in his room stained a deep brown from his incessant smoking, going for an occasional walk beside Lough Ramor with the help of a stick.

A local who knew McCabe believes that 'he was totally isolated' and was surprised that a cultured and well-educated man had no books in his room. Though some of the local clergy made efforts to include him in social outings, he was not capable of meeting them halfway. His interests were not theirs. He would say mass in the oratory in the morning and spend most of the rest of the day in his room. He seldom had visitors, except for the regular visits from his sisters whom he would entertain in his room. He was driven into Virginia to collect his old-age pension, his only source of income, from the post office.

His mind was still active and sharp, however, and he retained vivid memories of childhood and his time in Spain. He continued to jot down his thoughts about all manner of subjects, including literature, art, philosophy and history. Many aspects of modern life, not least Irish radio, vexed him: 'Though the Harp is our National musical instrument and emblem (one of several), most of the Music from Radio Éireann is

Jazz and Pop, with deadly variations of monotonous Tin Fifery, in the best Moorish style.'[4]

Professor Dermot Keogh, who interviewed McCabe while conducting doctoral research in the 1970s, paid him a handsome tribute in an essay for *Breifne*, the local history journal in Cavan. He wrote that McCabe was 'witty and sardonic', 'a gentleman' and not only did he represent 'all that was good in Irish Catholicism' but that his experiences 'gave him a deep insight into the human condition'. Keogh first met McCabe in Virginia in 1977. It took a while for McCabe to open up about his experiences during the 1930s, but during the historian's second visit, he read to him from his diaries.[5]

On 21 June 1986, the Bishop of Kilmore, Francis MacKiernan, concelebrated mass with McCabe in the chapel of the nursing home to mark the diamond jubilee of his ordination. His sisters, friends and some priests of the diocese attended.

On 2 July 1986, McCabe was invited to participate in the state visit of the king and queen of Spain to St Patrick's College, Maynooth. During their visit, the Spanish monarchs inspected a small exhibition drawn from the Salamanca Archive, including two sets of vestments that the queen of Spain, Maria of Braganza, had presented to the Irish College in Salamanca in the middle of the eighteenth century, and two autographed portraits of King Juan Carlos's grandfather and grandmother. During his address to the king and queen, McCabe spoke of the Irish College as a 'victim of the Spanish Civil War' and recalled meeting King Juan Carlos's grandfather, Alfonso XIII. He also remembered seeing King Juan Carlos's father, the then Prince of Asturias, in 1924. 'Rounding a corner in the town he came on us suddenly, and, recognising us as Irish, gave us a magnificent military salute.' McCabe's closing words were '¡Viva España! Long live the Spanish people and long live for many years the great King Juan Carlos, successor of so many distinguished monarchs.'[6]

Two years after being accorded this honour, a fitting reflection of his connection to an older Spain, on 29 November 1988 Alexander Joseph McCabe passed away at the age of eighty-eight.

# ENDNOTES

Dates in English (at the beginning of each citation) refer to when an entry was begun. They do not always indicate when an individual quotation was written because McCabe would often add to an entry on subsequent days without creating a new heading. Dates in Spanish (for example, *enero 1*) indicate the page on which the reference is to be found and do not refer to when the entry was written.

AMP: Alexander McCabe Papers, National Library of Ireland
Ms: Manuscript
SP: Salamanca Papers, Russell Library, St Patrick's College, Maynooth

## EPIGRAPH

1    13 June 1946, Diary, Spain, *enero 20–21*, AMP, Ms 42,488/12.

## INTRODUCTION

1    Francis McCullagh, *In Franco's Spain: Being the Experiences of an Irish War Correspondent during the Great Civil War* (London: Burns, Oates & Washbourne, 1937), p. 158.

## CHAPTER 1

1    17 January 1949, Diary, *marzo 26*, AMP, Ms 42,488/18.
2    Ibid, *marzo 28*.
3    Ibid, *septiembre 19*.
4    Ibid, *marzo 27*.
5    Ibid.
6    Ibid, *marzo 27–28*.
7    Ibid, *septiembre 18*.
8    Ibid, *marzo 29*.
9    Ibid, *marzo 30*.
10   Ibid, *marzo 31–resumen de marzo*.

11    Ibid, *marzo 31.*
12    Ibid, *resumen de marzo.*
13    Ibid.
14    Ibid, *marzo 25.*
15    Ibid, *resumen de marzo.*
16    Ibid, *resumen de marzo–abril 1.*
17    Ibid, *abril 7.*
18    Ibid, *resumen de noviembre.*
19    Ibid, *diciembre 4–5.*
20    Ibid, *diciembre 2–3.*
21    Ibid, *diciembre 3.*
22    Ibid, *marzo 22.*
23    Ibid, *marzo 10.*
24    Ibid, *febrero 2.*
25    2 April 1930, Diary, *abril 25*, AMP, Ms 42,488/5.
26    17 January 1949, Diary, *enero 18*, AMP, Ms 42,488/18.
27    Ibid, *enero 19.*
28    Ibid, *junio 2.*
29    Ibid, *junio 10.*
30    Ibid, *junio 26.*
31    Ibid, *mayo 25.*
32    Ibid, *julio 2.*
33    Ibid, *julio 2–3.*
34    27 February 1930, Diary, *abril 4–5*, AMP, Ms 42,488/5.
35    17 January 1949, Diary, *agosto 8*, AMP, Ms 42,488/18.
36    Ibid, *agosto 9.*
37    Ibid.
38    Ibid, *febrero 15.*
39    Ibid, *febrero 15–16.*
40    19 April 1949, Diary, *mayo 24*, AMP, Ms 42,488/19.
41    Ibid, *mayo 27.*
42    Ibid.
43    1 January 1930, Diary, *febrero 26*, AMP, Ms 42,488/5.
44    19 April 1949, Diary, *julio 3*, AMP, Ms 42,488/19.
45    17 January 1949, Diary, *septiembre 1*, AMP, Ms 42,488/18.
46    Ibid, *septiembre 2–3.*
47    19 April 1949, Diary, *julio 4*, AMP, Ms 42,488/19; see also 17 January 1949, Diary, *septiembre 3*, AMP, Ms 42,488/18.
48    17 January 1949, Diary, *septiembre 3*, AMP, Ms 42,488/18.
49    Ibid, *febrero 28.*
50    19 April 1949, Diary, *julio 12–14*, AMP, Ms 42,488/19.
51    17 January 1949, Diary, *resumen de enero*, AMP, Ms 42,488/18.
52    19 April 1949, Diary, *julio 13*, AMP, Ms 42,488/19.
53    Raymond Dunne and Francis J. MacKiernan, *The College Boys: Students of the Kilmore Academy & St Patrick's College, Cavan 1839–2000* (Cavan: Cumann Seanchais Bhreifne, 2008), pp. xix–xx.
54    John Cooney, *John Charles McQuaid: Ruler of Catholic Ireland* (Dublin: O'Brien Press, 1999), p. 30.
55    17 January 1949, Diary, *febrero 8*, AMP, Ms 42,488/18.

56    5 May 1929, Diary, *enero 18–19*, AMP, Ms 42,488/5.

57    17 January 1949, Diary, *septiembre 9*, AMP, Ms 42,488/18.

58    John McGahern, 'Schooldays: A Time of Grace', in *Love of the World: Essays* (London: Faber & Faber, 2009), pp. 103–8 (p. 103).

59    23 January 1929, Diary, *resumen de enero*, AMP, Ms 42,488/4.

60    Ibid, *enero 22*.

61    Ibid, *enero 29*.

62    Ibid, *febrero 3*.

63    Ibid, *febrero 17*.

64    Ibid, *febrero 19*.

65    Ibid, *febrero 20*.

66    Ibid, *febrero 21*.

67    Ibid, *febrero 22–23*.

68    Ibid, *febrero 24–25*.

## CHAPTER 2

1    See Óscar Recio Morales, 'Not Only Seminaries: The Political Role of the Irish Colleges in Seventeenth-Century Spain', *History Ireland*, 9, 3 (2001), pp. 48–52.

2    Richard J. Glennon, 'The Irish College, Salamanca' *The Furrow*, 23, 1 (1972), pp. 48–52 (p. 49).

3    William O'Dwyer, from Bohola in County Mayo. O'Dwyer's mother had been anxious for him to become a priest but he was not cut out for the religious life and failed to pass his exams. Instead, he emigrated to the United States in 1910, enlisted in the New York Police Department and took a night course studying the law. During the early 1930s, he was involved in the fight against organised crime, first as a magistrate, then as a judge, and finally as a district attorney. During the Second World War, he enlisted in the US army and was commissioned a lieutenant colonel. In 1945, O'Dwyer was elected mayor of New York City. He resigned in 1950, following a scandal over police corruption. President Harry S. Truman subsequently appointed him US ambassador to Mexico. Later, O'Dwyer was accused of having connections to the Mob. Throughout his extraordinary career, O'Dwyer helped organisations involved in funding and arming Jewish emigrants to Palestine, including Irgun.

4    See George Gavan Duffy to Denis O'Doherty, Paris, 11 March 1920, SP/S/77/1/6 (1); Fintan Murphy to Denis O'Doherty, London, 19 March 1920, SP/S/82/5; George Gavan Duffy to Denis O'Doherty, Paris, 22 March 1920, SP/S/82/5; Seán T. O'Kelly, Paris, 30 April 1921, SP/S/82/5; Katherine Hughes to Denis O'Doherty, Paris, 2 October 1921, SP/S/82/12; George Gavan Duffy to Denis O'Doherty, Dublin, 21 February 1922, SP/S/77/1/8 (1); George Gavan Duffy to Denis O'Doherty, Dublin, 14 March, SP/S/77/1/8 (2); 'Hablando con un eminente patriota irlandés: Declaraciones del Doctor O'Doherty', SP/S/77/1/13.

5    Robert Brennan to Denis O'Doherty, Madrid, 17 November 1921, SP/S/82/12.

6    George Gavan Duffy to Denis O'Doherty, Dublin, 14 March 1922, SP/S/77/1/8.

7    Copy of Esmé Howard to Earl Curzon, British Embassy, Madrid, 13 June 1921 (facsimile sent by Dermot Keogh to Alexander McCabe on 21 November 1978), AMP, Ms 50,555/31/8-9.

8    Copy of Esmé Howard to Earl Curzon, British Embassy, Madrid, 13 June, 1921, AMP, Ms 50,555/31/9.

9    22 January 1934, Diary, *mayo 17*, AMP, Ms 42,488/8.
10   See Regina Whelan Richardson, 'The Irish in Asturias: the footprint of the Irish College, Salamanca, 1913–1950', *Archivium Hibernicum*, 65 (2012), pp. 273–90.
11   Hugh Brady to Denis O'Doherty, Crosserlough, 17 January 1923, SP/S/82/2.
12   20 September 1933, Diary, *enero 19*, AMP, Ms 42,488/8.


CHAPTER 3

1    23 January 1929, Diary, *resumen de febrero*, AMP, Ms 42,488/4.
2    Alexander McCabe to Denis O'Doherty, Canning Town, 21 December 1925, SP/S/82/12.
3    Ibid.
4    23 January 1929, Diary, *marzo 12–13*, AMP, Ms 42,488/4.
5    Ibid, *marzo 13–14*.
6    Ibid, *marzo 21–22*.
7    Ibid, *marzo 24*.
8    Alexander McCabe to Denis O'Doherty, Canning Town, 21 December 1925, SP/S/82/12.
9    23 January 1929, Diary, *marzo 5–6*, AMP, Ms 42,488/4.
10   Ibid, *marzo 6*.
11   Ibid, *marzo 7–8*.
12   Ibid, *abril 9*.
13   Ibid, *marzo 16*.
14   9 October 1927, Diary, *enero 10*, AMP, Ms 42,488/1. AM attempted to redact the words 'put my fist through' in the original entry.
15   Ibid, *enero 11*.
16   23 January 1929, Diary, *enero 19*, AMP, Ms 42,488/4.
17   24 January 1929, *abril 17–18*, AMP, Ms 42,488/4.
18   Ibid, *abril 28*.
19   9 February 1930, Diary, *marzo 17–18*, AMP, Ms 42,488/5.
20   17 November 1929, Diary, *febrero 2*, AMP, Ms 42,488/5.
21   26 January 1930, Diary, *marzo 10*, AMP, Ms 42,488/5.
22   21 April 1930, Diary, *mayo 15–16*, AMP, Ms 42,488/5.
23   26 April 1929, Diary, *enero 7*, AMP, Ms 42,488/5.
24   26 March 1930, Diary, *abril 18*, AMP, Ms 42,488/5.
25   12 July 1930, Diary, *junio 21–22*, AMP, Ms 42,488/5.
26   28 February 1930, Diary, *abril 5–6*, AMP, Ms 42,488/5.
27   28 February 1930, Diary, *abril 7–9*, AMP, Ms 42,488/5.
28   11 July 1930, Diary, *junio 19–20*, AMP, Ms 42,488/5.
29   18 September 1930, Diary, *agosto 14*, AMP, Ms 42,488/5.
30   19 September 1930, Diary, *agosto 14–15*, AMP, Ms 42,488/5.


CHAPTER 4

1    15 December 1930, Diary, *septiembre 25*, AMP, Ms 42,488/5.
2    6 November 1930, Diary, *septiembre 8*, AMP, Ms 42,488/5.
3    Ibid, *septiembre 9*.
4    12 December 1930, Diary, *septiembre 20*, AMP, Ms 42,488/5.
5    Ibid, *septiembre 21*.

6   Thomas O'Doherty to Denis O'Doherty, 1 April 1926, SP/S/78/12.
7   12 December 1930, Diary, *septiembre 22–23*, AMP, Ms 42,488/5.
8   7 March 1931, Diary, *enero 5–7*, AMP, Ms 42,488/6.
9   17 March 1931, Diary, *enero 10–11*, AMP, Ms 42,488/6.
10  Ibid, *enero 11*.
11  13 April 1931, Diary, *febrero 20*, AMP, Ms 42,488/6.
12  14 April 1931, Diary, *febrero 21*, AMP, Ms 42,488/6.
13  Ibid, *febrero 22*.
14  Ibid, *febrero 23*.
15  Repr. in Hugh Thomas, *The Spanish Civil War* (London: Penguin, 2003), p. 46.
16  6 June 1931, Diary, *febrero 24*, AMP, Ms 42,488/6.
17  Ibid.
18  Ibid, *febrero 26*.
19  Ibid, *febrero 27*.
20  17 June 1931, Diary, *resumen de febrero*, AMP, Ms 42,488/6.
21  22 June 1931, Diary, *marzo 10*, AMP, Ms 42,488/6.
22  Ibid, *marzo 10–11*.
23  23 June 1931, Diary, *marzo 17*, AMP, Ms 42,488/6.
24  Ibid, *marzo 18*.
25  15 July 1931, Diary, *marzo 18*, AMP, Ms 42,488/6.
26  [No date] 1932, Diary, *marzo 24–25*, AMP, Ms 42,488/6.
27  19 June 1931, Diary, *marzo 3*, AMP, Ms 42,488/6.
28  [No date] 1932, Diary, *abril 15*, AMP, Ms 42,488/6.
29  Ibid, *abril 15–16*.
30  Ibid, *abril 29*.
31  Ibid, *mayo 7*.
32  Ibid, *mayo 13–14*.
33  4 April 1931, Diary, *enero 28–29*, AMP, Ms 42,488/6.
34  Ibid, *enero 29*.
35  Ibid, *enero 29–30*.
36  [No date] 1932, Diary, *junio 5*, AMP, Ms 42,488/6.
37  Ibid, *junio 7–8*.
38  Ibid, *junio 11*.
39  Ibid, *junio 10–11*.
40  Gerald Brenan, *The Spanish Labyrinth: The Social and Political Background of the Spanish Civil War* (Cambridge: Canto, 2008), p. 118.
41  Ibid, p.119.
42  [No date] 1932, Diary, *agosto 15–16*, AMP, Ms 42,488/6.
43  Ibid, *resumen de agosto–septiembre 1*.
44  Ibid, *septiembre 5*.
45  Ibid, *septiembre 12*.
46  Ibid, *septiembre 14–15*.
47  Ibid, *septiembre 15–16*.
48  Ibid, *septiembre 16–17*.
49  Ibid, *septiembre 18*.
50  Ibid, *septiembre 18–19*.
51  Ibid, *septiembre 19–20*.
52  Ibid, *septiembre 24*.

53   Ibid, *septiembre 25–26.*
54   Ibid., *octubre 4.*
55   [No date] 1933, Diary, *octubre 8,* AMP, Ms 42,488/6.
56   Ibid, *octubre 20.*
57   Ibid, *octubre 21–22.*
58   Ibid, *noviembre 2.*
59   Ibid, *noviembre 14–15.*
60   Ibid, *octubre 11.*
61   Ibid, *noviembre 16–17.*
62   Ibid, *diciembre 2.*
63   Ibid, *diciembre 2–3.*
64   Ibid, *diciembre 4.*
65   Ibid, *diciembre 5.*
66   Ibid, *diciembre 31–resumen de diciembre.*
67   Ibid, *resumen de diciembre.*
68   28 May 1933, Diary, *enero 27,* AMP, Ms 42,488/7.
69   Ibid, *enero 29.*
70   Ibid, *enero 31.*
71   Ibid., *enero 26.*
72   Ibid, *febrero 4.*
73   Ibid, *mayo 3.*
74   Ibid, *agosto 3–4.*
75   Ibid, *septiembre 16.*
76   Ibid, *agosto 9–10.*
77   Ibid, *septiembre 12–13.*
78   Ibid, *septiembre 14–15.*
79   Ibid, *septiembre 13–14.*
80   Ibid, *febrero 22.*
81   Ibid, *noviembre 4.*
82   Ibid, *noviembre 5.*
83   Ibid, *noviembre 16–17.*
84   20 September 1933, Diary, *febrero 18,* AMP, Ms 42,488/8.
85   Ibid, *febrero 5.*
86   Ibid, *febrero 7.*
87   Ibid, *febrero 10.*
88   Ibid, *febrero 16.*
89   Ibid.
90   18 September 1933, Diary, *resumen de diciembre,* AMP, Ms 42,488/7.
91   Ibid.
92   Ibid.
93   Ibid, *diciembre 4–5.*
94   Ibid, *diciembre 22–23.*
95   20 September 1933, Diary, *febrero 2,* AMP, Ms 42,488/8.
96   28 May 1933, Diary, *resumen de diciembre–resumen del año,* AMP, Ms 42,488/7.
97   Ibid, *resumen del año.*
98   Ibid.
99   20 September 1933, Diary, *febrero 3,* AMP, Ms 42,488/8.
100  28 May 1933, Diary, *diciembre 22,* AMP, Ms 42,488/7.

101 20 September 1933, Diary, *enero 31*, AMP, Ms 42,488/8.

102 Ibid, *enero 30–31.*

103 Ibid, *resumen de enero.*

104 Ibid, *febrero 24.*

105 Ibid, *marzo 13.*

106 11 February 1934, Diary, *julio 12*, AMP, Ms 42,488/8.

107 20 September 1933, Diary, *marzo 18*, AMP, Ms 42,488/8.

**CHAPTER 5**

1 27 January 1934, Diary, *mayo 29*, AMP, Ms 42,488/8.

2 Ibid, *mayo 30.*

3 Ibid, *mayo 31.*

4 1 January 1934, Diary, *marzo 23*, AMP, Ms 42,488/8.

5 27 January 1934, Diary, *junio 2–3*, AMP, Ms 42,488/8.

6 22 January 1934, Diary, *mayo 15*, AMP, Ms 42,488/8.

7 28 January 1934, Diary, *junio 14*, AMP, Ms 42,488/8.

8 Ibid, *junio 12–14.*

9 1 February 1934, Diary, *junio 17–18*, AMP, Ms 42,488/8.

10 9 February 1934, Diary, *julio 6*, AMP, Ms 42,488/8.

11 10 February 1934, Diary, *julio 11*, AMP, Ms 42,488/8.

12 22 February 1934, Diary, Spain, *agosto 16*, AMP, Ms 42,488/8.

13 Ibid, *agosto 15.*

14 18 February 1934, Diary, *agosto 2*, AMP, Ms 42,488/8.

15 Ibid, *agosto 2–3.*

16 4 March 1934, Diary, *agosto 25*, AMP, Ms 42,488/8.

17 Ibid, *agosto 27.*

18 Ibid, *agosto 31.*

19 28 April 1934, Diary, *septiembre 15*, AMP, Ms 42,488/8.

20 Ibid, *septiembre 18.*

21 8 December 1934, Diary, *noviembre 2*, AMP, Ms 42,488/8.

22 Ibid., *noviembre 1.*

23 Ibid, *noviembre 3.*

24 Ibid, *noviembre 3–4.*

25 Ibid, *noviembre 7.*

26 Ibid, *noviembre 10.*

27 Ibid, *noviembre 9.*

28 Ibid, *noviembre 14.*

29 Ibid, *noviembre 15.*

30 Ibid, *noviembre 15–16.*

31 Ibid, *noviembre 16.*

32 Ibid, *noviembre 16–17.*

33 15 December 1934, Diary, *noviembre 30*, AMP, Ms 42,488/8.

34 17 December 1934, Diary, *resumen de noviembre*, AMP, Ms 42,488/8.

35 2 March 1936, Diary, *febrero 4*, AMP, Ms 42,488/10.

36 [No date] 1935, Diary, *diciembre 5–6*, AMP, Ms 42,488/8.

37 [No date] April 1935, *diciembre 11*, AMP, Ms 42,488/8.

38  30 June 1935, Diary, *diciembre 14*, AMP, Ms 42,488/8.
39  23 June 1935, Diary, *diciembre 12*, AMP, Ms 42,488/8.
40  Ibid, *diciembre 12–13*.
41  Ibid, *diciembre 13*.
42  *The Rector's Report for the Academic Year 1935–36*, p. 4, AMP, Ms 50,555/36/1.
43  Ambrose Blaine to Denis O'Doherty, St Nathy's College, 12 September 1925, SP/S/82/12.
44  7 January, 1936, Diary, *enero 5*, AMP, Ms 42,488/10.
45  19 January 1936, Diary, *enero 15–16*, AMP, Ms 42,488/10.
46  20 January 1936, Diary, *enero 17*, AMP, Ms 42,488/10.
47  16 February 1936, Diary, *enero 30*, AMP, Ms 42,488/10.
48  17 February 1936, Diary, *enero 30*, AMP, Ms 42,488/10.
49  21 February 1936, Diary, *resumen de enero*, AMP, Ms 42,488/10.
50  22 February 1936, Diary, *resumen de enero–febrero 1*, AMP, Ms 42,488/10.
51  17 March 1936, Diary, *febrero 7*, AMP, Ms 42,488/10.
52  18 May 1936, Diary, *febrero 17–18*, AMP, Ms 42,488/10.

## CHAPTER 6

1   10 August 1936, Diary, *febrero 18*, AMP, Ms 42,488/10.
2   Ibid, *febrero 20*.
3   Ibid, *febrero 22*.
4   Ibid, *febrero*.
5   Ibid, *febrero 28*.
6   Copy of John O'Hara to Alexander McCabe, Pendueles, 11 July [*sic*] 1936, in 25 October 1936, Diary, *marzo 21*, AMP, Ms 42,488/10.
7   10 August 1936, Diary, *febrero 25*, AMP, Ms 42,488/10.
8   John O'Hara to Alexander McCabe, Santander, 5 August 1936, SP/S/88/1.
9   Copy of O'Hara to McCabe, Pendueles, 11 July [*sic*] 1936, in 25 October 1936, Diary, *marzo 21–22*, AMP, Ms 42,488/10.
10  Copy of O'Hara to McCabe, Asturias, 26 August 1936, in 25 October 1936, Diary, *marzo 25*, AMP, Ms 42,488/10.
11  25 October 1936, Diary, *abril 10*, AMP, Ms 42,488/10.
12  'El 19 de julio, salío el Ejército a la calle, declarando el estado de guerra, y en la Plaza Mayor, se oyeron algunas "vivas" contrarias y algún tiro de los otros, y entonces el Ejército hizo fuego, y mataron a seis o siete personas. Desde aquel momento, la ciudad ha estado siempre totalmente tranquila. Muchisima parte del pueblo se puso al lado del Ejército y dominaron por completo toda la provincia', copy of Francisco Ramos to Alexander McCabe, Salamanca, 15 September 1936, in 25 October 1936, Diary, *resumen de marzo–abril 1*, AMP, Ms 42,488/10.
13  25 October 1936, Diary, *abril 11*, AMP, Ms 42,488/10.
14  7 November 1936, Diary, *abril 29–resumen de abril*, AMP, Ms 42,488/10.
15  25 October 1936, Diary, *abril 18*, AMP, Ms 42,488/10.
16  Ibid, *abril 19*.
17  Ibid.
18  13 October 1936, Diary, *marzo 7–8*, AMP, Ms 42,488/10.
19  Ibid, *marzo 10*.
20  25 October 1936, Diary, *abril 11*, AMP, Ms 42,488/10.
21  Copy of Joseph MacRory to Alexander McCabe, 25 October 1936, in 25 October 1936, Diary, *abril 12–14*, AMP, Ms 42,488/10.

22    Manifesto of the Irish Christian Front. Repr. in Fearghal McGarry, *Irish Politics and the Spanish Civil War* (Cork: Cork University Press, 1999), p. 109.
23    25 October 1936, Diary, *abril 14*, AMP, Ms 42,488/10.
24    Ibid, *abril 21*.
25    Ibid, *abril 20*.
26    Ibid, *abril 16*.
27    Ibid, *abril 23*.
28    Ibid, *abril 25–26*.
29    Ibid., *abril 25–26*.
30    7 November 1936, Diary, *mayo 3–4*, AMP, Ms 42,488/10.
31    Ibid, *mayo 13*.
32    Ibid, *mayo 18–22*.
33    Ibid, *mayo 24*.
34    Ibid, *mayo 23*.
35    Ibid, *mayo 26–27*.
36    Ibid, *mayo 27–28*.
37    Ibid, *mayo 30*.

## CHAPTER 7

1    15 November 1936, Diary, *junio 20*, AMP, Ms 42,488/10.
2    13 November 1936, Diary, *junio 2*, AMP, Ms 42,488/10.
3    14 November 1936, Diary, *resumen de mayo*, AMP, Ms 42,488/10.
4    Ibid, *junio 5*.
5    Ibid, *junio 7–8*.
6    Ibid, *junio 8*.
7    15 November 1936, Diary, *junio 11*, AMP, Ms 42,488/10.
8    14 November 1936, Diary, *junio 4*, AMP, Ms 42,488/10.
9    15 November 1936, Diary, *junio 12*, AMP, Ms 42,488/10.
10    Ibid, *junio 12–13*.
11    Ibid, *junio 14*.
12    Ibid, *junio 14–15*.
13    Ibid, *junio 15*.
14    Repr. in Thomas, pp. 487–8. The authenticity of the speech has been challenged in recent years. See https://www.theguardian.com/world/2018/may/11/famous-spanish-civil-war-speech-may-be-invented-says-historian.
15    Miguel de Unamuno to Quintín de Torre, Salamanca, 1 December 1936. Repr. in Paul Preston, *The Spanish Holocaust: Inquisition and Extermination in Twentieth-Century Spain* (London: Harper Press, 2012), p. 195.
16    See John Horgan, '"The great war correspondent": Francis McCullagh, 1874–1956', *Irish Historical Studies*, 36, 144 (2009), pp. 542–63.
17    16 November 1936, Diary, *junio 30*, AMP, Ms 42,488/10.
18    McCullagh, p. 158.
19    McCullagh, p. 161.
20    15 November 1936, Diary, *junio 21*, AMP, Ms 42,488/10.
21    16 November 1936, Diary, *junio 25–26*, AMP, Ms 42,488/10.
22    Fearghal McGarry, *Irish Politics*, pp. 125–7.
23    16 November 1936, Diary, *junio 26*, AMP, Ms 42,488/10.

24  Ibid., *junio 22–23*.
25  Ibid, *junio 24*.
26  Ibid.
27  Ibid., *junio 28*.
28  Ibid.
29  17 November 1936, *resumen de junio–julio 1*, AMP, Ms 42,488/10.
30  Ibid, *julio 1–2*.
31  18 November 1936, Diary, *julio 25*, AMP, Ms 42,488/10.
32  Ibid, *julio 28*.
33  Ibid, *julio 31–resumen de julio*.
34  Ibid, *resumen de julio–agosto 1*.
35  Ibid, *agosto 2*.
36  Ibid, *agosto 8*.
37  23 November 1936, Diary, *septiembre 25*, AMP, Ms 42,488/10.
38  Ibid.
39  Ibid, *septiembre 27*.
40  Patrick Belton to Joseph MacRory, 17 February 1937. Repr. in McGarry, *Irish Politics*, p. 127.
41  Patrick Belton to Alexander McCabe, Dublin, 9 March 1939, AMP, Ms 50,555/24/6.
42  25 November 1936, Diary, *septiembre 30*, AMP, Ms 42,488/10.
43  27 November 1936, Diary, *octubre 6*, AMP, Ms 42,488/10.
44  5 December 1936, Diary, *octubre 8*, AMP, Ms 42,488/10.
45  9 February 1937, *enero 22*, AMP, Ms 42,488/11.
46  Ibid, *enero 21*.
47  4 December 1936, Diary, *octubre 7*, AMP, Ms 42,488/10.
48  12 December 1936, Diary, *octubre 16*, AMP, Ms 42,488/10.
49  11 December 1936, Diary, *octubre 14–15*, AMP, Ms 42,488/10.
50  McCullagh, p. 202.
51  Ibid, p. 203.
52  11 December 1936, Diary, *octubre 11*, AMP, Ms 42,488/10.

## CHAPTER 8

1   Eoin O'Duffy, *Crusade in Spain* (Dublin: Browne and Nolan, 1938), p. 12.
2   Fearghal McGarry, *Eoin O'Duffy: A Self-Made Hero* (Oxford: Oxford University Press, 2005), pp. 285–6.
3   17 June 1937, Diary, *junio 14*, AMP, Ms 42,488/11.
4   Composition of Irish Brigade, 21 May 1937, AMP, Ms 50,555/77/6.
5   17 June 1937, Diary, *junio 14–15*, AMP, Ms 42,488/11.
6   Joseph Mulrean to Alexander McCabe, Cáceres, 21 December 1936, AMP, 50,555/25/1.
7   4 January 1937, Diary, *noviembre 14*, AMP, Ms 42,488/10.
8   5 January 1937, Diary, *noviembre 12–13*, AMP, Ms 42,488/10.
9   Ibid, *noviembre 13*.
10  Ibid.
11  Ibid, *noviembre 15*.
12  Ibid, *noviembre 16*.
13  6 January 1937, Diary, *noviembre 17*, AMP, Ms 42,488/10.
14  Ibid, *noviembre 18–19*.

15   Ibid, *noviembre 19.*
16   Ibid, *noviembre 21.*
17   Ibid, *noviembre 20–21.*
18   Ibid, *noviembre 23.*
19   Ibid, *noviembre 21.*
20   Ibid, *noviembre 22.*
21   7 January 1937, Diary, *diciembre 2, AMP*, Ms 42,488/10.
22   Ibid, *noviembre 26.*
23   Ibid, *noviembre 29–30.*
24   Ibid, *diciembre 3–4.*
25   Ibid, *diciembre 5–6.*
26   Ibid, *diciembre 6–7.*
27   Ibid, *diciembre 7.*
28   Ibid, *diciembre 10.*
29   Ibid, *diciembre 9.*
30   Ibid, *diciembre 10.*
31   17 June 1937, Diary, *junio 18*, AMP, Ms 42,488/11.
32   7 January 1937, Diary, *diciembre 17*, AMP, Ms 42,488/10.
33   Ibid, *diciembre 11–12.*
34   17 June 1937, Diary, *junio 15*, AMP, Ms 42,488/10.
35   7 January 1937, Diary, *diciembre 13*, AMP, Ms 42,488/10.
36   Ibid, *diciembre 18–19.*
37   Ibid, *diciembre 21.*
38   17 June 1937, Diary, *junio 17*, AMP, Ms 42,488/11.
39   7 January 1937, Diary, *diciembre 24–25*, AMP, Ms 42,488/10.
40   Ibid, *diciembre 29.*
41   Ibid, *diciembre 30–31.*
42   Joseph Mulrean to Alexander McCabe, Cáceres, 2 February 1937, AMP, MS 50,555/
     25/2.
43   9 February 1937, Diary, *enero 15–16*, AMP, Ms 42,488/11.
44   Ibid, *enero 16–17.*
45   Ibid, *enero 18.*
46.  Robert A. Stradling, *The Irish and the Spanish Civil War 1936-1939: Crusades in Conflict*
     (Manchester: Mandolin, 1999), pp. 60–6.
47   O'Duffy, p. 143.
48   Joseph Mulrean to Alexander McCabe, Ciempozuelos, 26 February 1937, AMP, Ms
     50,555/25/6.
49   See Paul Preston, *We Saw Spain Die: Foreign Correspondents in the Spanish Civil War*
     (London: Constable, 2008).
50   9 February 1937, Diary, *enero 26*, AMP, Ms 42,488/11.
51   Preston, *We Saw Spain Die*, p. 136.
52   9 February 1937, Diary, *enero 20*, AMP, Ms 42,488/11.
53   17 March 1937, Diary, *febrero 19*, AMP, Ms 42,488/11.
54   Annual report from Leopold H. Kerney to Joseph P. Walshe, St Jean de Luz, 2 May 1938.
     Repr. in Catriona Crowe, et al. (eds), *Documents on Irish Foreign Policy (DIFP), Vol. V,
     1937-1939* (Dublin: Royal Irish Academy, 2006), pp. 288–90.
55   Confidential report from Leopold H. Kerney to Joseph P. Walshe, St Jean de Luz,
     6 March 1938. Repr. in *DIFP, Vol. V*, p. 37.
56   13 March 1937, Diary, *febrero 16*, AMP, Ms 42,488/11.

57  11 March 1937, Diary, *febrero 12*, AMP, Ms 42,488/11.
58  Ibid., *febrero 13–14*.
59  Ibid, *febrero 14*.
60  Ibid, *febrero 14–15*.
61  Ibid, *febrero 15*.
62  Stradling, p. 75.
63  O'Duffy, p. 154.
64. McGarry, *Irish Politics*, p. 41; Stradling, pp. 75–80.
65  O'Duffy, pp. 158–9.
66  O'Duffy, p. 162.
67  Stradling, pp. 77–9.
68  Stradling, p. 79.
69  Stradling, pp. 94–5.
70  25 March 1937, Diary, *febrero 25–26*, AMP, Ms 42,488/11.
71  2 April 1937, Diary, *marzo 5–6*, AMP, Ms 42,488/11.
72  3 April 1937, Diary, *marzo 11–12*, AMP, Ms 42,488/11.
73  Ibid, *marzo 12*.
74  21 April 1937, Diary, *marzo 30–31*, AMP, Ms 42,488/11.
75  Ibid, *resumen de marzo*.
76  See Ben Macintyre, *Operation Mincemeat: The True Spy Story That Changed the Course of World War II* (London: Bloomsbury, 2010).
77  Salvador Gómez-Beare to Alexander McCabe, Madrid, 31 January 1940, AMP, Ms 50,555/11/9.
78  21 April 1937, Diary, *resumen de marzo*, AMP, Ms 42,488/11.
79  Ibid, *abril 3–4*.
80  Ibid, *abril 4*.
81  Ibid, *abril 5*.
82  Ibid, *abril 6–7*.
83  Ibid, *abril 7*.
84  Ibid, *abril 7–8*.
85  29 April 1937, Diary, *abril 10*, AMP, Ms 42,488/11.
86  Ibid, *abril 11*.
87  See Alexander McCabe memo, 30 April 1937, AMP, Ms 50,555/77/4; Alexander McCabe memo, 30 April 1937, AMP, Ms 50,555/77/5; and Alexander McCabe memo, 1 May 1937, AMP, Ms 50,555/26/2.
88  30 April 1937, Diary, *abril 11–13*, AMP, Ms 42,488/11; see also Alexander McCabe memo, 30 April 1937, AMP, Ms 50,555/26/1.
89  1 May 1937, Diary, *abril 14–15*, AMP, Ms 42,488/11.
90  30 April 1937, Diary, *abril 13–14*, AMP, Ms 42,488/11.
91  1 May 1937, Diary, *abril 14*, AMP, Ms 42,488/11.
92  Ibid, *abril 16*.
93  O'Duffy, p. 112.
94  1 May 1937, Diary, *abril 16*, AMP, Ms 42,488/11.
95  1 September 1937, Diary, *agosto 8–9*, AMP, Ms 42,488/11.
96  1 May 1937, Diary, *abril 16*, AMP, Ms 42,488/11.
97  Ibid., *abril 16-17*.
98  17 June 1937, Diary, *junio 22–24*, AMP, Ms 42,488/11.
99  1 May 1937, Diary, *abril 17*, AMP, Ms 42,488/11.
100 Ibid, *abril 17–18*.

101  2 May 1937, Diary, *abril 21*, AMP, Ms 42,488/11.
102  3 May 1937, Diary, *mayo 9*, AMP, Ms 42,488/11.
103  Alexander McCabe memo, 5 May 1937, AMP, Ms 50,555/77/2.
104  4 May 1937, Diary, *mayo 11*, AMP, Ms 42,488/11.
105  1 September 1937, Diary, *agosto 7*, AMP, Ms 42,488/11.


**CHAPTER 9**

1    Thomas, pp. 614–24.
2    21 April 1937, Diary, *marzo 27*, AMP, Ms 42,488/11.
3    3 June 1937, Diary, *resumen de mayo*, AMP, Ms 42,488/11.
4    8 June 1937, Diary, *junio 5-6*, AMP, Ms 42,488/11.
5    19 June 1937, Diary, *junio 25*, AMP, Ms 42,488/11.
6    O'Duffy, p. 195.
7    25 June 1937, Diary, *junio 26-28*, AMP, Ms 42,488/11.
8    6 July 1937, Diary, *julio 5*, AMP, Ms 42,488/11.
9    Ibid, *julio 6*.
10   2 July 1937, Diary, *julio 1-2*, AMP, Ms 42,488/11.
11   Thomas Gunning to Alexander McCabe, Burgos, 6 April 1938, AMP, Ms 50,555/24/2.
12   Thomas Gunning to Alexander McCabe, Burgos, 6 May 1938, AMP, Ms 50,555/24/3.
13   McGarry, *Irish Politics*, p. 226.
14   Andrew O'Toole to Alexander McCabe, Salamanca Prison, Undated April 1939, AMP, Ms 50,555/24/8.
15   Leopold H. Kerney to Alexander McCabe, San Sebastián, 5 June 1939, AMP, Ms 50,555/13/1.
16   John Madden to Alexander McCabe, Pamplona, 20 November, 1937, AMP, Ms 50,555/27/3.
17   John Madden to Alexander McCabe, Vitoria, 29 November 1937, AMP, Ms 50,555/27/5.
18   Eoin O'Duffy to Alexander McCabe, Dublin, 12 April 1938, AMP, Ms 50,555/26/5.
19   Preston, *Spanish Holocaust*, p. 3.
20   4 July 1937, Diary, *julio 5*, AMP, Ms 42,488/11.
21   4 August 1937, Diary, *julio 23*, AMP, Ms 42,488/11.
22   Ibid, *julio 24*.
23   31 July 1937, Diary, *julio 20-21*, AMP, Ms 42,488/11.
24   1 September 1937, Diary, *agosto 6*, AMP, Ms 42,488/11.
25   See Boris Volodarsky, 'Kim Philby: Living a Lie', *History Today*, 60, 8 (2010), pp. 39–45.
26   6 July 1937, Diary, *julio 9-11*, AMP, Ms 42,488/11.
27   16 July 1937, Diary, *julio 11*, AMP, Ms 42,488/11.
28   3 June 1937, Diary, *resumen de mayo–junio 2*, AMP, Ms 42,488/11.
29   Ibid, *junio 1*.
30   23 August 1937, Diary, *resumen de julio-agosto 1*, AMP, Ms 42,488/11.
31   *The Rector's Report for the Academic Year 1937–38*, p. 4, AMP, Ms 50,555/36/1.
32   8 November 1937, Diary, *septiembre 6*, AMP, Ms 42,488/11.
33   *The Rector's Report for the Academic Year 1937–38*, p. 4, AMP, Ms 50,555/36/1.
34   29 October 1937, Diary, *agosto 26*, AMP, Ms 42,488/11.
35   Preston, *Spanish Holocaust*, p. 198.
36   Teodoro Rodriguez to Alexander McCabe, Burgos, 26 March 1939, AMP, Ms 50,555/24/10.

37 Joseph L. N. Wolfe to Alexander McCabe, St Gregory's Rectory, Philadelphia, 18 February 1939, AMP, Ms 50,555/5/3.
38 Charles O'Daly to Alexander McCabe, Enniskillen, 20 July 1937, AMP, Ms 50,555/23/13.
39 9 November 1937, Diary, *septiembre 8*, AMP, Ms 42,488/11.
40 13 November 1937, Diary, *septiembre 16*, AMP, Ms 42,488/11.
41 9 November 1937, Diary, *septiembre 8*, AMP, Ms 42,488/11.
42 22 November 1937, Diary, *septiembre 21*, AMP, Ms 42,488/11.
43 9 November 1937, Diary, *septiembre 7*, AMP, Ms 42,488/11.
44 27 December 1937, Diary, *octubre 19–20*, AMP, Ms 42,488/11.
45 *ASPA*, 15 June 1939, p. 3, AMP, MS 50,555/62.
46 4 July 1937, Diary, *julio 3*, AMP, Ms 42,488/11.
47 15 November 1937, *septiembre 18–19*, AMP, Ms 42,488/11.
48 12 November 1937, *septiembre 15–16*, AMP, Ms 42,488/11.
49 31 December 1937, *resumen de diciembre*, AMP, Ms 42,488/11.
50 *The Rector's Report for the Academic Year 1937–38*, p. 4, AMP, Ms 50,555/36/1.
51 Ibid.
52 See correspondence between AM and the Sanmartín family, AMP, Ms 50,555/17.
53 Copy of Alexander McCabe to Governor of Oviedo, 17 October 1938, AMP, Ms 50,555/43/2.
54 Author's interview with Concepción Sanmartín, 6 June 2014.
55 *The Rector's Report for the Academic Year 1938–39*, p. 3, AMP, Ms 50,555/36/1.

**CHAPTER 10**

1 Isidro Gomá y Tomás to Alexander McCabe, Toledo, 3 July 1939, AMP, Ms 50,555/2/2.
2 *The Rector's Report for the Academic Year 1938–39*, p. 3, AMP, Ms 50,555/36/1.
3 *The Rector's Report for the Academic Year 1942–43*, p. 6, AMP, Ms 50,555/36/2.
4 *The Rector's Report for the Academic Year 1944–45*, p. 3, AMP, Ms 50,555/36/2.
5 Ibid, p. 4.
6 Ibid.
7 Ibid, p. 6.
8 Richard Fitzgerald to Alexander McCabe, Gibraltar, 4 August 1945, AMP, Ms 50,555/1/5.
9 Richard Fitzgerald to Alexander McCabe, Gibraltar, 4 August 1945, AMP, Ms 50,555/1/6.
10 John O'Hara to Alexander McCabe, Kilbride, Co. Sligo, 22 August 1945, AMP, Ms 50,555/4/9.
11 Ibid.
12 Ibid.
13 Ibid.
14 John O'Hara to Alexander McCabe, 10 December 1945, Bohola, Co. Mayo, AMP, Ms 50,555/4/10.
15 Gonzalo de Aguilera Munro to Alexander McCabe, Carrascal de Sanchiricones, 26 February 1946, AMP, Ms 50,555/9/11.
16 Gonzalo de Aguilera Munro to Alexander McCabe, Carrascal de Sanchiricones, 30 August 1946, AMP, Ms 50,555/9/12.
17 Preston, *The Spanish Holocaust*, pp. 526–8.
18 13 June 1946, Diary, *enero 20–21*, AMP, Ms 42,488/12.
19 *The Rector's Report for the Academic Year 1945–46*, p. 4, AMP, Ms 50,555/36/2.
20 *The Rector's Report for the Academic Year 1946–47*, pp. 3–4, AMP, Ms 50,555/36/2.

21 Ibid, p. 4.
22 Michael Browne, 'Irish College at Salamanca – Last Days', *The Furrow*, 22, 11 (1971), pp. 697–702 (p. 699).
23 18 January 1949, Diary, *enero 12–13*, AMP, Ms 42,488/19.
24 Ibid, *enero 16*.
25 19 January 1939, Diary, *febrero 25–26*, AMP, Ms 42,488/19.
26 Browne, p. 699.
27 Ibid.
28 Browne, p. 700.
29 Browne, pp. 700–1.
30 Browne, p. 701.

### CHAPTER 11

1 Daniel J. Gallogly, *The Diocese of Kilmore 1800–1950* (Cavan: Cumann Seanchais Bhreifne, 1999), p. 358.
2 Anonymous interview with author.
3 Anonymous interview with author.
4 Personal notes, Jul. 1969, AMP, III.xiii, AMP, Ms 42,488/39.
5 Dermot Keogh, 'An Eye Witness to History: Fr Alexander J. McCabe and the Spanish Civil War, 1936–1939', *Breifne: Journal of Cumann Seanchais Bhreifne*, 8, 30 (1994), pp. 445–89.
6 Alexander McCabe, 'Address of The Very Reverend Alexander McCabe, Rector of Salamanca at the time of its closure during the Spanish Civil War', in programme for the 'State Visit of Their Majesties, the King and Queen of Spain' to St Patrick's College, Maynooth, 2 July 1986.

# SOURCES

*Archival material*

**National Library of Ireland, Dublin**
*Alexander McCabe Papers*

**Russell Library, St Patrick's College, Maynooth**
*Salamanca Archive*

*Articles, booklets, essays and pamphlets*

Browne, Michael, 'Irish College at Salamanca – Last Days', *The Furrow*, 22, 11 (1971), pp. 697–702.

Echeverria, Lamberto de, 'The Irish College, Salamanca', *The Furrow*, 23, 5 (1972), pp. 316–17.

Glennon, Richard J., 'The Irish College, Salamanca', *The Furrow*, 23, 1 (1972), pp. 48–52.

Henchy, Monica, 'The Irish college at Salamanca', in Felix M. Larkin (ed.), *Librarians, Poets and Scholars: A Festschrift for Dónall Ó Luanaigh* (Dublin: Four Courts Press, 2007).

—, 'The Irish Colleges in Spain', *Breifne: Journal of Cumann Seanchais Bhreifne*, 9, 35 (1999), pp. 140–56.

Horgan, John, '"The great war correspondent": Francis McCullagh, 1874–1956', *Irish Historical Studies*, 36, 144 (2009), pp. 542–63.

Keogh, Dermot, 'An Eye Witness to History: Fr Alexander J. McCabe and the Spanish Civil War, 1936–1939', *Breifne: Journal of Cumann Seanchais Bhreifne*, 8, 30 (1994), pp. 445–89.

McCabe, Alexander, 'Address of The Very Reverend Alexander McCabe, Rector of Salamanca at the time of its closure during the Spanish Civil War', in programme for the 'State Visit of Their Majesties, the King and Queen of Spain' to St Patrick's College, Maynooth, 2 July 1986.

McGahern, John, 'Schooldays: A Time of Grace', in *Love of the World: Essays* (London: Faber & Faber, 2009), pp. 103–08.

Mhic Aonghusa, Gráinne, 'The Parochial House' in *Rossinver Braes*, vol. 1 (Manorhamilton: Cumann Seanchaís Ro Inbhír, 1995).

Recio Morales, Óscar, 'Not Only Seminaries: The Political Role of the Irish Colleges in Seventeenth-Century Spain', *History Ireland*, 9, 3 (2001), pp. 48–52.

Richardson, Regina W., 'The Irish in Asturias: the footprint of the Irish College, Salamanca, 1913–1950', *Archivium Hibernicum*, 65 (2012), pp. 273–90.

Volodarsky, Boris, 'Kim Philby: Living a Lie', *History Today*, 60, 8 (2010), pp. 39–45.

**Books**

Beevor, Antony, *The Battle for Spain: The Spanish Civil War 1936–1939* (London: Weidenfeld & Nicolson, 2006).

Borkenau, Franz, *The Spanish Cockpit: An Eyewitness Account of the Spanish Civil War* (London: Phoenix Press, 2000).

Brady, Patrick (ed.), *St Mary's Parish Church, Crosserlough: Centenary 1888–1988* (County Cavan: Crosserlough, 1988).

Brenan, Gerald, *The Spanish Labyrinth: The Social and Political Background of the Spanish Civil War* (Cambridge: Canto, 2008).

Cooney, John, *John Charles McQuaid: Ruler of Catholic Ireland* (Dublin: O'Brien Press, 1999).

Crowe, Catriona, et al. (eds), *Documents on Irish Foreign Policy (DIFP). Vol. V, 1937–1939* (Dublin: Royal Irish Academy, 2006).

Cunningham, Terence P. and Daniel Gallogly, *St Patrick's College and the earlier Kilmore Academy: A Centenary History* (Cavan: St Patrick's College, 1974).

Dunne, Raymond and Francis J. MacKiernan, *The College Boys: Students of the Kilmore Academy & St Patrick College, Cavan 1839–2000* (Cavan: Cumann Seanchais Bhreifne, 2008).

Gallogly, Daniel J., *The Diocese of Kilmore 1800–1950* (Cavan: Cumann Seanchais Bhreifne, 1999).

Jeffery, Keith, *MI6: The History of the Secret Intelligence Service 1909–1949* (London: Bloomsbury, 2010).

Keogh, Dermot, *Ireland & Europe 1919–1948* (Dublin: Gill & Macmillan, 1988).

Macintyre, Ben, *Operation Mincemeat: The True Spy Story That Changed the Course of World War II* (London: Bloomsbury, 2010).

MacKiernan, Francis J., *Diocese of Kilmore: Priests and Bishops 1136–1988* (Cavan: Cumann Seanchais Bhreifne, 1989).

Manning, Maurice, *The Blueshirts* (Dublin: Gill & Macmillan, 2006).

Martín, José-Luis and Ricardo Robledo (eds), *Historia de Salamanca, Vol. V: Siglo Veinte* (Salamanca: Centro de Estudios Salamantinos, 2001).

McCullagh, Francis, *In Franco's Spain: Being the Experiences of an Irish War Correspondent during the Great Civil War* (London: Burns, Oates & Washbourne, 1937).

McGarry, Fearghal, *Eoin O'Duffy: A Self-Made Hero* (Oxford: Oxford University Press, 2005).

—, *Irish Politics and the Spanish Civil War* (Cork: Cork University Press, 1999).

O'Duffy, Eoin, *Crusade in Spain* (Dublin: Browne and Nolan, 1938).

Preston, Paul, *¡Comrades! Portraits from the Spanish Civil War* (London: Fontana Press, 2000).

—, *Franco* (London: Fontana Press, 1995).

—, *The Spanish Civil War: Reaction, Revolution, and Revenge* (London: Harper Perennial, 2006).

—, *The Spanish Holocaust: Inquisition and Extermination in Twentieth-Century Spain* (London: Harper Press, 2012).

—, *We Saw Spain Die: Foreign Correspondents in the Spanish Civil War* (London: Constable, 2008).

Robledo, Ricardo (ed.), *Esta Salvaje Pesadilla: Salamanca en la guerra civil española* (Barcelona: Crítica, 2007).

Stradling, Robert A., *The Irish and the Spanish Civil War 1936–1939: Crusades in Conflict* (Manchester: Mandolin, 1999).

Sullivan, Tom (ed.), *Drumkilly: from Ardkill Mountain to Kilderry Hill* (Cavan: Drumkilly History Committee, 2000).

Thomas, Hugh, *The Spanish Civil War* (London: Penguin, 2003).

# INDEX